Harvesting History

Harvesting History

McCormick's Reaper, Heritage Branding, and Historical Forgery

DANIEL P. OTT

University of Nebraska Press Lincoln

Portions of chapter 2 previously appeared in "Producing a Past: McCormick Harvester and the Producer Populists in the 1890s," *Agricultural History* 88, no. 1 (Winter 2014): 87–119.

Portions of chapter 3 previously appeared in "'The Reaper Is to the North . . .': The Genesis of a Lie," *Journal of the Illinois State Historical Society* 105, no. 4 (Winter 2012): 333–55.

The University of Nebraska Press is part of a land-grant institution with campuses and programs on the past, present, and future homelands of the Pawnee, Ponca, Otoe-Missouria, Omaha, Dakota, Lakota, Kaw, Cheyenne, and Arapaho Peoples, as well as those of the relocated Ho-Chunk, Sac and Fox, and Iowa Peoples.

♾

Library of Congress Cataloging-in-Publication Data
Names: Ott, Daniel P., author.
Title: Harvesting history: McCormick's reaper, heritage branding, and historical forgery / Daniel P. Ott.
Description: Lincoln: University of Nebraska Press, [2023] | Includes bibliographical references and index.
Identifiers: LCCN 2022018527
ISBN 9781496206985 (hardback)
ISBN 9781496234391 (epub)
ISBN 9781496234407 (pdf)
Subjects: LCSH: McCormick, Cyrus Hall, 1809–1884. | Harvesting machinery—United States—History. | Inventors—United States—Biography. | BISAC: HISTORY / United States / 20th Century | SOCIAL SCIENCE / Agriculture & Food (see also POLITICAL SCIENCE / Public Policy / Agriculture & Food Policy)
Classification: LCC HD9486.U44 M33 2023 | DDC 681/.7631—dc23/eng/20220819
LC record available at https://lccn.loc.gov/2022018527

Set and designed in Lyon Text by Mikala R. Kolander.

For Cassie

When the historian of the future comes to speak of the great Americans . . . who have succeeded the best in lightening the burdens of mankind, by the side of Franklin, and Fulton and Joseph Henry and Morse, they will not forget to mention Cyrus H. McCormick. Where the golden wheat rustles in the breeze, the panting toilers under the hot sun will hail him as their benefactor.

—S. C. P. Miller, *In Memoriam: Cyrus Hall McCormick*

Contents

Illustrations

Acknowledgments

This book is the result of eleven years of work, starting from my time as a graduate student at Loyola University Chicago and then as a historian trying to get published while making a living among adjunct jobs, nonprofits, and federal service. This project is a reflection of not only that decade of effort but also my preexisting love of history as a critical and thought-provoking craft. Throughout this journey I have always been inspired and supported by a large cast of teachers, professors, colleagues, co-workers, friends, and family. I am indebted to them all for making this book possible and for supporting my personal, scholarly, and professional growth.

I would like to thank everyone in the Department of History at Loyola University Chicago. The department and the graduate school not only provided the funding to make my academic journey possible but consistently challenged and supported me through the process. In particular my adviser, Ted Karamanski, was critical to my success. Dr. Karamanski offered me timely advice, insight, and encouragement as I navigated course work, exams, and my dissertation. Years later he has continued to be willing to talk about my project and the ins and outs of publication, as we have stayed in touch while discussing my varied career path or exchanging stories about Thursday morning pickup basketball games at the Halas Center. Professors Patricia Mooney-Melvin and Elizabeth Fraterrigo were also invaluable to my graduate career, providing constructive criticism as they challenged me in my course work and brought the best out of my dissertation. I would also like to thank Tim Gilfoyle for his help in focusing early iterations of two of my chapters during his research seminars.

Beyond the faculty I would like to thank my numerous colleagues. Erin Feichtinger and Amelia Serafine entered Loyola's history doctoral program as my cohort-mates in the fall of 2010. Through the joys and pains of scholarly life we became very close, often enjoying rigorous and sometimes ridiculous debates, engaging with one another's very different scholarship, and enjoying friendly companionship beyond the confines of academia. I especially appreciate the time and energy Amelia and Erin generously offered me, graciously reading and rereading my chapters while continually offering editorial corrections, fresh insight, and tough criticism. I would also like to thank my numerous colleagues who engaged with my scholarship and enjoyed coursework and shared the graduate student experience with me, including Rachel Boyle, Steve Catania, Devin Hunter, Will Ippen, Nate Jeremie-Brink, Pete Kotowski, Katie Macica, Amy Oberlin, Chris Ramsey, Matt Sawicki, and Hope Shannon.

Any historical research project requires the support of many librarians and archivists. The archival staff at the Wisconsin Historical Society was crucial to this project's success. At Madison the head of the McCormick–International Harvester Collection, Lee Grady, was instrumental in pointing me toward the history-making agenda of the McCormicks and their corporation as well as helping me to approach the massive collection. Staff at Loyola's own Cudahy Library, as well as the Newberry Library and the Indiana University–Purdue University Indianapolis Special Collections, were also incredibly helpful in facilitating my research.

My editor Bridget Barry and the staff at the University of Nebraska Press have also been wonderful to work with. I greatly appreciate the press's investment in my project as well as Bridget's insights and patience over the five years I've been in conversation with her. Along with the press I would like to thank two anonymous reviewers for their generosity and thoughtful comments, which have certainly improved the book. I would also like to recognize *Agricultural History* and the *Journal of the Illinois State Historical Society* for granting permission to reprint portions of chapters 2 and 3, respectively, which had been previously published as articles.

I would also like to acknowledge the people who have supported me in my historical career outside of graduate school. Tim Hoogland, my mentor at the Minnesota Historical Society, and Bob Ferguson, my eighth-grade history teacher, played crucial roles in fostering my love of history. Along with them I would like to thank Steve Gross, Paula O'Loughlin, Donna Gabbacia, and Andy Urban at the University of Minnesota–Morris and Twin Cities, who strengthened my understanding of public history as well as the historian's craft and helped me navigate my undergraduate experience. I also need to acknowledge the importance of my dear friend and former co-worker at History Day in Minnesota, Laura Zeccardi, who passed away at far too young an age in 2013. Laura encouraged me to go after my doctorate before I was sure I really wanted to and understood the power of public history to transform people's lives and the world.

I owe many thanks to my friends and family for their loving support of my historical interests and encouragement throughout my life. My mom and dad, Lynda and Peter Ott, provided me with an appreciation for education and have always nurtured me personally and academically. I would also like to thank my brother, Nate, and sister-in-law, Naira, as well as their kiddos, Annalise and Luca. My extended family of Otts, Bonsells, and Bielkes have also been great sources of encouragement, especially Oldemor and Oldefar, Lucy and Tom Ott, and Grandma Audrey Bonsell, who has passed. I would also like to thank my close family friend Jakob Erickson, who may as well be the third Ott brother.

Finally, I would like to thank my life partner, Cassie, and our children, Adelaide and Bennett. Addie and Benny were spared much of this decade-long experience, as they showed up after the dissertation was complete, though they have had to deal with the occasional missing dad as I worked on making revisions. Cassie, however, has endured the whole experience. She uprooted her life and came with me to Chicago for four years of late nights, existential crises, inconsistent academic schedules, and far too much information about the McCormicks. Cassie has been my biggest cheerleader and motivating force, knowing just when to encourage me to take a break to preserve my sanity and how to get me outside of myself to enjoy doing anything other than reading, writing, grading, or any other form of work. For the seven years since Loyola, Cassie has continued to be the steadying force in our partnership as she completed her graduate degree and we began our family, changed jobs and moved numerous times, dreamed and redreamed our lives together, bought a house, and continued to survive a pandemic for two years and counting. I could not have completed this book, or really much of anything, without her love and encouragement. This book is dedicated to her.

Harvesting History

Introduction

> The reaper, a horse-drawn machine that greatly increased the amount of wheat a farmer could harvest, was invented by Cyrus McCormick in 1831.
>
> —Eric Foner, *Give Me Liberty!*

> The automatic reaper, the invention of Cyrus H. McCormick, took the place of sickle, cradle and hand labor. . . . The reaper enabled a crew of six or seven men to harvest in a day as much wheat as fifteen men could harvest using the older methods.
>
> —Alan Brinkley, *Unfinished Nation*

> Inventions revolutionized not only manufacturing, but the age-old methods of farming. Cyrus McCormick, twenty-two-year-old son of a Virginia blacksmith-farmer, made his first reaper in 1831, a two-wheeled, horse-drawn chariot that harvested grain.
>
> —Daniel Walker Howe, *What Hath God Wrought*

Cyrus McCormick invented the mechanized reaper in 1831. This ubiquitous "fact" has been referenced in U.S. history textbooks and syntheses but has been a part of the historical canon only since the 1930s. Before that time the "fact" of the reaper's origins was a highly controversial and hotly debated matter. Far from uncontested truth, the question of the machine's inventor was valuable cultural currency in the incredibly competitive and heavily capitalized harvesting-machine industry of the late nineteenth century. To the minds of reaper-selling rivals, the heir of the true inventor was the crown authority of the industry, setting its products apart from its counterfeit competitors.

The settling of the reaper's history in the 1930s coincides with the consolidation of corporate economic and cultural power as well as the rise of professional historical authority within academia. The contest for the past was not resolved, however, by academics brandishing a smoking gun of conclusive evidence, as might be expected (although they would play a role). Instead, the historical battle was closed by the formation of International Harvester Company, the behemoth trust that consolidated 85 percent of harvester manufacturing into a single firm in 1902. In the same way that the corporation gained dominion over the industry and customers, it also solidified control over narratives of agricultural and national development. International Harvester prioritized McCormick as the inventor of the machine and utilized this heritage as the centerpiece of its brand, righteously justifying its domineering scale as the fair and natural rewards of real ingenuity. With McCormick's invention as a keystone, the harvester trust reframed corporatization as an inevitable and righteously benevolent step in the march of U.S. history toward material progress, innovation, and abundance. Its new past served as a cultural bulwark against seething antitrust sentiment that despised big businesses as undemocratic infringements on American independence. Parallel to this historical branding, the corporation and its first family, the McCormicks, mobilized incredible resources, including hiring academic historians, to reinforce its heritage with scholarship and exercise historical knowledge control by silencing dissent.

This story of an elite family and corporation's conscientious fabrication of a single "fact" offers insight about the foundations of the larger historical canon forged by the profession's founders around the turn of the past century. Crucially, it suggests that the scholarship produced by these early "scientific" scholars was a history that made the development of corporate capitalism align with American traditions of democracy and independence as well as newer ideas regarding national identity that hinged on prosperity and progress. These professionals participated in this hegemonic process somewhat unconsciously; unaware and unreflective about their subjective positionality as new educated workers seeking a place within the developing corporate order. Hoping to demonstrate the value of their historical expertise as well as secure salaries and philanthropic support from wealthy elites, new scholars created archives and advanced scholarship that legitimized corporate promotional heritage as historical fact. Only with greater distance from the profession's establishment and public financial support would scholars become critical of corporations, but not before a foundation had already been laid that culturally sanctified those same forces.

The connection between historical knowledge control and hegemonic power has been theorized by deconstructionists and relativists since the 1980s. Many scholars have studied this process as it has operated culturally, politically, socially, and racially in a variety of contexts. *Harvesting History* focuses on one well-documented example to reveal explicit connections between the historical profession and economic power as part of the history of capitalism. This one history suggests processes at work throughout the discipline during the formative period of its professionalization. To fully illustrate the process of history making requires following McCormick's invention as it was transformed from a mythical piece of private heritage into an industrial brand and then a historical fact over a fifty-year period.[1]

The story of McCormick's invention as history originated from his heirs. According to them, their patriarch was a mechanical genius, who invented the reaper in 1831 at the ripe age of twenty-two. He inherited his ingenuity from his father, Robert McCormick, who conceived and built many laborsaving farm tools in their Virginia plantation's workshop. Beginning in 1816, Robert attempted to build a horse-drawn implement to cut grain but had failed. Puzzling over his father's grain contraption for many years, in 1831 young Cyrus was struck by divine inspiration while on a journey through the mountains. As he was riding to a nearby foundry, his horse stopped for a drink in the middle of a considerable stream. "Just then, as he looked up, his eye fell on a fertile tract of land brightened by sunshine, and the blended thought of the vast future of the country in agriculture, and the possibilities of his invention for reaping grain, struck him." In that beautiful and dramatic moment, he conceived the horizontal reciprocating blade as the key to the machine's success. He went home and began fashioning his vision into wood and iron. Six weeks later he successfully unveiled his machine in front of a small audience of interested onlookers in a neighbor's field of oats near Steele's Tavern. And the rest, as they say, "is history." He began selling the machine, continued to improve it, moved to Chicago in 1848 to erect a reaper manufactory amid the prairies of the West, earned numerous accolades at world's fairs, and, by the time of his death in 1884, had built a vast industrial empire while revolutionizing agriculture.[2]

This origin story came from the pen of Cyrus Hall McCormick II shortly after his father's death. While the McCormick Harvesting Machine Company had begun advertising their founder's 1831 invention several years before, this "memoir," introducing a memorial volume on his father's life, is the first full publication of the McCormick invention story. Fancying himself an amateur historian, Cyrus McCormick II included heroic details of his father's life, his unimpeachable Christian character, and his monumental impact on the progress of the world. While he had great ease locating sources about his father's success as a businessman once he moved to Chicago, where the family and his company preserved relevant historical documents and artifacts, the story of the invention itself is a product of oral tradition. He was only twenty-five years old at the time of his father's death, and these details about the moment of invention are most likely Cyrus II's recounting of the story that his father had told him and his siblings when they were children.[3]

For this wealthy industrial family, their patriarch's invention was an important part of their identities. The story of his genius and revolutionary impact on agriculture was a righteous explanation of their elite status. Their massive reaper works, authority over armies of employees, mansions, luxury goods, and high standing as members of Chicago's Gilded Age society all stemmed from his 1831 invention. These were the privileges and rewards for their father's monumental contributions to agricultural progress and American civilization. As McCormick's widow, Nettie Fowler, reiterated to her daughter, their company was "an honor to your father, as one of the best known Institutions in the country" and their wealth was an "ornament" of his success. On another occasion Cyrus McCormick II explained that their fortunes and reputation were earned through their paterfamilias's "tenacity, energy and consistency of purpose" over years of "toil," inventing the machine and building the business that allowed farmers to flourish. In essence, the story was their family's celebratory "heritage," which exclusively explained where they came from and justified all the social, economic, and material realities of who they were without consideration of any other parties or larger cultural contexts. In a self-congratulatory vacuum they held this romance of their exceptionalism dear without regard for historical evidence, which, in the instance of their father's invention, was sorely lacking.[4]

Regardless of the family's private heritage, during the late nineteenth and early twentieth centuries, the fact of Cyrus McCormick's invention was far from consensus knowledge. Rather, ideas about invention, progress, civilization, and capitalism were debated in a period of incredible social and economic change that included fierce industrial competition within the harvesting-machine industry. Business rivals attempted to use history-based advertising to cultivate desire for their wares among rural farmers who did not passively accept the "natural" logic of capitalism or mechanization. Competing claims about the origins of the reaper were prevalent in advertising literature, sales scripts, public relations materials, and corporate branding projects. In the harvester industry the emphasis on invention was initiated by Cyrus McCormick's Chicago-based McCormick Harvesting Machine Company and used as evidence of the superiority of its product line. Competitors countered that many different inventors, mechanics, and tinkerers played a significant role in the gradual development of the reaper over many decades. Most often they pointed to the fact that Obed Hussey had patented a reaper in 1833, a year before McCormick patented his own in 1834. In the context of this industry-wide contest for the past, the public was inundated with a wide variety of conflicting histories about the machine's origins and was generally aware that the story of the reaper's invention was far from a settled fact. Moreover, Cyrus McCormick's own siblings, nieces, and nephews contested his supposed invention and resented his company's advertising. Alternatively, they argued that his father, Robert McCormick, was responsible for imagining and building the revolutionary farm implement, entrusting the machine to Cyrus to manage for the entire family's financial benefit.[5]

From a twenty-first-century perspective, historians have raised questions about the African American slave Jo Anderson's involvement in inventing the McCormick reaper, but none of the competing white inventors, family members, industrialists, or corporations advanced this possibility during the nineteenth or early twentieth century. While Anderson's assistance to both Cyrus and Robert McCormick at different times over the years was acknowledged in narratives supporting those competing claims, neither group suggested that Anderson's participation was crucial to the reaper's creation. Indeed, the province of invention was reserved for white men among white industrial competitors rather than an enslaved Black man who collaborated with his white "inventive" masters Robert and Cyrus on the reaper's creation from the late 1810s to the early 1830s.

The conflicting claims for Robert McCormick, Cyrus McCormick, and Obed Hussey as the inventor of the reaper all have their merits and solid supporting evidence. Obed Hussey's reaper was operational and officially patented before McCormick's. The story advancing Robert McCormick as the inventor after decades of experimentation is more believable than the twenty-two-year-old Cyrus inventing the reaper in 1831 after a flash of insight and six weeks of applied ingenuity. The Cyrus McCormick story is supported by an ocean of advertising literature, courtroom testimony and oral history, all of which came into existence at least a decade and a half after his supposed invention.[6]

Meanwhile, the evidence of Jo Anderson's inventive contributions can be read against the grain only in the margins of McCormick family stories. There is no archive of Anderson's innovation, no diaries of his thoughts, no patents or court records to support his competing claim, only references to his "mechanical genius" and ever-present support for the McCormick father and son's inventive efforts. As an enslaved man and later a freedman who remained connected with the McCormick family in Virginia, Anderson is largely silent in this debate as a man without status or wealth beyond his connections to the elite family. Historians can only speculate about his contributions, thoughts, and feelings on the topic.[7]

With this in mind the purpose of this book is not to rehash "who invented the reaper." That point has been exhaustively debated in advertising campaigns, the press, and history books beginning in 1884 and continuing well into the twentieth century. Rather, the purpose is to analyze the historical debate and the history-making process to get a glimpse of why invention and history mattered so much to one of the United States' most important corporations and elite families during the Gilded Age and Progressive Era. Through recounting the transformation of one piece of private heritage into a fixture of the historical canon, *Harvesting History* explains why history was worth fighting for during this era and reveals how the emerging historical profession participated in the process of corporate promotion and naturalization. This story of a seemingly innocuous bit of trivia demonstrates history's function as both a valued cultural resource and a malleable, producible material at the turn of the past century.

The inclusion of Cyrus McCormick's invention in history textbooks is a lasting artifact of the successful efforts of one family to shape the past to sanctify their role in the modern corporate order. Over the course of more than five decades, from 1878 to 1936, McCormick's heirs and their companies spent millions of dollars on an evolving variety of means to secure their patriarch's history beyond reproach. The cultural importance of history during the period is a salient thread of this book's central argument. In an era obsessed with progress and civilization, accomplishments of the past were seen as the crucial building blocks of modernity. Monumental, historic contributions teleologically explained the present social, political, and economic order. Within this cultural context a close association with the milestones of progress were celebrated marks of masculine leadership in the superior Anglo-American civilization. For this reason the invention of the reaper was more than just a "fact." Rather, it was pinpointed by the McCormick family as the righteous seed of their wealth and a justification of their supremacy in the harvester industry and the modern order.

Over time the story of McCormick's invention was adapted by the family and their employees as valuable cultural ammunition to meet a variety of emerging challenges. Initially, the story was promoted as the brand of the McCormick Harvesting Machine Company during the late 1870s, when many competitors were offering similar or better machines. At that time McCormick's invention was used to claim the company's paternal dominion over the entire industry, reprimand industry newcomers, and boast the superiority of its goods. The narrative of invention and progress proved eminently malleable. During the populist revolt of the 1890s, the story was altered to emphasize McCormick's personal origins as a farmer and to suggest his company's kinship with agrarian producers and long-term commitment to the welfare of farmers. After the company merged with competitors to form International Harvester, the story was spun again to meet the challenges of antitrust litigation during the opening decades of the twentieth century. In this context McCormick was credited with initiating the agricultural revolution that had provided cheap bread for the masses and allowed all of civilization to flourish in its wake. International Harvester used the story to recast itself as a benefactor of the nation rather than a parasitic industrial octopus leeching away wealth from the general public.

Along the way the family and its company encountered resistance to its heritage branding and historical sanctification efforts. The greater the emphasis family members placed on Cyrus McCormick's 1831 invention of the reaper, the more retaliation they provoked from competitors and their own relatives. It became that much more important to safeguard McCormick's legacy as the inventor of the reaper to protect the company's cultural legitimacy and, on a more personal level, the family's identity and status. Alternative histories of the reaper's origins could damage the general public's perception of the company and potentially impact the family's fortune. During the period beginning in 1897, dissenting historical narratives in advertising successfully diminished their brand, and the McCormick family was convinced that this "cultural warfare" undermined their sales and industry dominance. Industrial counternarratives ceased only when the family led their company into a merger with its mudslinging competitors, forming International Harvester in 1902. After that point the invention story was almost continuously challenged by McCormicks' relatives, who argued that the honor of inventing the reaper belonged to Robert McCormick. Crucially, that story was their heritage and part of their collective identity. They felt Cyrus McCormick's heirs had besmirched Robert and were unjustly stealing what should have been their shared glory. By the 1930s, however, International Harvester and the Cyrus McCormick family had drowned out contradicting voices in a crushing sea of historical scholarship, public relations narratives, and advertising, which successfully shaped public perception of the past.

As the McCormicks, their company, and the general public were confronted with conflicting histories of the reaper, the family and later their corporation utilized increasingly sophisticated means to promote its interpretation of the past and to silence dissent. These efforts began with historical-based advertising in the 1870s but moved on to public relations education in the 1910s. By the 1920s they implemented a plan to influence the budding historical profession. A variety of historical laborers were crucial to helping the McCormicks secure dominion over the past during this fifty-year period, including salesmen, inventors, advertisers, lawyers, clerks, librarians, and a host of trained academics. While only trained academics seem like "historians," these other professionals dabbled in historical research, analysis, production, and public education in an effort to demonstrate that they could help the McCormicks attain their objective and that their historical labor was in turn worthy of monetary rewards.

Trained academics were a part of the family's historical project as early as 1900; however, they were in direct competition with advertisers, public relations specialists, and lawyers for historical authority and remuneration until 1930. During this period academic historians held a tenuous and vulnerable position as laborers within an unestablished profession. In a competitive labor market, they were anxious to demonstrate the concrete value of their training and historical imaginations to claim greater monetary and cultural compensation. With their middle-class aspirations on the line, historians employed by the McCormicks were willing to promote and fortify the family's narrative of the past despite historical dissent. Their choices to do so were not as unethical as they might seem but were reinforced by the McCormicks' sustained historical presence in advertising and public relations. Utilizing a variety of mediums over decades, the company had indelibly marked public memory of the reaper. Historical propaganda on the company's and the family's behalf not only made the public receptive to academic sanctification of their past but also shaped academics' historical knowledge of the invention before they engaged the subject.

In pursuit of financial security and authority over the past, academic historians preserved and created a wide variety of lasting historical materials that solidified the heritage of McCormick's invention as history. The most important of these academics was Herbert Kellar. A university-trained historian, Herbert Kellar was employed by the family from 1915 to 1955, collecting a world-class archive on the history of agriculture, frontier America, and the farm-implement industry within the family's McCormick Agricultural Library. Including materials that shed light on a wide spectrum of agricultural and frontier topics, Kellar broadly promoted scholarly use of the library within numerous historical organizations to further spread the family's historical influence. With this collection assembled in 1928 the family commissioned William T. Hutchinson to write the two-volume authoritative biography of Cyrus H. McCormick, which proved McCormick invented the reaper in 1831 and quashed nonconforming narratives. Beyond fulfilling this direct purpose, however, the archive also became the foundation for a variety of other historical studies that prominently placed McCormick, his family, and his company and its successors in history books—ensuring that his contributions would never be forgotten.[8]

This book is not the first study to consider the process of mythmaking around the topic of an agricultural invention. Angela Lakwete's *Inventing the Cotton Gin* similarly identifies the cultural origins of the false "fact" that northerner Eli Whitney invented the machine that led to the expansion of slavery across the antebellum South. While Lakwete focuses on the technologically complex and deep history of the gin's development outside of the myth, however, *Harvesting History* sets technology aside to peel back the layers of how a myth is conscientiously popularized and transformed to meet changing cultural needs and challenges. In common both myths illustrate the American fascination with seeing history and invention as the simple outcome of exceptional individuals rather than its substantially longer and more complex reality.

Harvesting History speaks to several overlapping historiographies of the Gilded Age and Progressive Era. The history of capitalism and corporations, the new rural history of the progressive movement and agribusiness, and the history of the historical profession are the key literatures that underpin this study. This book demonstrates that these histories are connected in previously unappreciated ways. It shows how some within the nascent historical profession actively participated in supporting the new and embattled corporate order. They utilized their training to craft a usable past that sanctioned one corporation's activities in exchange for sponsorship of scholarly aims and middle-class lives.

For the past fifty years, historians of capitalism and business have demonstrated how corporations were actively built by white-collar employees along a variety of organizational, economic, cultural, and political lines. Middle managers, office workers, lawyers, marketing specialists, and others created profitable bureaucratic structures for new international businesses through the rationalization of markets. These white-collar workers built the corporate order in exchange for the trappings of middle-class life. Along parallel lines to the bureaucratic revolution, corporate advertisers developed cultural and political tools that assuaged popular anxiety about the massive scale of new monopolistic businesses and the disruption of traditional forms of economic interaction. Marketers, public relations specialists, executives, and advertisers utilized image making through advertising, philanthropy, and corporate welfare programs to convince employees and the general public that their businesses were compatible with American values and operated as moral institutions in society.[9]

Harvesting History builds on this work to demonstrate academic historians' involvement in this public relations process as another subsection of the "collar-line" middle-class workforce. As the McCormick Company and later International Harvester sought cultural legitimacy, a handful of historians offered professional services to meet corporate needs, while securing financial support and legitimacy for their own scholarly endeavors. These academics became engaged in the project of creating an authoritative precorporate U.S. history that offered a teleological justification of the rising corporate order in line with American values. At a time when the historical professional was still forming, the McCormicks recognized the value of the historical authority these academics sought and invested heavily in them. The family philanthropically supported professionalization and institution building through financing scholarly journals, supporting historical organizations, and placing trained academics on their payroll. All these efforts served to strengthen their claims to the past and legitimize their corporations, while bolstering the emerging historical profession.

Scholars have generally not considered academic historians as a part of the corporate workforce. While corporate history along with corporate archives have been recognized since the 1930s, these avenues of historical work have been perceived as isolated from the academic pursuits and intellectual development of the profession as a whole. Most scholarship of the profession focuses on changes in historiography and institution building in academia, giving short shrift to the influences of wealth and sponsorship on scholarly direction.[10]

Since the 1990s historians of public history have begun to reconnect the evolution of historical thought with professionalization efforts and institution building beyond the halls of academia. They have argued that "prairie historians" at midwestern universities and state historical societies became empowered by Frederick Jackson Turner's frontier thesis, which made the Midwest the center of U.S. history, democracy, and historical inquiry. They were inspired to preserve the history of the American interior, as well as to focus historical societies on improving civic life through "applying history" to government policy making and public education. These histories place the emergence of public history in government institutions in the early twentieth century.[11]

Harvesting History recovers another portion of these prairie historians' larger encompassing vision, demonstrating that the expansive outlook of this cohort had roots in using historical knowledge in the corporate world along with other relevant institutions. Within patron relationships prairie historians exercised a measure of agency to pursue their own goals. Early historical professionals that touted the "new history" and midwestern history accommodated corporate needs, like those of International Harvester, because they emphasized the importance of the midwestern experience to national identity and U.S. history. The history that the McCormicks wanted scholars to write seemed to be universally supported by the material realities of agrarian life that midwestern historians were most interested in chronicling. Historians were receptive to messages about the importance of progress and technology to modern life, because they had embraced careers within the new world of professionalization that ran parallel to the corporate order.[12]

Harvesting History also places historians within the context of the rural Progressive Era and the cultural conflict surrounding agricultural modernization. Historians working for the McCormick family and their businesses were participating in the larger agricultural complex of agribusiness, government agencies, and universities. They worked with these allies to convince reluctant farmers to abandon traditional agricultural practices and adopt modern farming as part of the natural logic of progress. Academic historians assisted the agricultural complex in promoting new forms of consumption and production by proselytizing a very particular vision of U.S. history as technological progress.[13]

The historical efforts of the McCormick family and their evolving corporate empire shed light on these overlapping histories in a unique manner that unites these three historiographies. McCormick Harvester was at the center of increasing the scale of American business, and its participation in industrial consolidation by creating International Harvester occurred at the height of the turn-of-the-century merger movement. During this moment the McCormicks were embattled on all sides: from their competitors, their customers, and the federal government. They repeatedly referenced their long history as evidence of their just moral standing in industry and made this past the cornerstone of their brand. As their version of history was contested, they invested in the emerging historical profession to bolster their brand against producer populism, broader antimonopoly sentiments, and antitrust prosecution. When midwestern historians rose to prominence during the high-water years of the frontier thesis, the McCormicks seized on the opportunity to inject their heritage of mechanical innovation into the frontier narrative of democratic civilization. For their part midwestern historians obligingly received support in their quest to free U.S. history from the East Coast. All these connections suggest historians' involvement in the creation of corporate cultural authority in rural America that have been previously overlooked.

As a cultural history, *Harvesting History* studies the abundant artifacts of people involved in producing a particular past of the reaper's origins and curating its larger meaning in American life. With a focus on preserved papers of the McCormick family and their corporation and the various historians they interacted with, it is possible to unpack the personal, social, economic, and professional anxieties wrapped up in the question of the reaper's provenance. Moreover, these collections of tightly manicured advertising, public relations, and scholarly materials offer a window for glimpsing the shifting and multifaceted meaning of the reaper's history, which was widely distributed to public audiences.

In considering these artifacts this book studies the gendered and racial discourse of civilization within them to understand why history was so important to the McCormicks and the reaper industry more generally. The cultural discourse and materials of civilization were utilized as demonstrations of cultural order by wealthy elites to shore up their cultural authority, legitimize new forms of business, discipline workers, and sell goods throughout the Gilded Age and Progressive Era. The language of manly progress and civilization was pervasive in McCormick representations of Cyrus McCormick. The family believed and promulgated that his invention made him a hero of progress and civilization, justifying its later authority in the harvester industry. The discourse of civilization offers a lens for understanding the McCormicks' investment in history and advertising, as well as the historical profession, as they authoritatively defended their past as a cornerstone of their company's brand.[14]

Additionally, this study makes use of two methodological avenues of analysis found in the historical scholarship of advertising. Historians of advertising have demonstrated how the material culture of advertising was arranged to guide consumer decisions and garnish consumer desire. They suggest that advertisements presented a "distorted mirror" of reality, which prioritized the values of the creators through images and arrangement that cultivated consumer demand. Beyond material culture analysis, they also analyze the labor and culture of advertisers and artists to capture their perspectives as middle-class workers, ambivalently creating the tools of mass culture.[15]

Emulating these approaches, *Harvesting History* considers historians not only as academics but as laborers and culture brokers. Similar to advertisers' "distorted mirror" of society, historians participated in distorting the past to make it usable for contemporary needs. The demands of the McCormick family and its company on the nascent historical profession reveal that the family perceived their heritage as the essence of their company's brand and a consistent and malleable defense against evolving criticisms. Simultaneously, academic historians and other historical laborers were in vulnerable positions as workers seeking to demonstrate the value of their expertise and historical authority to their employer in exchange for financial security. In such a context academic historians assisted the McCormicks in forging a usable past built on flexible family lore rather than rigorous objective study of historical evidence.

While the McCormicks eventually endorsed trained historians as authorities over the past by 1930, academic historians throughout the period of study were always working within a wider spectrum of historical laborers. The family and its corporation utilized a variety of agents and mediums to sanction its version of the past. These efforts began with journalists, advertisers, and world's fair judges but evolved to include lawyers, librarians, lobbyists, and mercenary historical biographers. The escalation of historical effort was brought about by direct contests for the past. Interestingly, the narrowing of the historical profession to an academic core paralleled the narrowing of the reaper industry into the single harvester trust.

Further borrowing from the history of advertising, *Harvesting History* analyzes the influence of cultural productions through considering readership among cultural producers. Academic historians make a concerted effort to reference every piece of evidence that informs their work. This makes tracking the genealogy of historians' concepts, evidence, and specific turns of phrase uniquely possible, revealing the spread and change of historical ideas over time. When applied to the McCormicks' history-making endeavors, changes in the narrative—including details, evidence, and points of emphasis—can all be charted and analyzed in light of particular historical contexts and challenges. In the end these shifts and changes in the official story allow us to catch a glimpse of why history mattered so much during the Gilded Age and Progressive Era and to understand how the McCormicks' private heritage became accepted historical fact.

At best, writing history has always been an educated approximation of the past. Archival resources are far too uneven, mentalities of historical actors are too multifaceted, and writing is too linear to perfectly capture the complex and infinite entirety of past experience. Historians, faced with such a daunting task, make crucial decisions about what to study based on personal beliefs, contemporary needs, and available material. The corpus of the profession's choices and labor impart "legitimate" knowledge about the past for public consumption. Importantly, the groundwork for the historical canon of key events, dates, and people was laid by historians in the early twentieth century, who strove to make studies "objective" but did not consider the subjectivity of their own positions within modern society. Informed by anxieties about financial security, professional status, and a Progressive Era worldview, early academic historians were open to elite support and wrote histories that reinforced the status quo. *Harvesting History* is the story of how one family worked hand in hand with a variety of historians to make one such "fact" a part of the historical canon. It is a reminder that scholarship is never isolated and pristine in an ivory tower but, like all cultural productions, influenced and molded by the society around it.

1

Every Salesman, a Historian

The morning of July 25, 1877, Samuel Peterson and George Brewster stood beside a ripe field of golden winter wheat in Brown County, Minnesota, near New Ulm. They looked on while their expert mechanic, Mr. Johnson, tuned up a McCormick Automatic Wire Binder and Harvester. All three were employees of the Chicago reaper manufacturer, C. H. and L. J. McCormick. Johnson had been "starting" McCormick binders all summer, beginning in Texas and following the ripening of grain northward. Nearby, a crowd of local farmers was forming, curious to witness the mechanized cutting and binding machine that they had heard so much about. For his part Peterson anxiously awaited the success of the machine he had so vigorously sold but that he had never actually seen work.[1]

Most of these farmers were aware of wire binders and their hand-binding predecessors operating in fields outside of Brown County during previous harvests. The Walter A. Wood Mowing and Reaping Machine Company had introduced wire binders into the Minnesota Valley three years before, and similar machines were being sold by numerous other firms such as Deering, Osborne, and Champion throughout the state and the upper Midwest. For three years McCormick lagged behind without access to a patent or its own version of the wire-binding mechanism—selling a machine that still required binding to be done by hand.

Despite the availability of technology and access to markets, McCormick's competitors could not sink roots in Brown County. The county seemed perfect for mechanized harvesters and small-grain agriculture because of its rich soil, temperate climate, abundance of water, and removal of the Dakota people in 1863. Its location along the Minnesota River and the arrival of the Winona and Saint Peter Railroad in 1872 also allowed cheap access to the national grain market. Moreover, most of these farmers were in good financial standing and owned their farmsteads. But these factors and the appearance of automatic binders nearby were not enough to convince Brown County farmers to become masters of machines.[2]

Peterson had been successful in drumming up interest among these farmers where others had failed because he spoke German and Norwegian. Most of the county was inhabited by first- and second-generation immigrants from northern Europe and Scandinavia. These people had risked migration for the rewards of the prairie's fertility in hopes of supporting their families and ethnic communities for generations to come. Unlike their Yankee counterparts, they did not necessarily perceive of the land as a strictly profit-oriented venture. These were people that Peterson knew and shared much in common with as a first-generation immigrant himself—having made the voyage from Norway at the age of three and grown up in transplanted communities.[3]

The crowd that July morning in 1877 was composed of Germans whom Peterson had canvassed repeatedly over the preceding months. Making numerous house calls every day with a grip full of sales literature, he read through McCormick catalogs and *Farmers' Advance* newspapers with them in German. He told these farmers about Cyrus McCormick's association with the origins of the implement and the establishment of the mammoth reaper works in Chicago in 1848 and its ballooning production since then, as well as the perfect evolution of harvesting machinery over time that resulted in that day's modern automatic binder. Peterson recounted McCormick's "world beating" victories at international expositions, fairs, and countless field trials over the course of the preceding generation as proof of his employer's competitive and lasting quality. He traveled the roads of Brown County with a harvester affixed to his wagon, explaining the intricacies of the machine and its economic value as farmers were invited to see and to touch for themselves. Connecting the machine in front of them with history, Peterson explained how the machine's progress was directly involved with the creation of American civilization, allowing farmers to enjoy better lives as masters of machines rather than mere toilers in the soil.[4]

Peterson was not particularly unique in his storytelling, only in his lingual ability. Hundreds of McCormick agents across the country utilized the same practices and stories, integrating their machines, employer, and customers into the active historical imaginations of nineteenth-century Americans. Compared to other salesmen, Peterson may have mixed in more references to family well-being to appeal to German communalism rather than Yankee notions of adventuresome independence. His sales pitch, however, was aimed at orienting farmers within a national story about the United States' past, present, and future, inviting these prospective customers to embrace new identities as risk-taking Americans who reaped profits while paving the way to the future. He presented Brown County Germans with the opportunity to join in the march of progress through buying a harvester or to face the certainty of being left behind without the tools of modernity.

Harvester salesmen needed to animate their product with cultural meaning to solicit sales. The contraption's bizarre mechanical aesthetic did not offer an uninitiated bystander any hints of inherent value or economic potential. The machine's mere presence and availability did not generate a farmer's desire to own it. The salesman cultivated customers' desire, exciting a change in their imagination and cultural identities by not only offering mechanization but also expounding on what ownership of such a machine would mean for themselves as members of progressive civilization. In this regard they created demand for their goods through popularizing self-serving, celebratory memories of mechanization as national history and inserting customers into that narrative as relevant historical actors in the present. They preached to the masses as both salesmen and de facto public historians.

Peterson drew a crowd of farmers to the field that morning because he was able to connect the importance of owning harvesting machinery to a sense of their personal identities as Americans in words they could understand. His multilingual ability and salesmanship were in fact his only good qualities as a salesman. His boss, George Brewster, found him to be utterly incompetent in matters of bookkeeping, asset management, final settlement, logistics, and order preparation. Brewster needed to constantly double-check Peterson's work to prevent damage to the company's reputation and finances. Despite this, Peterson successfully "bulldozed" a higher commission rate than any other subagent in Minnesota. Through his effective salesmanship he had "taken ahold" of the Germans and the Scandinavians in Brown County, and Brewster knew that McCormick could not stand up to Peterson there if he became employed by "the opposition."[5]

After conferring with Johnson and confirming that the machine was ready, Peterson approached his customer in the crowd. Exchanging pleasantries, Peterson reaffirmed the agreement—if the machine worked after a fair trial in the field, they would settle for $297 cash. Grandstanding a bit more to the modest crowd about the merits of the machine and its value to civilization, Peterson instructed Johnson to start the binder. As Johnson urged his team of horses to "come-up," the harvester clattered to life: the sickle blade clipping back and forth, the reel pushing wheat to the blade, the apron and elevator collecting the cut, and the wire binder snapping the wheat into perfect sheaths before dropping them softly on the ground. Peterson breathed a sigh of relief. He invited the crowd to follow along and witness the reaper's progress through the field, while he and Brewster began shocking the bundles. They marched alongside the machine all morning and into the afternoon, cutting and binding an acre an hour. Eventually the new owner tried his hand at driving the machine and, fully satisfied, settled with Peterson for cash. Brewster reported back to Chicago that the morning's trial was going to be good for fifty binder sales in cash with those Germans the following year.[6]

Samuel Peterson, like salesmen and businesses throughout the country, utilized flexible interpretations of history as a means to "take ahold" of customers and sell machines. As the nation rapidly changed during the late nineteenth century—increasingly interconnected, with growing businesses, larger cities, more immigrants, changing ideas and laws regarding citizenship, more dynamic and accessible markets, and new and frightening technologies—notions of progress and history were tethered to products by salesmen and advertisers hawking their wares. They used a sense of the past, present, and future as a means to offer customers the possibility of purchasing stability, fulfillment, and prestige through their products in an age of increasingly rapid change. In this regard in 1877 Samuel Peterson and McCormick Harvester more generally were no different than their competitors or any other businesses during the era. A few short years later, however, in 1879, McCormick Harvesting Machine Company would go further, creating an aggressive narrative brand that claimed mythical historical dominion over the entire harvesting-machine industry as a means of setting itself apart from its competitors.

When Samuel Peterson and other harvester salesmen invoked history to "take ahold" of customers and sell machines, they tapped into the American infatuation with progress and history. As Americans looked backward from the years following the national centennial of 1876, they were consumed by a self-congratulatory sense of U.S. achievement and divine destiny. Since the nation's founding, the democratic experiment had flourished (at least for white men) unbound from the strictures, hierarchy, and deference of Europe. In the new United States' society of equals, white men participated in politics and pursued their own fortunes—creating economic abundance, inventing new machines that "annihilated space and time," and "taming" a continent, while pursuing their supposed "Manifest Destiny." While there had been the uncertain years of bloodletting during the Civil War, in retrospect God's providence had seen them through and ensured that the democracy belonged to freemen rather than slaveholders and would not perish from the earth. In the Gilded Age decades of industrialization, geographic expansion, and technological innovation following the fiery trial, Americans celebrated new material abundance pell-mell as the physical embodiment of national progress and destiny. In such a context salesmen of all sorts, and reaper men in particular, did their best to tether their products to progress.[7]

Americans' triumphant sense of progress was built on fused secular notions of Protestant millennialism and social Darwinism. According to long-standing Protestant tradition, God shaped human history as a struggle between good and evil that overtime would result in evil being vanquished from the world through Christian purity and effort. This eventual victory would bring about the Christian millennium—the second coming of Christ and a thousand years of peace on earth. During the late nineteenth century, Americans secularly blended this Protestant millennialism with popular readings of Darwinism, which held that human history was the story of evolution and random conflicts in which the fittest survived. From this new perspective, evolution and "survival of the fittest" through competition became the key mechanism by which God was perfecting civilization toward an inevitable material and spiritual millennium.[8]

In this cultural concoction the course of human history was not random chance but rather God's cosmic plan of progress that included civilizations, nations, and individuals. Successes and failures became divine evidence of forthright and manly character: piety, bravery, honesty, frugality, and industry at all levels. Material outcomes thus reflected someone's morality as well as the divine Watchmaker's design. In some sense bourgeois Americans celebrated history, because when they looked back they recognized God's hand in shaping the present and looked forward to the continued blessing of progress in the future. Victorian Americans not only applied this cultural worldview to themselves to celebrate how far they had come but also used it to assess racialized and gendered "others." In such a mindset those who possessed the latest tools of mechanical invention—the newest sewing machine, harvester, or electric dynamo engine—were the most progressive, godly, and civilized, while those who trailed behind or failed in competition were deemed lesser on the spectrum of progress, potentially more savage than civilized. Progress served as a grandiose justification for the Victorian white, male-dominated status quo but also created anxiety about the present and the future for that same significant minority. If they had been blessed as the vanguard of progress through Darwinist survival to the present, it was possible that they could falter and savagely fall behind the cutting-edge in the future.[9]

Crucially, while the march of civilization proceeded as a seemingly unstoppable heavenly force, the majority of Americans witnessed providential progress by *visually* interpreting *physical material*. In an era of rapid industrialization and expansion, progress was *self-evident* and obvious to the naked eye. Progress could be seen in the faster and stronger railroads and steamships that annihilated space and time, replacing the slower carriages and sloops. Hand-delivered mail had been superseded by electricity, carrying news at the speed of light on telegraph lines. The wizardry of Thomas Edison had further mastered the forces of electricity to vanquish darkness with monofilament lightbulbs and dynamos that magically transformed coal into the mysterious substance of current. Belching smoke, industrial factories, and new machines efficiently replaced skilled workshop artisans, spreading consumer plenty far and wide. Americans could see the nation's progress westward and the "civilizing" of the frontier as "savage" wilderness gave way to farms, towns, and cities. In these ways and more, people believed they could *see* the material progress of their world in new technologies, expansion, and abundance, recognizing its clear superiority to what had come before.[10]

Throughout the United States businesses and their salesmen seized on the cultural significance of progress and its visual nature to sell their wares in a fiercely competitive national marketplace. Peddlers and agents compared their merchandise favorably to ancient predecessors as well as their competitive peers, ubiquitously claiming that their goods were on the leading edge of progress. They roused anxiety in potential customers as well, inviting them to stay in lockstep with the march of civilization by buying their "new," "improved," "progressive," and "advanced" product. Failure to buy progress was to risk savage marginalization by falling out of step with their civilized neighbors and the deific drumbeat.[11]

In the hands of the huckster, subjective ideas of progress were easily manipulated through a cultural mass alchemy—in which they transformed saleable goods and technologies into gold standards of civilization by utilizing a matrix of physical comparisons to rivals and "others." Gilded Age advertisers and salesmen compared technological innovations, industrial machinery, factory sizes, market shares, efficiency, and territorial expansion, among others like aesthetic refinement and cleanliness, as "merits" of civilization and indications of progress. The mass alchemy functioned because progress did not require a specialist or intellectual to chart. Progress was deemed visually and physically *apparent* to the average American, and the salesmen simply endeavored to direct a customer's attention to the relevant points of comparison to transform ordinary wares into cultural gold. Not solely practiced by the commercially minded, the mass alchemy of progress was performed by Victorian Americans for all manner of purposes as they were eager to see themselves in the marvelous vanguard of progress by measuring themselves favorably against racialized "others" as well as their more or less "civilized" peers.

While the alchemy of progress (and indeed the entire discourse of civilization) hinged on making evidence of physical materials, the comparative pseudoscience was intuitively animated by a haphazard *sense* of the past. Nebulous memories of mythical moments, technology, and expansion as well as military and commercial competition enabled bourgeois Americans to see material progress in the present and understand the divine teleological thrust of civilization toward perfection. From this perspective historical particulars of the development of steam power, for example, were not as important as modern outcomes and the hitherto unknown marvelous abundance conveyed by railroads, steamboats, and factories. Plain for all to see, steam was superior to waterpower or horsepower, and Americans were elated to have surpassed the technological constraints of their forebears. In the same way a western town could celebrate the twenty-fifth anniversary of its founding, because it had come so far from its pioneering origins in the wilderness. Likewise, a Singer sewing-machine salesmen could easily compare the efficient economy of mechanized stitching to the hand-sewing drudgery of the past. A sense of the relatively recent or obvious material past made notions of progress function.

Bates Harrington's 1879 book on rural salesmanship, *How 'Tis Done*, provides a clear example of historically minded rhetoric and the alchemy of progress at work in the hands of the traveling salesmen. Intended to help the savvy reader detect silver-tongued confidence men hocking useless wares across rural America, Harrington's book is as much an exposé as it is a how-to manual on the art of peddling. Covering products as varied as lightning rods, legal protection of patent rights, fruit trees, and jewelry, the book explains step-by-step how wandering canvassers appealed to "public vanity," a "vision of wealth," and personal "fear" to provoke desire and close sales.[12]

Harrington's first chapter, on rural subscription-book agents selling county histories and atlases, best demonstrates the huckster methodology of progressive comparison and invocation of the historyesque. Working for urban publishing houses, subscription-book salesmen canvassed rural Americans during the late nineteenth century. Selling advance subscriptions for county and state histories and atlases, peddlers invited customers to pay for the prestige of "see[ing] ones names in print"; putting their homes on the map; placing their lives within local, state, and national history; and comparing themselves favorably with their neighbors. While sales rhetoric was seemingly high-minded, these books merely featured local maps, illustrations, and formulaic biographies literally within the same binding as antiquarian chronicles of local history as well as unchanging presidential biographies and national narratives. The paginated proximity to celebrated patriotic achievement bestowed shades of that national glory on the local subscriber.[13]

The canvasser's sales pitch demonstrates the alchemy of progress in practice. To every potential customer, canvassers noted the need for good "white men" who were "intelligent and public-spirited" to subscribe to make the project viable. They frequently mentioned the threat of uncivilized "foreign elements" (the "Irish" and "Bohemians") throughout the county who would not support the endeavor and "thereby deprive the county of the greatest blessing that has ever been proposed in that region." These commercial travelers assured potential customers that subscribing to such a work was necessary for "men of education or knowledge . . . to keep up with the progress of the times." Furthermore, the invaluable knowledge within the book would place the owner on "equal footing with the early pioneer, who has made the settlement, progress and development of the county his life study." Canvassers transformed the publication into a talisman of progress, promising prestige for the county and boosting the owner's local stature equal to being a pioneer blazing the first trail into the wilderness. The pitch boiled down to loaded cultural comparisons between the customer and his "pioneer" neighbors, "whites" and the "foreign elements," and ignorance compared to "knowledge."[14]

Further playing on anxiety they had created through the alchemy of progress, canvassers pushed customers to pay additional money to have their personal biographies and pictures of themselves or their homes included in the books. Salesmen casually recalled that settlers of the East had failed to record their histories and had been forgotten. These men with the "gift of gab" related to farmers the importance of their new geography and noted that the story of the West must be preserved for posterity. In the West settlers had embraced the "general scheme of advancement," with specific reference to frontier improvement, increased scale of farming, modern technology, and social and civic institutions. Subscribers did not deserve to be forgotten, because their lives were too important to the greatness of the nation. They explained that the book would ensure that premium subscribers would be remembered "for years to come" and that the histories and atlases would be "cherished" by their children as well as "handed down through future generations." Functioning as historians, canvassers sold these products through orienting customers within a historical narrative of the past and present, further implying its critical value to the course of their future—as people worthy of being remembered but who might be forgotten.[15]

The result of such efforts met with great success and profit as local and county histories were ubiquitously published from the 1870s through the 1910s. As historian of American biography Scott Casper stated, these histories were "permanent evidence of their [local and individual] achievements in cultivating the land and establishing social institutions in formerly frontier places." County histories did include narratives of county, town, and township history, but these emphasized white "firsts" and accomplishments in physical terms of people, settlements, institutions, and business. In a fashion typical of the genre, the 1881 *History of Dakota County* in Minnesota rattled off a fantastic list of "firsts" associated with Fort Snelling that made the location significant: "[Fort Snelling] is now the historic landmark for the state and north-west. Here was the first settlement, the first birth, first marriage and first death. Here was organized the first church, here was the first farming, first milling and first enterprise of every kind. Around Fort Snelling cluster all the early associations of the state." Offering an emblematic sense of antiquarian history deemed significant in Gilded Age minds, Fort Snelling's firsts for white settlers were points of origin for the physical progress that was to come. This was the content that was deemed historic.[16]

Such local histories were surrounded by oceans of formulaic biographical repetition, recounting the brief self-made stories of the migration, settlement, struggle, and success of paying subscribers. The most substantial portions of these abbreviated historical profiles were subscribers' contemporary institutional affiliations with politics, churches, or municipalities and the size of their family and farm or business. What mattered about history was not the past but the outcome in the present. This was the same history of improving wilderness through civilized progress that was celebrated nationally, writ small. The physical essence of progress and history was internalized and preserved by individuals across the country, encouraged not only by their cultural milieu but also by the progressive discourse and historical alchemia of salesmen.[17]

In the late nineteenth-century decades of seemingly limitless innovation and material abundance, Americans "celebrated the past" as a means of "praising the present," as memory scholar Michael Kammen has pointed out. Thanks to the seemingly self-evident material nature of progress and history, as well as an unfounded democratic self-confidence in personal intellect, anyone could be a historian, including farmers or salesmen. While the "scientific" and "objective" study of history was beginning to percolate in academe during the late nineteenth century (with only twenty-four academically employed historians in the country by 1886), the public's history outside was boiling over, unrestrained by authority and uncritical of "historic truths."[18]

In such chaotic historical anarchy, the narratives that gained the most traction in the United States were those championed by regional and national businesses utilizing the alchemy of progress as a basis for claiming significance. Samuel Peterson and the rest of McCormick's canvassing sales force were not alone in their profit-motivated invocation of history. Salesmen, entrepreneurs, advertisers, and peddlers from all manner and size of businesses utilized the alchemy of progress to make history pervasive in the public mind as their primary tool for generating desire and anxiety within potential customers. These salesmen created a national market for their goods in some measure through popularizing narratives of the past and teaching Americans to perceive themselves through selective schemes of national memory.[19]

During the second half of the nineteenth century, the harvester industry grew exponentially, from producing and selling several hundred machines in the mid-1840s to hundreds of thousands of machines by the 1890s. As early as the 1850s, companies developed regional sales networks, which gradually came to include thousands of canvassers across the country to generate demand for their new and expensive machinery. These sales agents and their parent companies made history and the alchemy of progress a central part of their marketing strategy, actively inserting themselves, their machines, and their customers into the history of civilization. By and large, rival products evolved together at about the same pace during this era. New models and improvements were quickly duplicated throughout the industry, limiting technological advantages as well as making marketing and advertising very important to economic success. Cyrus Hall McCormick's various firms and partners did not necessarily create this marketing strategy, but his longevity in the field and his businesses' extant records provide the best evidence of the strategy's execution.

During the mid-1870s C. H. and L. J. McCormick published sales literature in the form of circulars, bulletins, and a house quarterly newspaper—*Farmers' Advance*—as well as annual catalogs. These were the all-important tools that filled the salesman's grip. This printed matter detailed the core of McCormick's claim to supremacy by laying out a narrative that tallied the firm's abundant progressive merits for potential customers. The annual catalogs were the longest and most thorough material. They provided the nucleus of the company's marketing narrative, offering a vantage point to observe the firm's changing use of history as an asset. The main text of the McCormick sales catalogs was formatted the same way from year to year. Every catalog included four basic elements: an annual letter from management to the customer, a list of noteworthy awards and premiums, descriptions of the machinery detailing the newest advancements, and testimonials from satisfied customers. As printing technology became cheaper, the catalogs gradually became longer and included more color chromolithograph illustrations, but their essence remained the same.[20]

The first annual catalog was published in 1859 and incorporated all four elements. The catalog evolved from single-page bulletins, phrased as letters from the manufacturer that incorporated tidbits of these same features in tiny font, along with an order form at the bottom of the page. The first catalog included only one print illustration of a reaper on its cover and sixteen pages of print. Ghostwritten for Cyrus H. McCormick by his brother and business partner, William, the heart of the 1859 catalog was an eight-page "letter" detailing the virtues of the machine. This letter made a mixed variety of claims to the progress of civilization and a detailed comparison of the McCormick Company and machine with the competition.[21]

The firm's first attempt at a long-form sales pamphlet was a response to other manufacturers' catalogs, which, William wrote, were "whole books" of "humbuggery and misrepresentations." The McCormick catalog was set on providing the "facts" and protecting farmers from being "misled" by the "gross fabrications" of others. William McCormick effectively compared his company to other firms utilizing the alchemy of progress as the standard of measure, finding McCormick "superior" in every instance. While somewhat clumsy, the 1859 McCormick catalog set out a format that was subsequently followed for the rest of the century.[22]

The greatest portion of McCormick's letter to the farmers in the 1859 catalog focused on clarifying McCormick's record in international trials. The catalog listed McCormick's achievements at world's fairs and other prominent international competitions as concrete evidence of progressive superiority, beginning with the Grand Council Medal at the London Crystal Palace in 1851 and continuing on to prizes from the Great French Exhibition in 1855 in Paris; the 1856 French Universal Exhibition; the Royal Agriculture Society of England in 1857; and, finally, the U.S. National Agricultural Society in 1857, which awarded a "Gold Medal and Diploma." The list was a correction of their opposition's catalogs. These competitors, unworthy of "public confidence," besmirched McCormick's record to "excite prejudice against my machine," while claiming false victories for themselves in all these prestigious settings. In a choppy style William then included two pages of fully cited newspaper quotations and testimonials from prominent citizens, politicians, and military officials supporting McCormick's claims to the "truth" as proven by his list of awards. In total this evidence was intended to convey that McCormick's reaper was "widely known throughout the civilized world," "a triumph of inventive genius," and "indispensable" to farmers.[23]

Correcting history was important to C. H. McCormick and Brothers because international trials and world's fairs were perceived as the highest venue of competition in the civilized world. These competitions, judged by international dignitaries, provided prolonged and closely monitored demonstrations in all manner of field conditions. Winners carried the torch of progress onward, while losers "died out." Spreading false results undermined the divine sanctification and "public confidence" that the "true" winner had justly earned. Company management regarded their machine's historical record of success in these events as the firm's highest endorsement.[24]

Beyond the trials William McCormick laid out more "facts" of "intrinsic merit" regarding reapers more generally in terms of material, geographic, and nebulously historical progress. Through prattling prose the author labored through a comparison of the reaper to the railroad and the threshing machine, emphasizing the technological progress that had replaced "the flail," "the cradle," and "the stage" to benefit "the wages of *harvest* hands." McCormick coupled material progress with geographic progress, emphasizing that older tools "had been almost wholly abandoned in the Western States." While such sweeping statements were hyperbole, McCormick's objective was to inspire farmers' comparative sense of progress in material terms, hoping to generate anxiety and sales from farmers that feared being left behind.[25]

William's catalog also outlined a history of the firm's manufacturing. The company's association with the "*very origin* of the Reaper" was mentioned, but more important was its business in the West and the establishment of their "extensive and superior" factory in Chicago in 1848. From this moment the factory had increased its production and sale of reapers year by year from 1848 to 1858. Like rural subscription histories, what mattered about McCormick's industrial past was the material outcome in the present. Great emphasis was placed on the sheer volume of raw materials "purchased in cash" for 1859, including weights and volumes of wrought iron, pig iron, cast steel, white and lead colors, lumber, chain, sheet zinc, tin and copper, oil and turpentine, lumber, coal and nails. Such materials would allow the factory to employ three hundred men to build five thousand machines later that year and was presented as "positive evidence of its [McCormick's] superiority," as if industry of scale denoted quality of product.[26]

The ad copy also indicated that the increased sales of machines, which mirrored the increased production of the reaper works, was proof of the farming public's approval. Customer demand was "constantly increasing," because it recognized the "benefit of my more than 20 years experience" and ignored the "*desperate efforts* of rival manufacturers." Such demand required the machine to be "shipped in all directions," because farmers recognized "the perfect simplicity, great strength and durability" that allowed them to use the machine "with as little risk as the plow." Encouraging customers to trust in their own mechanical competence, William reassured them that McCormick machines could be operated with "no attention at all" from agents.[27]

The catalog also included eight pages of testimonials and two pages of mechanical descriptions of the actual machines. The testimonials came from farmers across the country and supported the claim that the machine was simple, durable, and superior to competitors, while successfully functioning in a variety of conditions and cutting large acreages. Aimed at generating desire, the testimonials suggested that machine farmers were more progressive because they raised larger crops, had larger farms, and made more money. For its part the mechanical description detailed the improvements in the machines' design in fairly bland terms.[28]

Within the alchemy of progress, the scale of manufacturing, longevity of operation, and success in competition were easy points of comparison to score against competitors. Bigger was always better, and factories were monuments to progress and civilization. Victory in international trials was further proof of superiority. Historical longevity, however, was the ultimate indication of progress, because a firm's survival and growth over time indicated that it had flourished in the continual competition of the marketplace—where the customer was the judge. On the same scale farmers who embraced the most progressive machines were also rewarded with material success.

Catalogs throughout the harvester industry during the 1860s and 1870s embraced similar thematic features in the same basic format but became more concise over time. The bland mechanical descriptions became more narrative, touching on public popularity and trial victories rather than on technical details like the circumference of the drive wheel and the shape of the sickle blade. The section on international competition was reduced to a confident list of awards and locations rather than a thoroughly documented discussion of historical arguments. Descriptions of the factory became more intensive and included the dimensions of each workshop facility, proximity to rail lines, and inventories of manufacturing machinery as well as materials. As the lithography became cheaper, "bird's eye" illustrations of factory works adorned every catalog. Testimonials remained a mainstay, and there was increasing emphasis placed on the geographic extent of sales, especially internationally. Marketing strategies across the harvester industry evolved dialectically, and catalogs throughout the business were reminiscent of one another in terms of general content.[29]

McCormick literature became more selective in its invocation of history, as well as more forceful in its assertions about the meaning of the past. For instance, the 1861 catalog read, "The McCormick is the oldest Machine in existence, having any claim to *merit*, being the *first* practical development of power as applied to harvesting. Year by year, from infancy to the present manhood's prime it has grown in favor, till there is scarce a spot beneath the sun where its triumphs are not known." William dropped the esoteric details of industry debates and explicitly stated what their record meant. Oddly, despite claiming to have the "oldest Machine," the literature did not assert 1831 as the moment of invention. With the Civil War looming, the company instead emphasized its more recent "FOURTEEN YEARS in the city of Chicago" rather than its roots on an Old Dominion plantation. Cyrus McCormick had incurred popular wrath as a known Southern-sympathizing Peace Democrat. While he did not apologize for his views, his company's sale literature underlined the manufactory's connection to the progress of farmers in the Northwest rather than the South. This relationship would only be further stressed in the wake of the 1871 Chicago fire. McCormick advertising bulletins noted that the city and its works rose "from the ashes" because of the "teeming millions produced by the farmers of the vast Northwest," to which the firm had contributed through the "invention, as well as the manufacture of the Reaper."[30]

Significantly, the 1859 catalog was addressed to both farmers *and* salesmen. The catalog was intended to educate both groups about the merits of the company and the machines as well as the supposedly libelous claims of their competitors. Likely most farmers did not bother reading the long self-righteous treatise or the historical evidence; however, such information was useful ammunition in the hands of reaper agents as they sought to persuade customers and traded insults with their opponents. The annual catalog was the company's most important means for distributing information about itself and its products to its own employees, who in turn shared the material with customers by word of mouth in their sales pitches.[31]

Annual catalogs reached the customer only through direct interaction with traveling salesmen. Canvassers, like Samuel Peterson in

New Ulm, were employed seasonally on commission from the spring through the harvest and frequently changed employers from year to year. The best canvassers in the harvester trade were particularly well versed on the merits of all makes of machines, because rival companies vied for their labor. Every winter these salesmen wanted to see what tools the manufacturer would provide them and "call[ed] loudly for Reading matter." They made their choice of employer based on their commission rates but also on the quality of printed material available and the established reputation of the manufacturer. A better reputation and higher-quality advertising material enabled agents to close more customers and maintain higher prices. In direct competition for sales with rival firms, canvassers would rely on the manufacturer's published materials for important points of progressive comparison: including a firm's scale of manufacturing, its record in international trials, and its larger history of production and expansion.[32]

Canvassers from across the industry utilized similar methods to make their case and excite customer interest. As William J. Hanna, a sales manager at McCormick's Chicago office, explained to a recruit, being a subagent meant "active out door work, travelling and canvassing from house to house" rather than simply "staying in town and advertising!" Circular letters from Chicago to McCormick salesmen across the country regularly encouraged subagents to visit farmers "again and again" as the "only way to make numerous sales." The office managers believed that the "strong assertions" of "superiority" made by agents and advertising would be sustained by their machines and that the extensive canvassing effort would "show its results at harvest."[33]

Following instructions, McCormick canvassers drove homestead to homestead on horse-drawn wagons with bags full of sales literature, lugging a sample harvesting machine in the wagon bed. They delivered "into farmers hands" a wealth of printed matter. Making numerous trips, they always presented the farmer with something new—whether it was the annual catalog, the *Farmers' Advance*, or a shorter localized bulletin detailing the victory of the McCormick machine over another manufacturer's inferior contraption in a field trial. The Chicago office spared no effort in ensuring that their canvassers had ample material to share. The *Farmers' Advance* was published four times during the growing season. They also distributed national newspaper articles every summer, reporting their victories in major fairs and competitions. The firm was printing and distributing eight hundred thousand catalogs annually by the 1880s and exponentially more copies of the *Advance* and other ephemera, including colorful trade cards and eventually large chromolithograph posters. Furthermore, they encouraged their agents to carry the advertising material of their competitors, allowing them to make side-by-side comparisons between the McCormick machines and their rivals. All this material assisted the subagent in the important task of "getting before . . . [the farmer] the merits" of the McCormick machine.[34]

Sitting down in farmhouse parlors, McCormick's reaper men "sold" customers by making illustrative use of their literature. In these settings the canvasser was a storyteller alone. He could not demonstrate the operation of his machine until harvest. He could only invite farmers to see and touch a sample machine, and he could make promises, encouraging them to imagine what owning such a machine might mean for their lives. The agent might begin by asking about the farmer's family as well as how much land a farmer owned, how much was improved for planting, and what crops and livestock he raised, as well as the sort of tools he used. Such information provided important details for the yarn the agent was about to unfurl but was also valuable reconnaissance for assessing a farmer's creditworthiness. From there the agent would describe the great "prospects" for the coming year's wheat harvest. Every year the agent usually exclaimed, "We have seldom seen a season open better than the present." As he optimistically explained to prospective customers every spring, the winter had been favorable for a good growing season, and grain was fetching a high price in Chicago.[35]

The agent then pointed out that the farmer had the opportunity to take advantage of the ideal circumstances. The farmer simply needed to expand his acreage of wheat on the land that he already owned. Of course, the agent then emphasized how much time and labor it would take to cut that wheat using a cradle scythe (or an older harvesting machine, as the case may be) and binding the sheaths by hand. A man could cut and bind only an acre a day without the assistance of any machine at all, and a newer self-binding machine would free the farmer from the odious task of paying seasonal laborers to help at harvest. He was further limited by the short ten-day window when wheat was ripe for harvest. Furthermore, bad weather could further limit the period of harvest by making the grain wet and tangled and thus more difficult to cradle.[36]

After setting up the obvious solution, the agent suggested that purchasing a harvester would enable the farmer to seize the golden opportunity. Using a machine, one man could cut an acre an hour in any circumstance. He would need to be followed by at least three family members to bind the grain, but in the process he could increase his acreage from maybe ten acres to more than fifty. Fifty acres of wheat was the magic number to make the reaper pay. Not only would fifty acres allow the farmer to buy the harvesting machine "on time" (over two harvests, without a down payment) but also to make more money and afford the finer things in life. The agent might then refer to prominent neighbors who already purchased a self-binder or perhaps he would page through the catalog's testimonials to highlight others who had invested in a McCormick implement and enjoyed the fruits of civilization. On all counts the salesmen emphasized what mechanized reaping had "done, to lighten toil, to dignify farming, and to raise the farmer out of the dirt, into the purer better air of culture and refinement." One agent reminisced that such information was a "great education for the farmer, who would be back in the old rut if he did not know machines." They emphasized that the cradle scythe the farmer still used was the way of the past and that the machine at their fingertips was the way of progress, civilization, and the future. The customer could become a member of the "better class of farmers."[37]

Having established the importance of buying the newest implement, the salesman proceeded to explain why the McCormick was superior to all others. The agent tallied the merits of their machines according to the alchemy of progress, expanding on the points in the catalog. In particular, the canvassers relished telling the story of the company's victory at the London Crystal Palace in 1851. At this first international exhibition, the great nations of civilization displayed their magnificent objects of "luxury and ornament" as well as those of industry. The peddler explained that at the opening of the exhibition, the United States' department within the palace was seen as the "poorest and least interesting" exhibition, lacking in objects of culture and sparsely occupied, with tools rather than fine arts. It was derisively called the "Prairie Ground," surely a slap to the face of any midwesterner! The McCormick reaper was likewise "the butt of British . . . waggery," described as a "cross between an Astley's chariot, a flying machine and a treadmill." The storyteller joyfully explained that these sentiments changed as soon as the British saw the glory of McCormick's reaper working in the field. At an official trial McCormick's machine successfully cut wet and tangled grain in horrendous conditions, while defeating a longtime American rival, Obed Hussey, as well as a European manufacturer. At a follow-up trial, thousands thronged to see the machine in action, and ultimately McCormick was awarded the Grand Council Medal. His victory restored honor to the United States and was "recognized as the most valuable contribution" at the Crystal Palace. By the end of the exhibition, all had witnessed "American genius and skill, which convinced them in this age of progress and invention" that they may yet "learn" from the young republic.[38]

In telling this story, reaper men tapped into their customer's sense of patriotism as well as history. The McCormick triumph at the Crystal Palace demonstrated the promise of U.S. democracy as well as the nation's emerging imperial role in expanding the boundaries of civilization around the globe. The company's victories at later competitions were further evidence of its continued relationship with progress. Canvassers liked to point out that Obed Hussey had fallen behind in 1851 and had since ceased to manufacture machines. Likewise, they suggested that more recent losers would also soon be out of business and forgotten. McCormick salesmen had already explained why a new machine was important to a farmer's individual progress. Through regaling customers with these stories and the merits of their machines, canvassers convinced farmers that their product was both superior to and more prestigious than any other. Once harvest came the agent ensured that his noncommittal prospects witnessed the "starting" of a sold machine. Upon seeing that the machine functioned as well as promised, the customer paid for the machine and the spectators followed suit, placing orders for their own machines on the spot. The demonstration confirmed that the machine worked, but the sales talk and storytelling persuaded the farmer to see the machine in action and further cultivated the farmers' desire to own a McCormick.[39]

In many instances, by the time an implement salesman darkened a farmer's door in the 1870s, the prospective buyer was already thoroughly committed to commercial agriculture and the notion of "scientific farming." Indeed, the idea of "book farming" and the careful management of soil, crop selection, and livestock breeding, along with the concepts of investment debt, market orientation, and mechanization, had been gaining traction among old-stock Yankee farmers since the 1830s. Proselytized by ubiquitous agricultural journals, methods of "scientific farming" were thoroughly debated and tested by modernizing farmers inside and out of local agricultural clubs across the Midwest by the 1850s. With the exception of more recent ethnic arrivals, who made up sizeable populations in the upper Midwest (like Samuel Peterson's Germans in Brown County, Minnesota), and other derided "backwards" "dirt farmers," who were mired in old and futile ways, the lure of the expanding marketplace's profits, farming technologies, and consumer luxuries had already reoriented midwestern farmers toward commercial agriculture. The big question for these agrarians was not whether or not to pursue profits but rather which modern tools and strategies would help them take advantage of the market the most. Operating within such a context, the McCormick man may not have been selling a farmer his first harvesting implement. Instead, he was working to convince the potential customer that he needed to upgrade to the newest model of machine and that his particular make was the one to buy to have the most progressive and profitable farm.[40]

Beyond the isolated farmer's parlor and his field, reaper men peddled their past and hocked their wares at rural county and town fairs across their sales territory in direct competition with their rivals. Hosted by local farmers' clubs, rural fairs were key places for communities to socialize and learn about new farming methods and in particular to study and compare new agricultural machinery. Eager to participate in (and publicly underwrite) these popular rural get-togethers, implement agents displayed their machines shoulder to shoulder with their competitors in front of crowds of discerning potential buyers. Bringing their sales pitch and methods directly into the public sphere, salesmen encouraged farmers to size up every aspect of their machine to that of their rivals. They aggressively compared everything, from their machine's materials and dimensions to their company's historical resume in international trails, yearly sales, growing factory sizes, and geographic reach, as crucial means of setting their machine apart from those of their peers.[41]

Putting the idle chatter of festival barking and claims of superiority to the test, rural fairs were also important arenas of direct competition and field trials. Before a panel of select farmers as well as interested onlookers, machines were extensively evaluated and tested according to regulations set by the farmers' club or the larger state board of agriculture. Such trials were so popular that agricultural periodicals such as the *Prairie Farmer* printed score cards with standardized criteria for contest witnesses, prompting them to actively participate in the process by judging each competitor and debate outcomes among themselves.

After the trial winners were announced by the official panel and often received some cash award, but surely the accolades of besting a rival were more valuable to securing sales among the spectators.[42]

Outside of the organized rural fair, in particularly competitive districts, reaper men from opposing companies also competed and issued less formalized trial challenges. In these situations the challenge was usually for a particular farmer's business, and the farmer was free to buy "the machine *which he prefers*." The trial was usually well publicized in the neighborhood, and whole communities turned out to watch the competition. Taking advantage of the informal gatherings, salesmen made a big noise at these events, emphatically fighting among themselves, exchanging insults, and playing to the gallery of spectators. Generally, such commotion was mere posturing and showmanship, as opposing agents usually had little real animosity between them. Agents acknowledged that the real work of a trial was "well done before they commenced" during the canvas. What farmers saw at the trial tended to confirm what they already thought and had heard about at length. In some sense these trials, like those competitions at the rural fairs, were historical reenactments of international competitions. They were opportunities for local farmers to witness and partake in the progressive glory of head-to-head competition firsthand.[43]

After the trial opposing firms wasted no time in printing and distributing the nondefinitive results as overwhelming victories. "Who won" made "no difference," as varying newspapers, bulletins, and circulars claimed the day for every competitor, regardless of whether a trial had official judges or not. Most firms were actively engaged in "puffery," paying for newspapers to publish biased and imagined trial accounts as if they were typical newspaper articles. D. M. Osborne and Company informed its agents that such tactics were "the most profitable way to advertise," as the "science of advertising" allowed "false statements and misrepresentations" to be spread "just as easily as real truth." C. H. and L. J. McCormick was also engaged in such subterfuge from top to bottom. Salesmen as well as management in Chicago bought favorable press regardless of the actual results or the magnitude of the event. Beyond newspapers they also printed these stories in their own bulletins and the *Farmers' Advance* with headlines such as "Sweeps the Field!," "A Bad Day for Chokers!," and "A Grand Fizzle!" Salesmen distributed all this printed matter to customers, recounting the falsified stories as legitimate news and history in the making.[44]

Successfully selling harvesters meant that a salesman was able to tap into a customer's environmental and historical imagination as well as his pocketbook. Owning a machine required a farmer to reorganize his farmland and finances. In most cases farm families had to increase their overall improved acreage and raise more grain to pay for a new machine. They made this choice to incur more debt and more risk because salesmen were able to orient them within a specific historical rendering that equated their make of machine with the progress of civilization, enduring credibility, and future personal wealth. Harvester salesmen were colloquial historians, interpreting the past for the masses of rural Americans and explaining what their machines meant to that past as well as the future trajectory of both individual owners and civilization. In their sales talk they sowed the seeds of demand for their machines as well as the seeds of history.

Reaper salesmen and the industry at large succeeded in making their machine a touchstone of progress in the public imagination. *Scientific American*, among many others, regularly referenced the reaper alongside the telegraph, the railroad, the power loom, and the sewing machine as one of the "exponents of civilization" that "bring us nearer to that social millennium." The nationally known journalist-turned-politician Horace Greeley frequently shared his belief that the reaper had enabled the progress of urban manufacturing and the social uplift of the mechanic and laborer. The agricultural writer and rural tastemaker Solon Robinson, whose great mission was to "elevate the standing of the cultivators of the soil," believed that wheat was the great crop of civilization and "*must* be *cut* by machines." An 1851 *Chicago Daily Democrat* article summarized the value of the machine, stating that the reaper "conquers nature to the benign end of civilization," progressively transforming the continent as it pressed westward.[45]

Evangelical preachers too made ubiquitous references in their sermons to the reaping machine. They noted God's divine intention for both the land and man's invention of the reaper. The "All-wise Power" created the "Arable land" of the Midwest, which "prophesied grain-crops and these predicted reaping-machines." The reaper functioned as a "gospel worker . . . written over with the promise of a new Eden to be won out of the earth." One sermon held that the reaper, and indeed all progressive machinery, was "one of the world's great democratic forces," acting as a "mighty level placed under the lowest classes of society to raise them up." The reaper not only "doubled the crop of the country, but doubled its manhood." Beyond ringing endorsements of the country's divine progress, ministers also utilized the reaping machine metaphorically in their jeremiads. In 1859 Reverend J. A. James encouraged greater energy in proselytizing, stating that "God's harvest must be gathered with his own implement. . . . No reaping machine of modern invention can be supplied to us: the sickle of the gospel of Christ is still in our hands." These statements were tied to the already popular "spiritual harvest" metaphors within evangelical rhetoric but indicate the salience of the reaper's progress in American culture.[46]

Beyond politicians, preachers, and newspapermen, there is some indication that customers bought the history as well as the machine. In many instances county histories funded by local subscribers listed the first time such machines were used in their territory alongside the "first death," the "first birth," and the "first marriage." Some atlas patrons also paid to include depictions of harvesters in their idealized illustrations of their farmsteads. These people wanted to be associated with the reaping machine because it was a powerful material symbol of progress and a reflection on their own status as progressive farmers.[47]

From the late 1850s until the late 1870s, the marketing strategies in the harvester industry remained relatively static—relying on house calls, trials, and narratives based on the alchemy of progress. Throughout this time, however, the "industrial art" of reaping was constantly changing through the efforts of tinkerers, mechanics, and inventors at firms across the country. As could be anticipated, these innovations promoted greater efficiency of labor and value. Inventors lightened the draft, widened the sickle, combined the mower and the reaper into a single machine, mechanized raking, created an elevator and apron to collect the cut grain, attached a binding platform for laborers, and eventually invented apparatuses to bind the grain with wire and later twine. Specific articulations of these mechanisms were patented and then licensed to other manufacturers that operated in noncompeting regions. Competing patents could be secured to produce the same final outcome of a technology, such as binding grain with wire, but the process needed to be novel enough to avoid prosecutable patent infringement. Once a new outcome was patented, knockoffs emerged usually within a year. Machines incorporated many overlapping patented mechanisms within a single "modern" model, encouraging manufacturers to create "patent pools" with strategic allies to share technologies. Pooling patents with a distant manufacturer in a noncompeting region was an elegant way to market a more sophisticated machine and gain a local competitive advantage.[48]

Beginning in 1875, C. H. and L. J. McCormick faced a problem: the firm was on the outside of a "wire-binder" patent pool, looking in. William Deering, D. M. Osborne and Company, and Walter A. Wood Mowing and Reaping Machine Company, as well as several smaller firms, manufactured and sold the "Locke" or "Gordon" patented wire binders beginning in 1875. Denied a license to either, McCormick did not patent and sell a comparable product until 1877, and in that year their manufacture of wire binders was very limited. The wire binder was a complex mechanism attached to the side of a grain harvester, which tied grain into uniform sheaths. As a D. M. Osborne and Company catalog advertised, the self-binder "saves the wages and board of from five to eight men . . . doing better work than can be done by hand

and with none of the waste." These "self-evident" merits were great sales fodder. While the machine was expensive, it was easily sold as a tool that would allow the farmer to profit from larger crops free from the hassle and expense of itinerant laborers. Without an analogous product for two full seasons, McCormick's market share was slipping; however, their rhetoric of "superiority" continued unchanged.[49]

In 1879 twine binders were introduced by Deering and Wood, and again McCormick was on the outside. Advocating the obvious superiority of twine over wire was a bit more nuanced than advertising the advantages of automatic over hand binding. To make the case salesmen resorted to fearmongering. They labored to demonstrate that wire was counterproductive to the entire project of harvesting grain, either for personal or market consumption. Wire, they claimed, could not be successfully sorted out in the threshing process. The results were negative on three counts. The wire would damage the expensive threshing machine. Milling companies would not buy grain with wire in it. Finally, livestock would be killed by eating wire that was mixed in with their grain or left in the pastures. Such statements were debatable, but as a constant chorus of voices in rural America, these salesmen, traveling door to door and publishing newspaper "puffery" on the topic locally and nationally, planted potent seeds of doubt. These sentiments were difficult to correct in the public imagination because of the lack of established and unbiased public authorities on the topic.[50]

In response to these negative allegations and patent deficiencies, C. H. and L. J. McCormick developed an evolving branding strategy to claim authority over the harvester industry in the public mind and negate their competitors' touted mechanical advantage. Beginning in 1879, the company asserted a paternalistic authority over the entire industry based on its long historical record and invention of "the first successful reaper ever made." The catalog that year historicized the company's significance: "It is a well known fact, that ever since 1831, the name of McCormick has been inseparably linked with the recorded progress of the invention and manufacture of grain and grass-cutting machinery; and in all the years . . . the machinery bearing that name has been found to be in advance of anything in the field; for, in the ceaseless round of invention and improvement, year by year we have kept pace with the demands of a progressive age, so that the article of our manufacture have never yet been 'weighed and found wanting.'" The narrative went on to marginalize the rest of the industry, explaining that "whoever builds a mower, reaper or harvester, copies . . . the McCormick of nearly fifty years ago." The ad copy brushed off the company's technological deficiencies, instead proclaiming that "history but repeats itself," as the McCormick continually demonstrated "overwhelming proof" that it is "*foremost in the field*" through international trials and sales to farmers.[51]

The ad copy further utilized the firm's historical record as a trusted adviser to claim a recognized benevolent relationship with farmers. The invention "lightens their labors" and "curtails their expenses." Most incredibly, McCormick's invention bestowed civilization on farmers because it "relieves their wives and daughters of the odious slavery of harvest time." C. H. and L. J. McCormick were responsible for *all* of the economic and cultural benefits that owning any manufacture of harvesting machinery conferred. The 1879 catalog followed the usual conventions of the progress-centric marketing strategy, with the crucial twist of claiming absolute paternalistic credit for the entire history of the industry. Beginning in 1879 and continuing until the formation of International Harvester in 1902, every McCormick catalog cover included the simple declarative statement: "Established 1831."[52]

The shift to McCormick's "established 1831" brand can be attributed to the founder's oldest son, Cyrus McCormick II. Having graduated from Princeton in 1878, he immediately joined his father and uncle's family business and became the assistant to the president. He also became deeply involved in writing the company's advertising copy. To that point writing advertising copy had been done on an ad hoc basis among the firm's executive board. McCormick II was fascinated by his father's role in the development of the United States. He was a young man captivated by "the contrast between the old and the new" and pushed for greater recognition of his father's accomplishments in an industry that had recently become dominated by the automatic binder, someone else's invention. He fashioned his father's mythical innovation into a brand utilized in all advertising matter, from the annual catalog to the *Farmers' Advance*. Eventually, he made his father's portrait the symbolic logo of the company, posted in all advertising material and hung on a sign at every McCormick sales agency across the country.[53]

McCormick salesmen were encouraged to seize on the new branding strategy by smearing their competitors as irresponsible swindlers rather than progressive innovators. They told customers that competitors' twine binders were fundamentally "untried" "experiments at best." The strong "talk" of Wood and Deering agents was an effort to "effect premature sales" of a machine that had not "gone through at least *one* harvest in all kinds and conditions of grain." The "opposition" sold their untested implements at the expense of farmers' financial "safety." Farmers "foolish" enough to buy the machine would be met by "endless annoyance" and lose both "time and money." Moreover, they would be required to buy twine, which was both "*expensive* and *scarce*." McCormick's canvassers further argued that twine binders were sold only by "manufacturers who have a *poor* wire binder or perhaps *none at all*." Affecting their position as trustworthy advisers, salesmen noted that McCormick was responsibly "perfecting" a twine binder in harvests from Texas to Manitoba and assured farmers that "we will have a successful Twine Binder as soon as anyone can do it safely."[54]

Such talk was mostly bluster and a skillful hedge against a potential sea change in public opinion toward a machine that McCormick did not sell. While other manufacturers claimed that new twine binders were the most advanced and progressive machines on the market, as had been the advertising practice for decades, McCormick utilized its self-proclaimed authority to suggest that the new contraption was not a part of the "march of progress" at all. In reality, throughout this time the company was busily experimenting with twine binders and met with little success. Desperate to close the technology gap, the Chicago office instructed its agents "to keep your eyes wide open" and "examine closely . . . the working of every twine binder." The agents were then to report back just "exactly how they are constructed" in an "unprejudiced way." In 1881 they were finally able to release a twine binder to the public that was "as good or better" than any twine binder on the market. Maintaining their previous position, for that first season they continued to claim that their wire binder remained superior to any twine binder on the market.[55]

Coupled with the new "established 1831" brand narrative, McCormick began printing chromolithograph posters that elegantly illustrated their version of the past for the general public. They freely distributed thousands of these elaborate color posters to socially aspiring rural Americans, inviting them to beautify their homes with historically branded art, which approximated the sophisticated trappings of the upper classes. Using chromotechnology, in 1883 the company printed *The Testing of the First Reaping Machine Near Steele's Tavern,* VA. *A.D. 1831,* which was the first piece of company advertising to illustrate the supposed first trial of a working reaping machine in 1831 (fig. 1). An article in the *Western Rural*, potentially puffed by the company, praised the "Historical Picture," because the historic moment was of "momentous importance to the world" and "one of which every American citizen must feel proud." The author further explained the importance of the imagery because it "tells the story more forcibly than any written description . . . and will have a tendency to fix in the public mind, and perpetuate in the pubic memory, the fact that the

1. *The Testing of the First Reaping Machine Near Steele's Tavern,* VA. *A.D. 1831,* advertising poster, 1883. The McCormick Company illustration depicts the first reaper trial of 1831, showing the machine in operation in front of a crowd of onlookers. The poster was widely distributed by salesmen to potential customers as a form of heritage advertising and popular art to be hung in the home. Wisconsin Historical Society, WHI-2497.

THE TESTING OF THE FIRST REAPING MACHINE NEAR STEELE'S TAVERN, VA. A.D. 1831.

first practical reaper the world ever saw was the 'McCormick.'" At a "glance" the poster summarized the invention of the reaper as a simple "fact," to be hung on walls across the country and admired for its beauty and historical significance.[56]

Competitors soon responded to McCormick's new branding campaign of images and celebratory heritage, fully aware of its power to damage their own reputations. D. M. Osborne and Company simply refuted McCormick's chirping, stating that its "Self-Binding Harvester is not an experiment" and asking that customers trust their innovations, because of "our record of the past." William Deering and Company went significantly further, waging war against McCormick's entire claim to authority and defending its own record of progress. Without mentioning McCormick by name, the Deering 1881 catalog stated that the "howl of disapproval" about twine binders came from "'old and established manufacturers,'—old and established in non-progressive notions and methods—who were alarmed by this bold step in invention." They attempted to marginalize the McCormick fearmongering and claims to authority by implying that such statements were simply the sentiments of traditionalists and ungracious losers. The copy further mocked McCormick for its "modesty and truthfulness . . . trumpeting themselves . . . as the chief benefactors of the world."[57]

Undeterred by competitors, McCormick II continued to develop the company's historical 1831 brand. Moving from a historical assertion to a full-fledged narrative, the 1886 catalog began with a nine-page "short history of wheat and wheat reapers." The objective of the narrative was to demonstrate that "very little progress was made in its [wheat] culture during all the ages past" until 1831, when McCormick "constructed the first reaper that ever successfully harvested grain." The history included illustrations of ancient sickles found during archaeological digs—stressing that such "methods were employed before the time of the Pharaohs" and were "quite like the sickle our fathers used." The copy also compared ancient means to those utilized in the less civilized world, like India, where the farmer "sits upon his heels, cuts a handful of straw . . . and then waddles on without rising, cutting in this way about one-twelfth of an acre a day." The catalog further related the humble origins of the reaper in McCormick's quaint "Old Reaper Workshop in Virginia" in 1831 to the massive and smoke-belching McCormick reaper works in Chicago, which produced over fifty-four thousand machines annually. Narrowly interpreting the past through the material framework of the alchemy of progress, the catalog emphasized that McCormick's invention was of "incalculable value to the human race" because of the increase of grain and industrial production capacity since 1831, with scarcely any discussion of technological or economic developments in the interceding fifty-five years. Accompanying the catalog, trade cards were also printed, illustrated with the same imagery as the catalog, teleologically summarizing the history of harvest pictorially as an obvious Darwinian hierarchy of the past and present history (see figs. 2 and 3). Through such imagery and comparisons the McCormick Harvesting Machine Company made clear that the civilized farmer rode a grain harvester to profits, while those who did not may as well be "waddling" like "Indians."[58]

Beyond metanarratives of civilization, McCormick II steered company advertising toward bolder claims and imagery regarding the nation's past. In particular he emphasized the company's role in settling the West and "Manifest Destiny" throughout the company's advertising material. While the connection was made in company catalogs, the best examples are seen in their increasingly elaborate chromolithograph posters. The pioneer's Conestoga wagon became a ubiquitous symbol in these posters, even ahistorically showing up in an illustration of the first reaper trial in 1831 (fig. 1). More blatant than this, however, the company printed a poster titled *"Westward the Course of Empire Takes Its Way" with McCormick Reapers in the Van* (fig. 4), which was an explicit copy of Emanuel Lutzen's popular painting from 1862, *Westward the Course of Empire*. The McCormick poster depicts settlers caravanning in darkness to the top of a ridge, over-

2. "The Improvements of Fifty-Five Years," exterior of the McCormick Harvesting Machine Company trade card, 1886. The card offered colorful visual cues to accompany the salesman's "historical" narrative of the harvester's evolution. The images depict changes in harvesting technology in gendered and racialized tropes from ancient archaeological hand scythes to modern horse-powered riding machinery. The type across the bottom reads, "The Pioneer Reaper Manufacturers of the World. Originators and Leaders in All valuable improvements of the Art." Wisconsin Historical Society, WHI-36208.

3. "The Improvements of Fifty-Five Years," interior of the McCormick Harvesting Machine Company trade card, 1886. The back of the card also illustrates the change in the reaper's manufacturing from McCormick's humble blacksmith shop in 1831 to his family's massive Chicago reaper works in 1886. The comparison of scale was meant to suggest both the company's success over time and its close association with American progress. Wisconsin Historical Society, WHI-36369.

looking a bright field of grain, where a farmer is already harvesting with a McCormick self-binder. The reaper was a mechanized Daniel Boone.[59]

McCormick II also began to revise his father's infamous Civil War record and participated in reimagining the larger meaning of the war in general. Advertising and bulletins began to stress the company's Northern allegiance, utilizing pro-Union imagery. For instance, an 1883 bulletin referred to their customers as "the Grand McCormick Army," while another from 1882 stressed that the McCormick was "on the War Path! . . . All Along the Southern Line." Certainly, such military metaphors played in the masculine culture of the Gilded Age, but they also resonated with their key demographic—free-holding farmers in the upper Midwest. The company also created a series of Civil War–related posters featuring their product amid epic landscape battles including Gettysburg, Shiloh, Missionary Ridge, and, inexplicably, the ironclad battle of the *Merrimac* and the *Monitor* (see fig. 5). These historyesque advertisements were intended to hang in people's homes as reminders of the nation's military glory and the company's glorious achievements.[60]

Until the consolidation of the harvester industry in 1902, the McCormick Harvesting Machine Company continued to make grander claims to patriarchal ownership of the industry's past, with implications for the present. While competitors initially responded to McCormick with

4. *"Westward the Course of Empire Takes Its Way" with McCormick Reapers in the Van*, advertising poster, 1886. In the mid-1880s McCormick's advertising posters took on a particularly expansive historical perspective, boldly inserting their machine within iconic images and events to align their brand with both progress and U.S. history. For this poster—one of many possible examples—McCormick Harvesting Machine Company commissioned artists to create a knockoff of the famous Emanuel Gottlieb Leutze mural in the U.S. Capitol, placing their harvester on the frontier's leading edge. The business insinuated their product's close association with historical pioneers' aspirations as well as with manifest destiny. Wisconsin Historical Society, WHI-2496.

"WESTWARD THE COURSE OF EMPIRE TAKES ITS WAY" WITH McCORMICK REAPERS IN THE VAN.

·BATTLE OF SHILOH·APRIL 6th 1862·

THE McCORMICK MACHINES COME VICTORIOUSLY OUT OF EVERY CONTEST, AND WITHOUT A SCRATCH

·PRESENTED WITH COMPLIMENTS OF ·McCORMICK HARVESTING MACHINE COMPANY·

McCORMICK HARVESTING MACHINE CO.

·PANORAMA PAINTING·

ON EXHIBITION IN CHICAGO

corrective statements in their catalogs, they soon adopted the idea of branding themselves in similar fashion through their agents. William Deering and Company touted itself as the inventor of the first harvester in 1857, claiming it to be the real breakthrough in the progress of harvesting technology. In a similar manner the Walter A. Wood Mowing and Reaping Machine Company advertised itself as "the Pioneer" of self-binders, adopting the motto "Progress is our Watchword." D. M. Osborne and Company went in a different direction, attempting to reframe itself as the farmer's ally and educator—filling its catalogs with incredibly complex illustrations of binding mechanisms and operational instructions. In comparison to McCormick's bold historical narrative, pressing the monumental change from hand-cutting with scythes, which had been used for thousands of years, to mechanized reaping in 1831, opponents' branding and narratives seemed trivial.[61]

This era of branding and advertising wars, which McCormick initiated in 1879, was accompanied by increasingly stiff competition across the industry that ended only with corporate consolidation in 1902. The market became saturated with harvesting machines, as industry production surged from 133,000 machines produced and sold in 1880 to some 324,000 in 1890. McCormick on its own jumped from producing 20,000 machines in 1880 to nearly 90,000 in 1890 and almost 200,000 by 1900. As competitors improved their efficiency and the economy of production in the factory, they also expanded their sales and distribution networks across the country and began to work internationally as well. McCormick alone went from employing more

5. *Battle of Shiloh, April 6th, 1862*, advertising poster, 1885. One of several McCormick Harvesting Machine Company posters in its Civil War series, this illustration ahistorically features an 1880s harvesting machine in a shed surrounded by epic imagery depicting the Battle of Shiloh in 1862. Many of the posters in the series were approximate copies of the popular 1880s Civil War panoramas exhibited in Washington DC and at other locations around the country. The bottom of the poster reads, "The 'McCormick' machines come victoriously out of every contest, and without a scratch." Library of Congress, LC-DIG-pga-00540.

than one thousand district salesmen in fifty sales regions in 1880 to over twelve thousand district salesmen and two thousand canvassers in seventy-one sales regions in 1900. Within this intense competition marketing was crucial to commercial success. Thousands of McCormick salesmen crisscrossed rural America, distributing colorful posters and narrative catalogs in hopes of exciting sales. In this pursuit they tapped into Americans' obsession with the past and advanced self-serving histories that utilized the alchemy of progress to transform the McCormick harvester into the gold standard of civilized harvesting machines in the public imagination. At the same time as salesmen created a national market for their goods, they also popularized the fiction that Cyrus McCormick invented the reaper in 1831 as self-evident national history.[62]

2

Producing Invention for Producer Populists

Beginning in the late 1880s, the McCormick Company changed its marketing rhetoric in response to the growing economic and political activism of American farmers. The business stressed to insurgent rural producers that Cyrus McCormick as a farmer had *produced* technology through toil and ingenuity that allowed other farmers to prosper in his wake—equating the wealth-producing power of labor with the wealth-producing power of invention. The company rolled the "labor theory of value," which undergirded producerist criticism into their "established 1831" brand and narratives about its founder to create what I have termed a "technological surplus-value ideology." Instead of McCormick being a capitalist, parasitic leech on producers in the fields, the firm's ideology pronounced that his labor and invention made the company's relationship with farmers harmonious. The agency asserted that its laborsaving technology increased the individual prosperity of farmers in ways previously unattainable. The McCormick Harvesting Machine Company spread this ideology and its advertising to justify the McCormick family's elite position in the Gilded Age social order and the firm's leading role within the harvester industry.

The manufacturer's exhibit at the 1893 World's Columbian Exposition in Chicago offered the clearest perspective of how this advertising narrative and ideology operated. It also revealed the weakness of a brand based on history: their claim to priority in the marketplace could be threatened by alternative narratives of the past. The McCormick Harvesting Machine Company's exhibit prominently displayed the historical features of their advertising, stirring discontent among rivals and prompting protests to the exposition's officials on grounds of historical inaccuracy. At the same venue where Frederick Jackson Turner delivered his famous frontier thesis to the American Historical Association, harvester-industry millionaires relied on lawyers, patent officers, and inventors to protect their versions of the past.

The organizers, exhibitors, and sponsors of the 1893 world's fair ordered the entirety of humanity through the lens of civilization and the layout of Jackson Park. They projected their conceptions of social, racial, and gender hierarchies to visitors through architecture, displays, performances, and landscapes. The Court of Honor was the core of the White City, a reverent monument to white civilization's claimed accomplishments in art, science, and technology. Outside the White City, on the Midway Plaisance, other "savage" cultures were presented as subjects of amusement rather than knowledge. Through this structured spectacle, racial and gender differences were presented as natural products of evolution, which occurred through the drama of history, "scientifically" justifying social hierarchies and differences in the present. The 1893 exposition reinforced the existing social, economic, racial, and gender order of the United States while supporting the further expansion of Anglo-American dominance around the world.[1]

Within the buildings of the White City, businesses erected exhibits, staking claims in the great project of civilization. In the Agriculture Building, adjacent to the Court of Honor, the displays of American manufacturers were arranged around a massive globe at the center. Fair planners suggested that the agricultural technology of civilization had spread beyond the nation and literally surrounded the world. Inside this massive, high-ceilinged building, the energy of "civilization" bustled, as more than five hundred farm-implement businesses offered educational and attractive exhibits, while employees handed out trade cards, brochures, and catalogs to crowds of curious and awestruck visitors. These solicitors competed with their industry peers for audience attention, hoping to excite interest and future sales.[2]

As a leading business in the host city and a veteran of every world's fair since the London Crystal Palace Exhibition in 1851, the McCormick

Harvesting Machine Company spared no expense in presenting its machines and story. The company president, Cyrus McCormick II, took the lead in conceptualizing the exhibit, assisted by his senior patent officer and inventor, Rodney B. Swift, an authority on the mechanical development of the McCormick reaper. The display cases were created by local furniture makers under instruction from a Marshall Field and Company consultant, who further advised McCormick II on the exhibit layout and the use of text, flags, and banners. The exhibit and its visitors were attended to by knowledgeable salesmen, assisted by Ms. Keefer, a "good girl" from Indiana—mechanically minded, young, and single. As a bonus, she also spoke German, allowing the company to pitch their wares to some of the more "civilized" tourists from abroad.[3]

While most farm-implement businesses offered "sales floor" exhibits that presented machines and tools, the McCormick Company advanced a coherent narrative of its contributions to civilization. The McCormick exhibition was a genuine spectacle, a "constant magnet for a large and admiring audience." Visitors followed a carpeted pathway that wove through McCormick machines and display cases on a tour of reaper history. The tour began with a replica of Cyrus Sr.'s original 1831 reaper and included company machines that had won top honors at the 1851 and 1867 world's fairs, as well as its first wire binder, which took gold in 1878. The tour culminated with its line of 1893 models. Along the way the audience passed a display case of the awards won by the McCormick Company and its founder in international competitions and banners announcing these feats, along with flags from four continents. An oil portrait of the late Cyrus Sr. was prominently featured, adjacent to a glass display case that held the McCormick Company's superior quality twine—a mundane but contentious commodity in 1893.[4]

As fairgoers passed through the McCormick gallery, placards narrated the importance of McCormick machines to history and the success of modern agriculture. The replica of the 1831 reaper was labeled "the first practical reaper, invented and built by Cyrus H. McCormick." A label on McCormick's portrait reflected a similar sentiment. Along the way Keefer and other McCormick exhibitors regaled visitors with the tale of McCormick's invention. In their story Cyrus's father attempted throughout his lifetime to create a machine to cut grain but had failed after decades of toil. A twenty-two-year-old Cyrus resumed his father's work with inventive rigor in the spring of 1831. Later that summer, after a mere six weeks of tinkering, his machine cut standing grain in front of a small crowd of locals in a field near Steele's Tavern, Virginia. As the company spokesmen told it, from that point forward American agriculture was on the path of progress. Decorative shields affixed to structural pillars in the exhibit connected this early date with the company's continued success: "First in 1831, First in 1893." A large banner above the exhibit reduced competitors' products to McCormick's mechanical progeny: "All Harvesters of To-Day Are Based Upon the Features C. H. McCormick Invented and Built in 1831." The company ensured that all visitors knew McCormick possessed the "prestige of priority" in the harvester trade and that all the competitors surrounding them in the exhibit hall were docile followers and uninspired imitators.[5]

These messages of industrial primacy were nuanced and accentuated by the crown jewel of the McCormick showcase—a massive mechanized diorama. The diorama was set within a large case against a bird's-eye illustration of the McCormick reaper works in Chicago, with transparent glass signs that offered interpretation. In the distant background, at the top of the illustration, vessels crisscrossed Lake Michigan. Set along the base of the cabinet opening to the left, trains moved in and out of the works' busy warehouses and train yard. A label read, "These works produce more Harvesting machines annually than any others in the world." On the front right a farmer rode a tiny modern binder that clicked across a field of wheat, with the label "the sun never sets on the McCormick machines at work." Adjacent to this garden of wheat was a small model building, with a note simply stating, "In this blacksmith shop, near Steele's Tavern, Virginia, Cyrus H. McCormick made the first successful reaper in 1831."[6]

The ahistorical and spatially inaccurate McCormick display offered visitors a wealth of meaning, framing the company's relationships with customers and employees in historical terms. The exhibit expressed a worldview in which McCormick and the company's farmer customers and laborers were all interconnected producers contributing to civilization. The McCormick works, filled with "busy artisans" (according to McCormick exhibitors), produced more harvesters daily than any other manufactory. This industrial marvel in Chicago was connected to the entire world by railroad and ship, allowing McCormick to spread the tools of civilization. On the receiving end farmers everywhere were able to purchase harvesters, enabling them to produce greater quantities of grain for the world marketplace and create otherwise unattainable wealth. Most important, the diorama suggested that both the development of the factory and the modern farmer were possible only because McCormick "made" the first reaper in 1831. The positioning of the blacksmith shop along the field also suggested that McCormick was a farmer at heart, not an industrialist. Fair-going farmers and factory laborers could see that they were allocated representative space within the White City. As agents of civilization, however, they were not equal. McCormick was their superior and benefactor because his invention allowed others to prosper.[7]

An exposition souvenir book summed up the meaning of technological surplus value and its presentation within the exhibit for visitors: "The measure of Cyrus Hall McCormick's contribution to the welfare of men and nations cannot be estimated." The text further announced that McCormick's invention "distributed an annual income to the whole country of over fifty-five millions of dollars, which must increase through all time." The company underlined its ideological perspective that the wealth and surplus value generated by modern agricultural technology radiated from McCormick's inventive genius. As the organizers of the World's Columbian Exposition ordered society as a whole, so too did the McCormick Harvesting Machine Company depict the moral social hierarchy of its business relationships. The elaborate display established the firm as the moral authority within the harvester industry as well as the patriarchal figure over its customers and employees. On all counts McCormick's historical invention of the reaper in 1831 was the linchpin to his successors' mastery over others.[8]

The company's ideology and historical narrative not only were made available to those who attended the fair but were also distributed to homes across the country within the pages of the McCormick annual catalog. No stranger to teleological anachronisms, its catalog depicted Cyrus McCormick on the front cover of the 1893 issue as the "historical egg" that hatched civilized farming, differentiating the gardens of the nineteenth-century United States from the savage continent Columbus "discovered" in 1492. The advertising narrative supplied more intricate points of the ideology, emphasizing McCormick's origins as a farmer and his contributions to civilization. "In aiming to promote the honorable cause of those with whom he toiled in the field . . . Cyrus McCormick builded [*sic*] better than he knew. A benefactor to the farmer he became a benefactor to the world." The following page boasted that farmers "of every land" recognized McCormick's invention "as an essential factor in his race for individual supremacy." The copy further highlighted the company's acknowledged leadership in "the field his genius illumined." The 1893 catalog and company salesmen brought the McCormick messages of paternal authority and benevolence directly into parlors across the United States.[9]

Competing firms were galled by the McCormick Company's reductionist and insulting interpretation of history. Ultimately, they had no recourse against these advertised fabrications. Companies such as Deering; Aultman, Miller and Company; and Walter A. Wood held that the reaper had evolved through dozens of minor adaptations by a large number of inventors, which all materially contributed to making the machine practical for farmer use. Their grievances were on sound legal and historical footing. Obed Hussey had a patent on a reaper that was practically identical to McCormick's in 1833, while Cyrus McCormick did not apply for a patent on his own machine until 1834. His dissenters also pointed to Patrick Bell's 1829 reaper from England, indicating McCormick's 1831 reaper did not have historical priority on innovation either. These rivals made their nuanced interpretation of the past readily available to the public in trade journals and histories of the harvester industry. They could not, however, persuasively compete with McCormick's simplistic and epic past, ubiquitously repeated in all the company's advertising copy.[10]

Since the 1880s harvester firms had been locked in tight competition, and advertising had become increasingly important to success. With the arrival of twine binders in the late 1870s, the major harvester firms were selling very similar products in a mature technology line in which innovation no longer substantially altered the operation of the machine. During the same period well-capitalized manufacturers, such as Deering, McCormick, and Wood, became capable of selling their products on a national scale because of sophisticated sales networks and exponentially larger machine output at behemoth factories. Intensification led to greater competition throughout the United States, as more firms began to compete for traditionally "safe" single-company sales territories. Such competition, along with a groundswell of populist disapproval for big business, led to "price slashing," and profit margins began to shrink. In such a context advertising material and branding became particularly important for gaining an edge. While most of these companies advertised their special relationship with progress and farmers, the grand McCormick narrative of the past trumped all other claims.[11]

The 1893 World's Columbian Exposition offered competitors a rare opportunity to censure the McCormick narrative and overthrow its grandiose conceptions of the industrial order. During the fair an Inventors Congress, an international body of inventors and patent specialists, met to discuss the creation of international patent laws and to compare and contrast the merits of the many innovations presented in Chicago. This group also volunteered its services to act as a judiciary in cases of inventive dispute. Collectively, three rival companies seized the opportunity to rebut the lies of the "McCormick Thief," petitioning the congress. Inventors and patent officers took the lead in tearing down McCormick's public heritage. Lewis Miller, an owner and inventor at Aultman, Miller and Company, led the charge by publishing and distributing a pamphlet titled "The First Reaper: BE IT KNOWN and DISTINCTLY UNDERSTOOD THAT McCORMICK DID NOT MAKE the FIRST REAPING MACHINE." Russell Parsons of Wood and John F. Steward of Deering, both senior patent officers and inventors, published evidence in *Farm Implement News*. When Cyrus McCormick II was informed of the historical coup, he had his own officer, Rodney B. Swift, compile a defense, but their efforts fell short. Within weeks the Inventors Congress forced the McCormick Harvesting Machine Company to take down all of its placards claiming inventive priority. Without the labels it is doubtful that the intrinsic historical importance of the McCormick machines was apparent to the visitors as they walked through the exhibit. They likely only saw old machinery.[12]

The Inventors Congress reprimanded the company but could not force the firm to roll back its claims outside of the White City. While both sides published and distributed historical treatises in trade newspapers, the specifics of the Inventors Congress judgment were handled discreetly, unknown to the wider public. Many of the harvester companies from Illinois were involved in financing and planning the World's Columbian Exposition and probably had no interest in embarrassing the city or the industry on the international stage.

After the World's Columbian Exposition Deering began to more fervently dispute the McCormick claims to the past through its own sales force and advertising. Beginning in 1894, that company's catalog included John Steward's chronology of the reaper's origins, with portraits and descriptions of seven inventors who contributed to the creation of the modern harvester. The catalog stated that "the history of their inventions is one of persevering struggle against difficulties . . . and of systematic efforts on the part of others . . . to rob them of their well-earned laurels." Taking issue with the McCormick narrative of the past, the Deering catalog stated that its account was a matter of "truth versus fiction." Practical inventions were not conceived in whole form as the result of a divine moment of inspiration but instead were the result of generations of inventors building on one another's previous accomplishments.[13]

Compounding the troubles of industry competition, the McCormick Company and others also faced mounting criticism of radical populist producerism, beginning in the 1870s, which mushroomed to a fever pitch of unrest during the 1880s and 1890s. Producerists maintained that wealth was produced only through the labor of workers rather than through financial manipulation or owning capital. These producerist expressions originated from different positions in the economic order—workers as employees and farmers as business owners—but were unified by a common experience. Their articulation of producerism rejected the "harmony of interests" ideology that had been preached by capitalists since midcentury (and which was visibly evident in the McCormick world's fair diorama). The populists did not believe that capital and labor operated in a mutually beneficial relationship. Rather, the producer ideology of these groups—undergirded by the labor theory of value, that labor created wealth—combined with an antimonopolist perspective that framed big businesses and millionaires as parasites, unjustly leeching away wealth from producers. These ideas and groups, along with others, politically solidified in the 1890s within the ranks of the People's Party, creating no small discomfort for big-business owners.[14]

In identifying the producerist undercurrents of radical nineteenth-century resistance to capitalist hegemony, historians have rarely acknowledged the inherent contradictions some producer-goods industries negotiated in responding to the distinct antimonopolism of their workers and agrarian customers. Two massive literatures of labor and populism have discussed the republican rhetorical tradition of producerism in appealing to people from broad experiences and also producerism's lack of lasting, class consciousness–building grit among adherents. However, both veins of scholarship largely ignore how farmers and factory workers from materially different positions in the economic order embraced producerism. They required separate rebuttals from industries that built producer goods. Only labor historians have shown how capitalists formulated a response to producerism through reappropriation of the language and symbols of producerist freedom. They have demonstrated that as laborers claimed the right to the wealth created by their toil, so too did employers claim their right to manage their business toward higher productivity and profits through mechanization and efficiency schemes, undermining worker autonomy.[15]

Industrialists, like McCormick, could not use the same language of republican liberty and progress that they used with their employees to reject agrarian producerism. While they could tell their employees that they had the right to find a new place to work if they did not appreciate their wages or laborsaving machinery, they could not antagonize their customers with the rhetoric of republican liberty. Telling irate agrarian customers that they could buy another make of machine if they did not like company practices was clearly ill-advised. Instead, they created new ideological formulations and paternal justifications to assuage the producers' populist threats and morally reinforce their position atop the Gilded Age hierarchy.

The McCormicks recognized that both their employees and their customers criticized their industrial power through producerist antimonopolism. They attempted to leverage the difference between their employees and customers into increased authority over both groups. For example, in 1886 the McCormick Company installed new molding machinery at their factory to crush the highly specialized Iron Molders' Union, which had been a thorn in its side since the Civil War. During the spring the company hired less skilled factory hands to perform the task, prompting the molders' union to strike. Cyrus McCormick II claimed the freedom to select his own workers in the same way that workers had the liberty to choose employers. He dismissed the union and its objections as un-American and backward. In a February meeting with representatives from the union, he reported, "They had no cause of grievance against the molding machines, as that was solely our business, and that whatever suited us suited them. They said they were too intelligent to object to the use of machinery for any purpose any more than they would object to farmers using the harvesting machines which we manufacture." It seems unlikely that the molders' union arrived at McCormick II's office with no "grievance" against the machines. After all, the company purchased the machinery to regain control of the shop floor, drive down wages, and employ unskilled labor in pursuit of higher profits. This report suggests that when the union representatives arrived, McCormick II reframed union objections. He compared his own purchase of modern machinery with that of farmers buying the machines that the company and laborers produced. He demonstrated that the very source of the molders' employment was tied to manufacturing the sort of laborsaving machinery they were protesting. Intellectually outmaneuvering his employees, McCormick II used the symbols of modernity and producerism against the molders to make their critique untenable.[16]

At the same time McCormick Company management was aware that its customers perceived union busting as monopolistic abuse. In a circular distributed by its sales agents, the company sought to align its antiunion actions with those of farmers dealing with unruly seasonal harvest labor. McCormick agents reminded their customers that they too had the "difficulty of dealing with the help at harvest time, before the self-binder freed them from such trouble." Salesmen further asserted that "we are sure . . . that no independent farmer would . . . submit to be dictated to in regard to who they should hire or discharge." Such posturing reflects their cognizance of the shared antimonopolism of farmers and laborers. Alternatively, McCormick management and sales agents argued that farmers had more in common with the company as business owners than with the agitating union men. They especially underlined the point that their machinery had "freed" farmers from such problems.[17]

By the 1890s the company had successfully marginalized its employees on the shop floor. The manufacturer's investment in machinery and unskilled labor to break worker control of production had gained wider cultural salience in-line with the antiunion sentiment that followed the 1887 Haymarket Bombing. The McCormick family did not face any serious threats from workers within their factory during the following decade, but they were continually conscious of the potential for the working class to violently challenge their elite authority. Though factory management had successfully neutralized the labor threat within its own walls, they still harbored anxiety about the working classes at large, especially during turbulent times, such as the Pullman Strike of 1894. While the firm's power marginalized employees, it had less leverage to silence customer critiques of its wealth.[18]

The McCormick Company and family had concerns about populist farmers for decades. Radical rural populism threatened their position in the economic order, and the company was aware that it needed to work vigilantly to undermine agrarian producerism and strengthen its bonds with customers. As early as 1873, Grangers had specifically protested McCormick's use of "middle-men" sales agents, who artificially inflated the price of machines without adding value. Many Grangers published books and pamphlets that singled out McCormick for inflated machinery prices that were 50 to 100 percent higher than the cost of production. Grangers sought to secure lower prices through buying directly from the company. Later in the 1890s local branches of the National Farmers' Alliance would use similar tactics.[19]

Pricing was not the only front on which the company was maligned by agrarian discontent. The populist farmers also attempted to organize manufacturing to supply cheaper machines and tools. In this pursuit they attempted to overturn federal patent laws to allow populist manufactories to build the newest harvesting equipment without investment in research and development. Some state-level granges, like the one in Iowa, went as far as setting up their own farm-implement factories to provide cheaper machines to farmers. These efforts ultimately failed, because of a lack of access to capital and limited customers in any given state. In the early 1890s the National Farmers' Alliance joined with the National Cordage Company to secure cheaper twine and financial backing for a national wholesale warehouse, the National Union Company, in exchange for guaranteed patronage. This strategy undercut McCormick's international maneuvering to secure cheaper twine by contracting directly with the Yucatán plantations that produced the best fiber (sisal and henequen) for binder twine, as well as its twine distribution through its branch-house sales network. In 1891 elected Populists in Minnesota went so far as placing twine manufacture in the Stillwater State Penitentiary, ensuring that farmers in that state could pay a lower price for twine than was offered by any business in the harvester or twine industry. The populist farmers experimented with many strategies to overturn their dependence on big businesses, effectively challenging the economic authority and profits of established manufacturers.[20]

With the rising tide of antimonopolism among farmers, the company even had trouble forcing customers to pay past-due notes on machinery purchased on credit. By the late 1880s McCormick had initiated a policy restraining legal action on overdue notes and began to exercise more conservative lending practices. As one agent explained the difficulty of collecting through the courts, "Justice, equity law and everything else is on our side. The only thing that would be against is that in this day of Grangerism, *you can't always bet on a jury*, [and] law has very little to do with some of their decisions." Illustrating this sentiment, in 1884 the company took Ignatius Donnelly, later the "father of the People's Party," to court in Minnesota for $600 plus interest on two wire binders he had purchased in 1878. Donnelly had not paid because the machines did not work as well as advertised. The jury decided in Donnelly's favor, ruling that the company pay him $25 plus court fees. Donnelly warned the company of its folly in advance, stating that juries "realize that machines are sold for three times their cost, and that patent laws are breeding great and injurious monopolies." Populists were successfully carrying out their vision in some localities, threatening to turn the nature of the economic and political system upside down.[21]

Company officials like McCormick II, Swift, and general manager of operations, Earl K. Butler, discussed agrarian populists in broad disdainful terms as backward farmers who did not understand the principles of qualitative value or order. They rarely perceived nuanced differences among agrarian populist groups such as the National Farmers' Alliance, the Agricultural Wheel, or the Patrons of Husbandry. Rather, they grouped them all as "granger organizations" that "demoralized" prices and the harvester industry more generally. "Populists," they thought, made no distinctions for quality and were "ready to be gulled" by lower prices. Meanwhile, "intelligent people" were ready to pay more for the "best" machines. Factory officials resentfully labeled anyone who questioned the company's authority as "populists"—especially local tax commissioners. To the McCormick Company, populism did not represent specific people or organizations but existed as a groundswell abstraction of the lower classes, menacing the Gilded Age social order.[22]

The producerist undercurrents of labor and farmer discontent converged as the People's Party in 1892, representing the national political embodiment of producer-populist challenges. The 1892 Omaha Platform pronounced a program of action to "restrain the extortions of aggregated capital" that plundered the "fruits of the toil of millions." As a proclamation of producerist unity, the Populists declared, "'If any will not work, neither shall he eat.' The interests of rural and civic labor are the same; their enemies are identical." The platform called for the permanent union of labor forces of the United States, nationalization of natural monopolies (such as railroads and telegraphs), redistribution of railroad land grants, and illegalization of private police (such as the Pinkerton Detective Agency), among others. However, the party's ultimate support of free silver was perhaps the most frightening plank of the platform to the wealthy.[23]

While many of the Populist planks targeted specific groups and offered governmental protection of producer interests, the issue of loose money, such as greenbacks and to a lesser extent silver coinage, was particularly alarming to Gilded Age capitalists. "Gold bugs" believed the gold standard was central to a stable economy and also their authoritative role within society. Loose money allowed greater social mobility and also the repayment of debt with less valuable currency—a shift that would erode elite economic authority and that they feared might topple the entire system. The McCormicks perceived that the People's Party unified their producer populist laborers and customers against them and that such an event, coupled with bimetallism, could lead to their ruin.[24]

To make matters worse for themselves, the industry's "big six" firms, including McCormick, Deering, and Wood, briefly created a Harvester Trust in 1890 to collectively raise prices, garnering still greater popular antagonism. Devoted to the idea of making the business more profitable, the American Harvester Company was formed in November 1890. Nationwide newspapers were filled with stories about the formation of the company, including its monumental scale, justifications for its existence, and critiques of its monopolistic abuses. Its creation invited immediate legal and political challenges from farmers and Populists throughout the United States. Finding these threats credible, owners of the trust disbanded in mid-January 1891, only a month and a half after it had been founded.[25]

Companies involved in the Harvester Trust tried to spin its dismantling as public benevolence, while their competitors seized on the debacle for their own advertising. In 1891 the Plano Manufacturing Company made hay of their exclusion from the Harvester Trust, moralizing on the evils of the trust while illuminating its own sanctity for staying aloof of the parasitic evil. Its catalog that year began with a four-page "word to our customers about the late American Harvester Company," detailing their competitors' "gigantic and mercenary 'Harvester Trust,'" aimed at fleecing farmers. Plano educated customers about the "nefarious organization" as an "unlawful tribute upon farmers" through reprinting a long scathing article about the trust published in the *Chicago Inter-Ocean*. Juxtaposing itself against the trust, Plano was "engaged in no unlawful combination" and had "been concerned with nothing excepting its legitimate business." Presumably such muckraking excited greater animosity among populist farmers and benefited Plano at the expense of conspiring rivals.[26]

In response to the challenges of agrarian producerism, the later People's Party, and rival smear campaigns, McCormick copywriters reoriented the firm's "established 1831" brand, incorporating the technological surplus-value ideology. The company's heritage and founder's invention was positive evidence that its interests were compatible with the interests of farmers. Others also attempted to assuage producer criticism by highlighting the productive power of technology and ingenuity as well. In 1893 *Labour and the Popular Welfare* by William Mallock asserted that both labor and "ability"—shorthand for technological ingenuity and efficient management—created wealth. Mallock argued that radical producerists advocated stealing the fruits of "ability" in the same way that slaveholders stole labor from men. The book was well received by the Chicago elite, and the *Chicago Daily Tribune* wondered, "Have the socialistic labor agitators given a thought to this?" In 1894 leaders of the National Association of Farm Implement Manufacturers couched their argument against producerist criticisms in similar terms of technological surplus value, stating that "labor of brain and hand" created wealth. McCormick copywriters utilized these ideas in tandem with the company's heritage to present a coherent narrative of the past and the present to its customers, mollifying populist antagonism while continuing to claim patriarchal authority over the industry during the reaper wars.[27]

The company's annual catalogs demonstrate the firm's use of history and technological surplus-value ideology. In the decade after Cyrus McCormick's death in 1884, the "established 1831" advertising developed a more aggressive edge. The narrative implied that McCormick was the "Father of Reapers," and all competitors were mere childlike followers. The 1885 catalog pronounced, "We glory in the undisputed fact that the McCormick is the original of all grain and grass cutting machines . . . admitted to be 'the type and pattern after which all others are modeled.'" The company's longevity in the industry was evidence of "the inexorable law of the survival of the fittest," which crowned the McCormick machine "unapproachable and alone." The company further implied that competitors did not contribute to the progress of the modern harvester industry but merely "anxiously follow[ed]" its lead. The 1892 catalog made this charge directly, labeling industry peers as "followers . . . who can copy, can rob and pattern" but could not match the ingenuity or quality of the house of McCormick. The company's "priority of invention" was equated to its "superiority of construction."[28]

The firm also utilized the past to place its machine among the great inventions of civilization and progress. The 1887 catalog compared McCormick's reaper to such important inventions as the railroad, steamboat, and telegraph, which had "set the world in a blaze of excitement and upon a career of marvelous prosperity." Ad writers went further the next year, declaring the advent of the reaper to be *the* event that prompted modern ingenuity and progress. Claiming authority over modernity, the company boldly stated itself the leader not just of the harvester industry but of progress in general: "from no other institution in any land has the spirit of progress . . . received such an impetus as ours." Tapping into Gilded Age and Progressive Era infatuation with progress, civilization, and technology, the company included their founder among the pantheon of great inventors that brought about modernity.[29]

The McCormicks also applied their brand to command higher prices from farmers during the competitive reaper war, thanks to their supposed higher moral value. The literature and sales agents referred to these traits when explaining why a McCormick machine cost more than a Wood harvester or a Deering binder. Customers would "cheerfully" pay more, because of McCormick's "historical record" and the "intrinsic merits" of their machines. Tellingly, McCormick sales management in Chicago acknowledged that "the very fact that our goods are sold for more money than our competitors' . . . increases their popularity with the farming community." The "McCormick prestige" of history coupled with the comparatively higher price translated into the perception of McCormick machines as being a higher qualitative value, allowing the company to "get the bulk of the best farmers" and capture a sizeable market share.[30]

Beyond justifying McCormick supremacy in the harvester industry and more expensive machinery, the sales narratives also asserted that the technological surplus value of their founder's invention allowed farmers to prosper. These messages to farmers about their own relationship with the company mark the change in the advertising appeal of the "established 1831" brand, which originally only signified McCormick's superiority to its industrial competitors. In contrast, the 1885 catalog emphasized the relationship between farmers and the company, reminding customers that McCormick's invention "released the

6. McCormick annual catalog, front cover, sketch draft, 1890. The cover conveys the idealized meaning of owning McCormick's updated harvester-binding machine. Farmers would no longer harvest the grain by hand, as they had in 1830. Rather, they and their families would enjoy a life of relaxation and leisure as farmer-capitalists while wage laborers using the McCormick binder profitably harvested their fields for them. In this advertised imagining, the machine was the customer's gateway to upward social mobility, a better life, and wealth. Wisconsin Historical Society, WHI-86968.

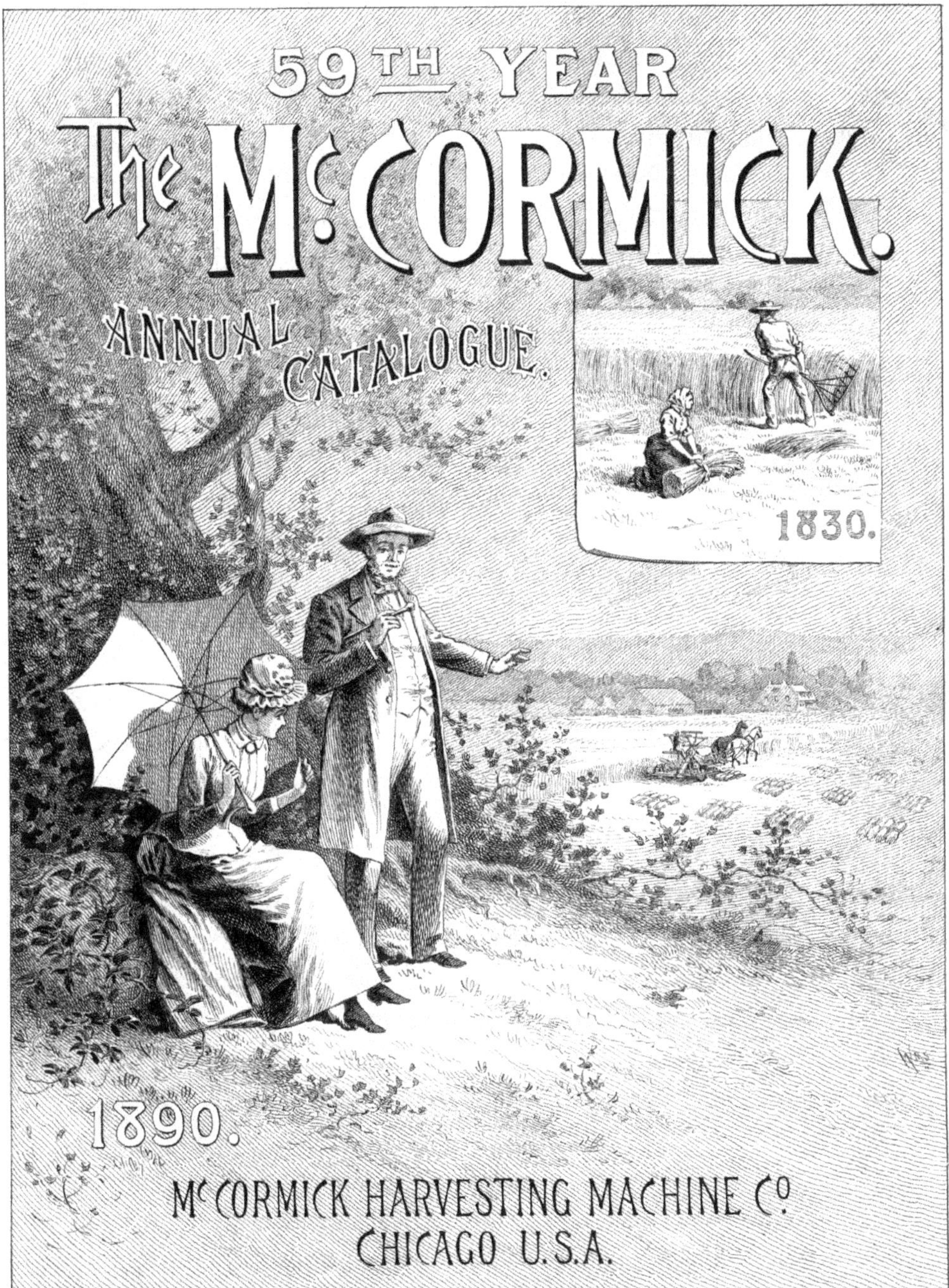
59TH YEAR
The McCORMICK.
ANNUAL CATALOGUE.
1830.
1890.
McCORMICK HARVESTING MACHINE Co.
CHICAGO U.S.A.

farmer from the drudgery of life, [and] almost miraculously increased production." The company's ingenuity conferred substantial benefits on customers, as it reminded farmers "as heretofore we shall make your interests our interests."[31]

The cover art of the 1890 catalog summarized the concept of technological surplus value. On the front cover a farmer stands next to a fashionably attired woman wearing a stylish hat and holding a parasol beneath a hilltop tree (fig. 6). He is gesturing to a harvester cutting a field of grain in the background. An inset picture in the top right corner of the illustration, labeled "1830," shows a man raking grain by hand in front of uncut fields and a bonneted woman binding grain by hand. The image implied that the modern farmer and his wife were no longer toilers as their predecessors had been in 1830. Rather he was an owner of producer-good capital—operated by wage laborers—which accumulated such wealth that he and his wife could enjoy a life of leisurely consumption.[32]

The back cover drew out the concept further by incorporating mechanized farmers into middle-class consumption and the project of civilization (see fig. 7). Set in a parlor, the picture shows a well-groomed, bow-tied man sitting in an armchair with a foot on an ottoman, pointing a pencil at North America on a globe. A boy leans across the man's lap to get a good look at the globe, and a girl looks up from her book on the plush carpeted floor. There is a large mirror on the wall, revealing Asia on the literally darker side of the globe as well as a miniature marble bust atop a bookcase. A painting of a mower cutting through a field hangs adjacent to the mirror. Text across the globe reads, "My children, on this globe you see the harvest fields of the earth where the McCormick is ever king." The illustration is labeled "Teaching Object Lessons."[33]

The 1890 cover art, combined with the narratives in the catalog pages, conveys the core of the technological surplus value within the brand. The founder's invention signaled a monumental jump forward in the progress of civilization and the circumstances of farmers

7. McCormick annual catalog, back cover, 1890. Similar to the front cover, the back cover of the catalog invited potential customers to imagine themselves as landed gentry with comfortable parlors full of luxurious consumer goods. Wisconsin Historical Society, WHI-4413.

everywhere. The McCormick Company continued in its founder's footsteps as a cutting-edge leader in agricultural progress, blazing trails where others merely followed. Investing in a more expensive McCormick machine not only guaranteed that the purchaser had the highest-quality machine on the market but also promised that the farmer would rise in status and material wealth. No longer would the farmer be a toiler, but rather he would transform into a capitalist, owning producer goods and hiring laborers, both of which produced the wealth necessary to enjoy the consumer goods and leisure of the Victorian middle class. McCormick machines were branded as a status symbol, an idea intrinsically connected to the company's "prestige of priority." Butler bragged that the 1890 catalog was "the best advertising matter that was ever put out." He recognized that selling harvesters was about convincing would-be customers to dream of the material benefits that owning such an expensive machine would confer on them. As farming men and women gazed through the pages of the catalog, they saw "better" machinery as a pathway to having "better" lives.[34]

With the rising tide of radical agrarian producerism in the later 1880s and into the 1890s, the McCormick Company sought to harness its supposed authority over farmers to defuse their hostility. In 1889 the firm sent out literature to its agents, advising them on how to deal with "the Farmers Grange Movement"—its blanket term for all agrarian organizations that sought communal solutions to social and economic problems. The pamphlet outlined why the McCormick Company was not a monopoly and could not bear to reduce the price of its machinery because of the rigorous competition in the harvester business. Its tone was patronizing, as it warned "against the *politicians* who are . . . political demagogues who care little for the farmers' Granges or the farmers' interests." The company attempted to separate its customers from the radical elements. Furthermore, this circular seemed to encourage reform efforts: "Wherever extortion or monopoly or combination rings exist, we hope the farmers will strike hard blows to eradicate them." Indicating the smarminess of their public relations rhetoric, the next year they attempted to create a "Harvester Trust" along with five other manufacturers.[35]

Reflecting populist rhetoric of modernization and economic liberty, McCormick advertising further stressed that farmers' shrewd management was necessary to reap the rewards of the land. An 1893 advertisement began, "The Pleasures of Toil are unknown to many thousands in the world's grand army of toilers. It's because so few of them labor with their heads as well as with their hands. Thinking pays; ideas are so much capital." The advertisement stated the literal wealth production of thought, suggesting a similarity between the productive methods of farmers and the harvester firm. Manual labor alone was not the best way to obtain "the Pleasures of Toil"; clearly producer goods were necessary to the production of wealth as well.[36]

Alongside the campaign of marketing literature, McCormick officials consistently solicited newspaper editors to publish glowing articles that reflected their history and its just rewards. These pieces more openly justified the company's elite position in society and the merits of technological surplus value. A mechanical journal explained "that immense wealth came to the inventor for the benefits conferred." Some more explicitly placed Cyrus McCormick among the canon of great inventors. An article in *Greater Chicago* claimed that McCormick's "fame in the agricultural field was gained solely through the fact that not unlike Thomas A. Edison, his was a mastermind in mechanics. . . . [He] was one of the world's greatest benefactors to mankind." The text went on to state that his reaper was "the greatest labor saving device of the century." The reading public, and farmers in particular, received the message of Cyrus McCormick's inventive prowess from many sources.[37]

The apex of the company's efforts to generate consumer empathy with the brand and restore their authority over their customers was the 1894 catalog. Looking radically different from previous catalogs, the cover read, "The Farmer—Our Country's Defender—The Builder of Our National Prosperity and the Guaranty of Our Future Greatness" (see fig. 8). Betraying anxiety about the agrarian political movement, it displayed two illustrations. The first was of a courtroom bordered by a U.S. flag, captioned "The Balance of Power." The second was of a farmer riding a McCormick and titled "The hand that drives the Binder is the hand should rule the world." The cover set the tone for the catalog, shifting away from the company's usual celebration of the reaper in years past toward a rejoicing paean to the farmer. Company management knew that their customers were the same populists that threatened to topple the economic order. In response they tried accommodating the insurgents.[38]

Within the catalog's pages, the narrative labored to establish the parallels between the farmer and the manufacturer. The connection was drawn from their supposedly similar relationship to technology and producerism: "The practical farmer of today is a theoretical mechanic." A few pages later the text reads, "No workman can perform as much labor and do his work as well as the American mechanic." Following the narrative's rationale, the farmer was not a toiler, but neither was he a capitalist, as the catalogs had inferred in 1890. Rather, the farmer was a modern mechanic running finely tuned machinery, which made him more productive. The company implied that it played a special role in allowing the farmer to reach this evolved state because of its relationship with mechanical ingenuity.[39]

For the first time the sales magazine included historical biographies of prominent farmers. The new feature introduced a rhetorical question: "What does not the world owe to the farm?" The biographies presented important business and political figures with agrarian roots,

8. McCormick annual catalog, front cover, 1894. Reflecting concern about the rise of the People's Party, the catalog's imagery and messaging dramatically shifted in 1894. Instead of encouraging potential customers to view themselves as soon-to-be farmer-capitalists, the 1894 catalog celebrated farmers as the core of national values and political power. The text within further highlighted the role of famous farmers, like Cyrus McCormick, in bringing about progress as vanguards of civilization and agrarian allies. Wisconsin Historical Society, WHI-4415.

1894
THE FARMER
OUR
COUNTRY'S DEFENDER.
THE
BUILDER OF OUR
NATIONAL PROSPERITY
AND
THE GUARANTY
OF
OUR FUTURE
GREATNESS.
The Balance of Power
McCORMICK
The hand that drives the Binder
is the hand should rule the world.

including George Washington, Henry Clay, Leland Stanford, and Phillip Armour. Predictably, the catalog also lionized Cyrus McCormick. His biography demonstrated "how a farmer boy worked his way up to be one of the greatest and richest manufacturers of the country." The entire performance of the narrative suggested McCormick was a farmer hero. In all, the house of McCormick, then, was not leeching wealth away from producers whom populists targeted but rather acting as an ally in the pursuit of individual success. The biographies as a whole, and McCormick's in particular, implied that farmers could rely on political and industrial elites to act in their best interests. The advertising copy stressed that these leaders had risen through the economic and political ranks from origins as farmers themselves.[40]

The McCormick Harvesting Machine Company's publications leading up to 1894 were public messages to potential customers aligning the two parties' interests and justifying a position of dominance. The change in promotional literature from the original "established 1831" advertising in 1879 indicated the company's accommodation of the prominent grassroots challenges it faced. These messages were no longer only about superiority to competitors but also about harmonious relationships with customers. By 1896, however, the radical populist sentiments, which the McCormicks sought to alleviate, were sweeping the nation in anticipation of the upcoming presidential election.

By early July the populist movement seemed to be influencing the Democratic Party at the National Convention in Chicago and was making Cyrus McCormick II anxious. The populist uprising was reorienting the party his family had supported since the 1850s, away from his economic interests. His business dealings with farmers and laborers had made him familiar with the threats that populism posed, but as these radical ideas seeped into mainstream politics, he worried that it signaled more drastic changes to the existing economic order. While stumping for bimetallism, Ohio bonanza farmer and Democratic leader John Bookwalter compounded McCormick II's fears by proclaiming that mechanized harvesters did not share the wealth in the ways that the industry implied, but only increased productivity in exchange for increased debt. When Democrats adopted the People's Party plank on bimetallism, McCormick II sought to translate the authority created by his technological surplus value and brand into real political capital against the radical movement.[41]

McCormick II publicly took a stand against the radical movement, urging the Democratic Party to abandon the free-silver platform. His gold-bug appeal seemed to be economic suicide because it went directly against the core of his agrarian customer base. An incredulous newspaper telegraphed McCormick to confirm the quote, "believing that the news would create a strong prejudice against product of your company." McCormick confirmed the report and presented himself as a trusted adviser to the farmers: "The present silver sentiment is a delusion, put forward for political purposes and for individual personal gain by a few at the expense of the masses." He confirmed his commitment to the Democratic Party but qualified it by saying he could not support free silver, "which I firmly believe to be disastrous to the highest interests of the Nation." As in earlier public statements against the Grangers, McCormick II attempted to separate his customers from the agitators who led them astray. This exchange garnered national attention but did not stop the Democrats from nominating William Jennings Bryan for president after his famous Cross of Gold speech. Following his failed appeal to curb the Democratic adoption of free silver, the harvester magnate abandoned his family's political legacy as staunch Democrats and endorsed Republican William McKinley for president.[42]

McCormick II continued his campaign against Bryan and free silver through his sales network. In mid-August Butler surveyed all 7,500 McCormick agents, asking them to provide information on the political leanings of their regions. Butler warned, "We have never before been so at a loss to lay out our plans and work for the next season as we are at this time. If we felt sure the election would go for sound money and reasonable protection, we should push ahead with our manufacturing." He implied that if free silver won, the company would cease manufacturing machines because of resulting monetary instability. The memorandum was widely published by conservative papers as evidence of the economic apocalypse that would reward free-silver monetization. Undoubtedly the message was an attempt by McCormick II to claim a leadership position among his clientele and employees. The company made clear that if Bryan won, they would have to curtail production of reapers. Sales agents reminded customers that if the company had to cut back, the farmers would no longer have access to the technology that allowed them to prosper.[43]

McKinley utilized McCormick II's message and endorsement in his stump speeches, predicting that free silver would destabilize the economic order of the nation. "This uncertainty makes every businessman pause, makes every business enterprise halt; and while they pause and halt the home of every workingman is filled with despair." McKinley interpreted the message as McCormick II planned, implying that anything that negatively impacted capital would dynamically harm farmers and laborers.[44] McCormick II's public stance against free silver was a calculated gambit. In taking the stand, he relied heavily on his company's prestige as a respected source of authority in the agrarian mind. He hoped the brand would be resilient enough to prevent a consumer backlash and sought additional means to reinforce the company's public image as the great agrarian liberator and forerunner of progress. The U.S. Department of the Treasury provided him with just such an opportunity.

In March 1896 the Treasury began to print a new "education" series of silver certificates. The new bills artistically represented the progressive themes of the 1890s. In allegorical classical style, the images depicted "Electricity Presenting Light to the World" and "History Instructing Youth," among others. For the first time federal currency was pressed with images of nonpolitical leaders, including the inventors Samuel Morse and Robert Fulton on the two-dollar bill. The

Department of the Treasury planned to issue five-dollar and ten-dollar bills later that year. After bimetal exchange had been prohibited in 1893, silver certificates plummeted in value because they were perceived as intrinsically inferior to gold-backed currency. Secretary of the Treasury John G. Carlisle—a gold bug himself—recognized the legitimacy of silverite demands for an increased money supply and attempted to shore up the cultural and moral value associated with silver without "freeing" it, to encourage its circulation. The printing of inventors and machines on the "education" series was to remind people that silver was associated with the superiority of American civilization, even if the certificates could not be exchanged for gold. Despite these efforts, gold-bug capitalists and most bankers would not accept silver-backed currency as a means to repay debts, so Carlisle's gesture was fruitless.[45]

Regardless of this, the McCormicks learned of the new silver-certificate series and sought to have their patriarch's likeness printed on the new currency, as a pillar of progress. McCormick II wrote to their agent in Washington DC, Louis Dent, to "ascertain who is it that decides [on the designs] . . . and from them could you not inquire whether the development of the agricultural resources of the country are not equal in importance to the development of the steamship or the telegraph. . . . The name of the inventor of the Reaper might find a place with those of the pioneers upon other lines." If the family could have their father definitively presented as the inventor of the reaper on the silver certificate, the government would effectively brand their version of history onto the currency most associated with agrarian interests. The meaning would seem to be that wealth accrued by farmers using McCormick's technology was literally printed as "McCormick" money—a profound statement of elite hegemony. McCormick II began his lobby of the Treasury office three days before his sales agents began pressuring farmers to abandon free silver. He considered his ability to make a political stand against populists without injury dynamically linked to the intellectual debt he perceived farmers owed his father's company. He hoped that placing his father's image on currency would remind them of that relationship.[46]

Louis Dent was the family's first historical laborer who did work resembling that of the modern historian. Smarting from the debacle at the 1893 world's fair, the McCormick family had employed Dent to compile evidence in Washington DC at the Congressional Library and Patent Office that would verify their history. Dent was college educated and had worked as a stenographer, a journalist, and a freelance researcher beginning around 1890. He came into contact with the McCormicks because he had provided research assistance to James G. Blaine's (Anita McCormick Blaine's father-in-law) for his memoirs of his experience as an elected representative to Congress.[47]

Dent's lobbying efforts proved successful. The Department of the Treasury released the new design in late December 1896. The *Chicago Daily Tribune* ran the headline "New $10 Silver Certificates: Will Bear Vignettes of C. H. McCormick and Eli Whitney." McKinley had already won the presidential election by that point, and undoubtedly the chorus of dire predictions by gold-bug capitalists played some role in defeating Bryan, even if the exact degree is immeasurable.[48]

Competitors throughout the harvester industry had long contested the McCormick origin story as an oversimplification of the past and a direct slight to their own credibility. They too had been faced with discontented agrarian customers and endeavored to temper their criticism. As a whole, the harvester industry advertised an amicable relationship between farmers and industrialists that aided in their pursuit of wealth. These attempts at fostering a harmonious partnership with farmers were constantly undercut by McCormick's "bombastic advertising," which derided them as "followers" that "rob[bed]" McCormick of its intellectual property and peddled "second-rate" machines that were "trash."[49]

Steward, an inventor and patent officer for Deering Harvester, was the most outspoken crusader against the McCormick narrative. He sarcastically summed up the success of the McCormick advertising campaign as a result of its longevity: "Popular belief that Cyrus H. McCormick invented the reaper and thus laid the foundation for Harvesting Machinery is as deeply rooted as the child's faith in Santa Claus. . . . It is a half-century since Cyrus H. McCormick began advertising and claiming he was the inventor of the reaper. It has been dinned into the ears of the press, into the ears of editors, has found its way into Encyclopedias and has loaded the shelves of our libraries with false biographies." Steward further lamented the inability to counter fictitious advertising: "While business houses cannot be seriously censured for this kind of advertising, it is censurable to mold advertising talk into history." Regarded as the utmost authority on the reaper's true mechanical evolution, he saw it as his duty to correct the "historical injustices to real inventors."[50]

As previously detailed, rival harvester manufacturers corrected the history at the 1893 world's fair through presentation of historical evidence to the Inventors Congress. News of the victory, however, did not reach their agrarian customer base. In 1897, when the rivals contested the placement of Cyrus McCormick's likeness on the silver certificate, they were more successful in publicly revealing the McCormicks' fictionalization of history. Upon becoming aware of the McCormick scheme at the Department of the Treasury, competing manufacturers organized a cooperative refutation. The arguments and the results were covered extensively in farm-trade journals as well as many national newspapers. The public would finally bear witness to the contest for the past.

The Illinois-based harvester manufacturers of Deering Harvester Company, Plano Manufacturing Company, and Warder, Bushnell and Glessner responded to the initial report from the Department of the Treasury, collectively sending a letter to Treasury secretary John Carlisle. Their letter offered a history of the reaper's development, and they pleaded to be seen in a hearing on the topic. They were prepared to present "overwhelming proof that the popular belief that McCormick was the inventor of the reaper is a fallacy." The rivals believed that placing McCormick on federal money—whose likeness was also the official symbol of his family's company—would serve as a government endorsement of the "falsehood . . . which injustice would result in corresponding financial injury to all competing manufacturers." After sending their letters, the companies recruited other firms to join their cause—successfully gaining the support of at least the Walter A. Wood Mowing and Reaping Machine Company in Hoosick Falls, New York. The companies began immediate preparations to send Steward and another lawyer, Henry S. Robbins, to Washington to argue their case to Secretary Carlisle. Wood Harvester also recruited the U.S. senators from New York, David Hill and Edward Murphy, to assist Robbins and Steward.[51]

The legal brief that Robbins and Steward presented to Carlisle laid out the injustice of promoting the McCormick brand over others as well as the historical inaccuracy of such a decision. Robbins described the stalemate of the reaper war and the importance of advertising to the industry, telling Carlisle that "the actual merit of those manufactured by the different makers are so nearly equal that the selection of the purchaser is generally decided by some outside consideration." He further argued, "The [government] indorsement [*sic*] . . . of C. H. McCormick will attract universal attention . . . and will ensure to them great profits which they would not otherwise enjoy." He disclosed what those throughout the industry had known for years: the McCormicks had fabricated history. The rest of the industry salivated at the opportunity to refute that past publicly in front of an official arbiter.[52]

McCormick II responded by writing a letter to Carlisle that ostensibly restated years of branding and advertising. He argued that his father deserved recognition because his efforts "resulted in such benefits to mankind," allowing farmers and other manufacturers to substantially contribute to the progress of civilization. McCormick presented the central tenets of technological surplus value and underlined his father's efforts as a producer. "My father toiled as few men have toiled and with remarkable perseverance. . . . You will understand the pride

I naturally feel in his invention and especially in the tenacity, energy and consistency of purpose that animated him during his early years of hardship and toil." He further listed his father among other great inventors and the meaning of this invention to civilization: "At the beginning of the century agriculture was almost the sole occupation but with the tremendous energy of American invention progress in lines of manufacture has led our people into the workshop and the cities. . . . The reaper . . . has enabled the production of crops that have more than kept pace with the growth of the centers of population, and though the young man of the farm has gone to the city still the labor saving farm tools have kept up production." Concluding his letter, he justified federal endorsement of his company's brand because it was "impossible to dissociate my father's name from the invention which he made and the business which he founded."[53]

McCormick also sent Swift to Washington to assist Dent in arguing the facts of their case to Secretary Carlisle, but their efforts came up short. Undoubtedly, Carlisle was surprised by the uproar caused by his decision to place McCormick on the silver certificate. He, like many others, had recognized the company's advertised past as truth and so accepted Dent's early lobbying as a clear choice for inclusion on the proposed silver certificates. Once the other harvester manufacturers contested this decision, he decided it was easier to leave well enough alone rather than bother with such things. He instructed his chief of engraving to substitute other vignettes for Whitney and McCormick before any of the bills went into circulation. National and local newspapers reported Carlisle's decision, creating widespread doubt regarding the McCormick narrative.[54]

The rival harvester companies wasted no time in generating press to spread the news of the Treasury's rejection of the McCormick fabrications of the past. They sent out essays and articles across the country, and their sales agents reminded customers of the decision. One article, written by the Deering Company and printed in *Farm Machinery*, began by crediting Hussey with the invention of the reaper. After revealing the "true" history of the reaper, it then concluded, "It seems very strange that his [McCormick's] successors should claim that he ever invented any detail that lasted, or in fact, any that was ever used by any manufactory." Deering implied that the McCormicks knew the true history of the machine all along and played the role of the despised confidence man, willfully lying to the public to boost sales.[55]

The McCormicks were aware that the events at the Department of the Treasury threatened to undermine their credibility in the public mind and waged a countersmear campaign. Immediately, Butler telegraphed *Farm Machinery*, ordering them to issue a retraction of the article or be sued for libel. This worked to silence one paper, but on the whole irreparable damage had been done to their reputation by the entire incident at the nation's capital. The company used their in-house paper, the *Farmers' Advance*, and networks of sales agents to reassure their customer base that the allegations were untrue. The paper proposed that the McCormick Company's status as the leading producer of reapers was evidence that McCormick invented the machine: "Had Hussey really demonstrated to the world that he was the inventor of the successful reaping machine, and had McCormick been forced as Hussey was, to recognize his failure and retire from the field . . . Hussey would be, to-day, the leading manufacturer of harvesting machines and McCormick would be comparatively unknown." Hussey could not have been the inventor because he did not have the rewards that would befit invention. While this seems like a desperate argument, it reflected the power of the alchemy of progress in national culture, using success in the present as direct evidence of Cyrus H. McCormick's marvelous invention in the past.[56]

Shortly after Carlisle changed his mind, both sides published documentation of their arguments for public consumption and advertising material. The inventors, Steward, Miller, and Parsons, assembled *Overlooked Pages of Reaper History*, a republication of three pamphlets from the 1850s, which demonstrated that Hussey invented the reaper before McCormick, through detailing the mechanical operation of each. Steward wanted to have the title "placed in every library in the world and perhaps translated into foreign languages." Rodney Swift at McCormick countered with an April 1897 article in *Implement Age*, "Who Invented the Reaper," an incredibly long and detailed mechanical description of the difference between Hussey's and McCormick's reapers. Swift's argument (and perhaps even the entire text of the article) was based on historical research that had been compiled by Louis Dent, who had found an 1850 advertisement in which Cyrus Sr. directly compared his machine with Hussey's on both its mechanical and historical merits for the purposes of patent extension. Dent presented this document and others, along with his own analysis, to the family in a bound volume. Dent's volume, which Swift reprinted as his own for the company's purposes, can be considered the family's first in-depth historical study.[57]

The editor of *Implement Age* reviewed the arguments provided by McCormick and the opposition later that month and found neither to be conclusive or compelling. He felt that others "who have time and patience to wade through the tediously long *ex parte* pleas of both" would agree. Despite this finding, Steward and Swift and several other inventors—paid clandestinely by both factions—carried on a running argument in the journal for two more years. The printed exchange degenerated from a discussion of the mechanical evolution of the machine to personal attacks on each other's character. "I have stated that John F. Steward, who in this controversy has been attempting to make a record to suit his own sinister motives," wrote Swift, "has been guilty of mutilating and misrepresenting well established historical facts." Steward ultimately threatened to sue Swift for libel, forcing *Implement Age* to stop publishing the heated exchange.[58]

The 1897 silver-certificate victory emboldened William Deering and Company to make greater hay out of history as a way to cut into the McCormick brand. Deering had made its own 1850s connection with the evolution of the binder a part of its advertising as early as 1886, practicing the McCormick historical advertising strategy for its own ends. The company's success in contesting McCormick's past, at both the 1893 world's fair and then more publicly during the silver-certificate controversy of 1897, led Deering management to advertise a counterhistory of the reaper that, although it that had no connection directly to their own company, was a single-minded assault on McCormick's brand and history.[59]

Deering's historical aggression is best demonstrated by its activities at the Paris Exposition of 1900. Mirroring the McCormicks' efforts at the 1893 world's fair, Deering staged a historical coup and secured an exclusive right from French officials to create a "retrospective exhibit" of harvesting technology for the fair-going public. Covering fifteen thousand square feet, the Deering exhibit included ninety-five reproductions of historical harvesting machine models (dazzlingly electrified to demonstrate each machine's mechanical operation), thirty large watercolor paintings of historical reapers in various landscapes, and portraits of eighteen inventors. Digging as deep as the Roman Empire, the exhibit included a model of the "semimechanical means of harvesting resorted to by the Gauls, as told by Pliny," flattering the French by referring to it as the first civilized attempt at mechanized reaping. Deering set out to muddy the waters, telling a more complicated narrative of technological evolution, which the McCormicks resented as an attack on their brand, business, and family.[60]

Ultimately, the prolonged historical advertising battle tarnished the reputation of the McCormick Harvesting Machine Company as the most prestigious manufacturer of reapers. The McCormick works produced an estimated 150,000 machines annually by the 1890s—about 88,000 fewer machines than the Deering Company—an acceptable difference when their brand was a status symbol and their machines commanded higher prices. Once their competitors had dispelled the "prestige of priority," however, the McCormick market share dwindled in the face of comparable and cheaper harvesters supplied by competitors. In private conversation the Deerings offered to cease their counterhistory advertising if the McCormicks would eliminate their claims to the past. The McCormicks, however, could not sacrifice the "historical feature of the harvesting machine business" because it would be "against the interests of the Company" as the cornerstone of their brand.[61]

Faced with a declining market share, the McCormicks were forced to mark down their prices and began pursuing opportunities to eliminate the Deerings through a merger or an acquisition beginning in 1897. Advertising played a key consideration in this decision. As the family matriarch, Nettie Fowler McCormick, put it, the Deerings' successful "cultural warfare" on her deceased husband's prestige and the company's brand demanded that they either "buy" or "kill" their competitor's company. Feeling that the Deerings' "enormous" price was too high, despicably implying that they were "the equal of our business in its prestige in the country," she resolved that the McCormick Company must bury the Deering Company through price slashing. She was certain that her family would emerge victorious if they sold at prices "as low or lower than anyone," because McCormick machines were better and "have the greater [public] respect due to . . . longer standing." Following her advice, the McCormick Company engaged in price warfare for the next five years, determined to eliminate their competitors and the negative advertising campaigns that had tarnished their company's brand.[62]

Failing to destroy their rival through competition or restore their company's previous market advantage and historical prestige, in 1901 the McCormicks renewed negotiations to merge with the Deering Company. The fierce competition had proven too ruinous to their fortunes to continue onward. With the help of George Perkins from the House of Morgan, the Deering and McCormick Companies combined with the three other largest harvester manufacturers to create the International Harvester Company in 1902. Importantly, the McCormicks duped their new partners with the help of their in-law John D. Rockefeller, who secretly bought large portions of the "public stock." By 1903 the two families owned half of the total stock in the new corporation.

After the ten-year period of Morgan-guided leadership mandated by the merger agreement, the McCormicks gained complete control of the corporation and the very industry they claimed their father had created. Almost immediately, they resurrected their historical narrative as part of their public relations and legal defense to refute a federal antitrust case brought against them in 1912.[63]

In the last two decades of the nineteenth century, the McCormick Harvesting Machine Company was embattled on three fronts by its employees, its industry peers, and its customers. While the firm and its competitors recited economic theories of capitalist liberty to their unionizing employees, none dared antagonize their customers with the same language. In dealing with radical agrarian clients who sought drastic economic reforms, the McCormick Company was not unified with other harvesting companies but in direct competition. In response the McCormicks articulated a technological surplus-value ideology that offered a usable past for public consumption, creating a brand based on Cyrus Sr.'s invention of the reaper and aligning their supposed inventive energy with producer populists' labor. The McCormicks' technological surplus-value ideology helped the company maintain primacy in the harvester trade during the reaper wars and through the rise of the populist movement. Their brand, however, made protection of their history the same as protection of their profits—a critical chink in their armor of "prestige" that was ultimately exposed and led to the demise of the company's market dominance.[64]

3

Historical Laborers and the Manipulation of the Past

"Secretary of War Stanton said: 'The reaper is to the North what slavery is to the South. By taking the place of regiments of young men in western harvest fields, it released them to do battle for the Union at the front and at the same time kept up the supply of bread for the nation and the nation's armies. Thus, without McCormick's invention I feel the North could not win and the Union would have been dismembered.'"[1]

This quote came from a public relations history produced in 1931 by International Harvester as part of the centennial celebration of Cyrus McCormick's invention of the reaper. This history of McCormick's reaper was distributed to teachers, newspaper editors, and others. Edwin McMasters Stanton's quote dominates the brief section devoted to the U.S. Civil War. It is meant to suggest that one of the iconic figures of the Civil War recognized McCormick as a patriotic contributor to the Union cause, and without him Union victory and the emancipation of millions of slaves would have been in doubt. However, this noble, patriotic image of Cyrus McCormick is a myth.

The problem with Stanton's quote is that it has been taken out of context and grossly misrepresents not only McCormick's feelings about the Civil War but also his factory's production of reapers to support that righteous cause. Of course, Stanton's quote—and its misinterpretation—does not only appear in International Harvester's history publications but pervades the historiography of Cyrus McCormick during the Civil War. It has also been used in hundreds of books, articles, and historical documents about the Civil War and nineteenth-century America.

The ubiquity of Stanton's misleading quote is the result of a concerted effort by Cyrus McCormick's family to shape and protect Cyrus's legacy as the inventor of the reaper. The McCormicks had faced frequent threats to this legacy from competing reaper firms. These battles for the past were carried out in newspapers, advertisements, field trials, and world's fairs. Salesmen from across the industry carried the controversy into farmers' homes throughout the country as they compared their machines and their histories with those of the opposition. In the years following their patriarch's death, the McCormicks discovered that holding fast and repeatedly broadcasting their private memory of the past was not enough to certify their story as truth in the public imagination. Unwavering and outspoken about their historical beliefs, they gradually turned to historical professionals to discover, analyze, and publish evidence that would vindicate their claims. Sensitive to shifts in public perceptions of the past, the McCormicks also sought cultural institutions that would protect their father's legacy for all time. They ultimately set their sights on New York University's Hall of Fame for Great Americans, seeking their father's inclusion in that temple of honor for thirty-five years following its opening in 1900.

The family's sustained efforts focusing on the Hall of Fame provoked vehement resistance from their own relatives. Crucially, Cyrus McCormick's siblings, nephews, and nieces believed that his father, Robert McCormick, had invented the reaper and entrusted it to Cyrus to manage for the family's financial well-being. The relatives had long been offended by the company's advertising of the supposed "great inventor," who they knew had no mechanical instinct whatsoever. In fact, when Cyrus McCormick II began utilizing his father's heritage as the brand of the company in the late 1870s, the bold claim tore apart the ownership of C. H. and L. J. McCormick, resulting in the creation of the McCormick Harvesting Machine Company. Leander and his son, Robert McCormick II, demanded a buyout for their share of the company, because they would not be a party to detracting from Robert McCormick's legacy and their own heritage. The buyout was completed after Cyrus's death, for $2.5 million in 1889. As part of the deal, they informally agreed to let the company's advertising stand. This understanding was upset when Cyrus McCormick's heirs began campaigning for the Hall of Fame. In response the cousins began to make their own larger claims to promote Robert McCormick's legacy.[2]

Faced with fierce industrial challenges to their company's advertising, in 1900 Cyrus McCormick's heirs created the McCormick Biographical Association, which eventually spearheaded their Hall of Fame efforts as well. This organization was founded at a time when academic historians had not yet closed ranks as the sole professionals of historical merit. The McCormick Biographical Association's experience employing and consulting with a variety of historical laborers willing to do research, organize libraries, offer analyses, and write narratives inside and outside of academia indicates the breadth of the historical professional spectrum at the turn of the twentieth century. Employing historical laborers from across the spectrum, the McCormicks hired lawyers, advertisers, freelance researchers, librarians, clerical workers, and academics. Like many other new professionals in the emerging corporate order, these historical laborers strove to secure stable employment and middle-class salaries through energetic institutional organizing and relentless pursuit of their employer's objectives. Approaching their work from very different vocational backgrounds and with diverse professional identities, these historians adopted widely divergent conceptions of "objective" historical conduct in hopes of proving the value of their expertise. Their historical contributions were of varying quality, credibility, and style but became equalized and dynamically interwoven under the obscuring aegis of the McCormick family's elite status and historical enterprise.[3]

The full spectrum of historical laborers during the early twentieth century is largely ignored in the historiography of the historical profession. The most relevant work on the topic, Peter Novick's *That Noble Dream*, details the struggle of academically trained historians to gain professional authority and their quest for "objective" study of the past. Under the auspices of James Franklin Jameson and the American Historical Association, academics were able to wrest control of university historian positions from "literary" "gentlemen amateurs" by 1900 through creating peer-reviewed journals, standardized "scientific" training for students, and certified credentials in the form of the doctorate to control access to jobs. While Novick acknowledges that beyond the university "nothing approaching a thoroughgoing monopoly [over historical labor] by certified professionals was ever achieved," he fails to recognize that noncertified laborers had a substantial impact on academics' historical project.[4]

The McCormicks were able to reshape their father's Civil War legacy because of the uneven application of professional standards within this broad historical labor pool during this era. Historical laborers across the professional spectrum, including moonlighting and unemployed academics, were overly eager and willing to provide historical evidence and narratives that placed Cyrus McCormick on "the right side of history" in exchange for monetary rewards. Seeking middle-class earnings and professional stability, the family's historical staff and associated consultants actively conducted research, challenged dissenting historical opinions, produced historical works, influenced the scholarship of others, and created a world-class agricultural library. In this context "objectivity" was murky, and Stanton's quote became powerful ammunition for the McCormick Biographical Association as the primary proof of Cyrus's contributions to one of the United States' most formative moments.

Only after peeling back the layers of fictitious history can a clear picture emerge of Cyrus McCormick's real relationship to the Civil War. He was not the patriotic supporter of the Union cause that Edwin Stanton's quote implies; rather he was a Peace Democrat. Also mistaken is how prolific his reaper works was during the Civil War. From 1861 to 1865 reaper production at C. H. McCormick and Brothers can be characterized as turbulent at best.

Cyrus McCormick was deeply distraught by the outbreak of war within the United States and actively sought to end the conflict in peaceful reunification through both legitimate and clandestine means. As a native Virginian and a businessman of Chicago, he was uncomfortably torn between the two belligerents. Until the outbreak of war, he continued to remind Southern farmers that, despite the company's location in the North, "our heart still yields allegiance to the 'Old Dominion' and we claim a place as the representatives of your interests." McCormick's actions from 1860 to 1865 reflect the truth of that statement. He believed that the Union should be preserved and that the North should make the utmost concessions to the South. Determined to promote this perspective, McCormick purchased two newspapers in Chicago and combined them to make one strong Democratic paper. He also attempted to reconcile Stephen Douglas and Southern Democrats, became chair of the Democratic Cook County Central Committee, and unsuccessfully ran for a seat in Congress in 1864. Staunchly supporting conservative religious beliefs on the question of slavery, he provided monetary support to prop up Old School Presbyterianism when sectionalism was tearing the denomination apart. More damning than his party politics were his extra political affairs. Before his journey to Europe in 1862, Cyrus procured a note of introduction from Horace Greeley to William L. Dayton, the U.S. ambassador to France. The note suggested that McCormick wanted to convince Napoleon III to intervene in the conflict as a peacemaker. Late in the war he also hatched a desperate plan for Northern Democrats to negotiate a peace with the Southern Democrats in Richmond. McCormick went as far as petitioning President Lincoln to condone this plan. More blatant unpatriotic activities are implied by his conscious destruction of letters, which he wrote to Confederate officials operating in Canada.[5]

Once the war commenced Cyrus fled to Europe to cultivate a market for the reaper abroad, avoiding the war and leaving his brothers William and Leander to run the business. William summed up the family's opinion of the war in a scathing letter to his brother, accusing

Cyrus of "flee[ing] away from this land of blood and death—where we are trodden by abolitionism in the *North* without liberty of speech and with utter ruin in the south." His neglect of the reaper works and the U.S. market during the Civil War is perhaps the leading cause of the factory's flagging production.[6]

During the war C. H. McCormick and Brothers lost its dominating control of the reaper market as their production faltered. Manufacturing became inconsistent as a result of several factors working in concert: an antiquated mode of production, labor shortages, strikes, monetary inflation, and Cyrus's distracted initiatives to create a more complicated reaper that took twice the time to produce. The McCormick reaper-production statistics bear this story out. In 1861 the McCormick works produced 5,491 reapers. In the next two years, reaper production declined to as low as 4,312 in 1863, before shooting up to 6,090 in 1864 and dipping to a ten-year low of 2,503 in 1865. When compared to the 250,000 reapers produced nationwide by more than two hundred firms, the McCormick works produced only 10 percent of the reapers built from 1861 to 1865. For a comparison, during the 1850s McCormick annually produced over half of the reapers nationwide.[7]

In this light it is clear that McCormick was far from the patriotic, prolific contributor to the Union cause implied by those who use the Stanton quote. Torn by the outbreak of war, McCormick promoted peaceful reconciliation through newspapers, political participation, and covert activities. Moreover, his company's reaper production was inconsistent; the war marks the period when C. H. McCormick and Brothers lost their dominant position in the industry. This compels investigation as to why Stanton would make such an erroneous conclusion that "without McCormick's invention . . . the North could not win and the Union would have been dismembered." Obviously, the Union did win, but this was no thanks to McCormick, who was seeking peaceful reunification with the South throughout the war.

Prior to his family's historical activities in the late nineteenth century and even the crucible of Civil War, Cyrus McCormick was busy defending his machine against patent challenges in federal courts. In the 1850s he was famously engaged in fierce competition with other inventors and firms in international competitions and courtrooms. His earliest and most tenacious opponents were Obed Hussey and John Manny. Hussey had patented his reaper in 1833, one year before Cyrus received a patent on his own reaper. To maintain market control these parties engaged in frequent legal battles to contest one another's patents and patent extensions. One of these many legal battles came in 1861, when Cyrus applied for extensions of his 1847 and 1849 patents. Obed Hussey's family contested the extension, and the case went to trial in front of a U.S. patent commissioner.[8]

This is the context for "the reaper is to the North . . ." Edwin Stanton was acting as one of McCormick's attorneys in the 1861 patent-extension case. He argued that McCormick's *potential* contributions to the Union merited the extension of his reaper patent. The war was in its infancy in June 1861 when he was alleged to have made his famous statement. Stanton was thought to be one of the best patent lawyers in the country and would not become Lincoln's secretary of war until January 1862. Stanton's failure to gain a patent extension for his client allowed the reaper to be produced by many other manufacturers during the war, contributing to McCormick's declining market share.[9]

While this was the context for Stanton's quote, there is no direct primary evidence that the statement was ever made. The furthest back in history that any citation goes is Byron Levene's footnote from "Lincoln and McCormick: Two Emancipators," which references a 1905 biography of Edwin Stanton written by Frank A. Flower. In that biography Flower's contextualized version of the quote is noticeably different from how later historians would use it to demonstrate McCormick's support of the Union cause. Flower quotes Stanton as saying, "The reaper is as important to the North as slavery to the South. It takes the place of the regiments of young men who have left the harvest fields to do battle for the Union, and thus enables the farmers to keep up the supply of bread for the nation and its armies. McCormick's invention will aid materially to prevent the Union from dismemberment, and to grant his prayer herein is the smallest compensation the Government can make." What is clear from this version of the quote is that Stanton was referencing the probable value of the reaper to the Union effort and in the last sentence is explicitly making the plea for a patent extension. International Harvester's version of the quote, which leads this chapter, has been manipulated to make it seem as though Stanton was reflecting on McCormick's contributions after Appomattox.[10]

The inconsistent use of Stanton's quote may be attributed to a complete lack of primary documentation. Flower does not cite the quote but rather begins his discussion of it with this statement: "During the argument on these extension cases, which is still remembered in Washington, Stanton formulated his famous tribute to McCormick," which indicates that the entire quote may have been derived from word-of-mouth recitation rather than primary documentation.[11]

The conclusion that the quote lacks primary provenance is further substantiated by looking into the Patent Office records of the extension case, which does not have the quote on record. The documentation does set the tone for Stanton to make his bold statement. An "Argument for the Applicant" submitted in Stanton's name on June 20, 1861, to the commissioner of patents states "that while the country is in the midst of Civil War, and some departments of the government are contending against treason and rebellion, others are calmly pursuing the paths of peace, and wise judgment and judicious policy securing to authors and inventors due reward for whatever their genius may contribute for the happiness and prosperity of mankind." This excerpt might have created the framework for "the reaper is to the North . . ." by referencing the reaper's contributions to humankind. However, it is far from saying that McCormick's invention would save the Union.[12]

The excerpt from this "Argument for Application" also strongly suggests that if Stanton made his statement about the reaper in oral arguments, it was only to soften McCormick's well-deserved reputation as a Southern sympathizer. He wanted to paint McCormick as the man "pursuing the paths of peace," reframing the image of his client for the patent commissioner. The Northern public and the patent commissioner were likely aware of Cyrus's outspoken belief that the North should have made further concessions to the South to prevent secession. A letter to the editor in the *Chicago Tribune* indicated McCormick's dubious reputation among Northerners: "Who would think that at the very moment Mr. McCormick's press is preaching treason, Mr. McCormick is urging his petition at Washington. . . . He would bleed the North . . . and he would stab the Government." The author, "One of the People," further urged that McCormick's patent not be extended and that his invention be renamed the "*disunion reaper*." While this account may be an excessively colorful description of McCormick typical of the partisan press, it highlights the public awareness of McCormick's unpopular stance on the crisis. Historians' later use of Stanton's quote becomes ironic as the statement—meant to convince a patent commissioner to ignore all of Cyrus's unpatriotic activities—became the singular motto that historians used as proof of his Union support.[13]

Later historians took liberties with Stanton's quote, often neglecting the context; mislabeling him the secretary of war; and, in many cases, manipulating the quote for their own purposes. While the last of these charges may be a result of multiple and differing recollections and a lack of primary documentation, the first two are certainly an indication of poor and potentially unethical scholarship. The undoubted power of the quote makes it too good to pass by, especially if it reaffirms a sought conclusion.

With some perspective on McCormick's Civil War experience and having established the context for Edwin Stanton's declaration regarding the reaper, the focus of this chapter turns to how both of these became twisted together and rewritten. The genesis of Stanton's dubious quote reveals how the McCormick family's understanding of history and historical work had evolved. Reflecting their increasingly nuanced appreciation of the historian's craft, the McCormicks dealt with a wide range of historians from across the professional spectrum to rebuild the credibility of their father's legacy in the public imagination. Their efforts focused on bringing new evidence to light as well as finding credible groups and institutions to protect their patriarch's monumental past. The McCormicks' interactions with historians at this time demonstrates the fluidity of history and "objectivity" at the turn of the century and betrays the anxieties of an emerging group of middle-class laborers.

Coming out of the silver-certificate controversy of 1897, the best historical evidence of McCormick's priority of invention that the family could muster was found by Louis Dent, who had provided an argument and supporting evidence about the mechanical differences between McCormick's and Hussey's machines of 1850. Dent's analysis and material was printed ad nauseam—titled "Who Invented the Reaper?"—in newspapers and in pamphlet form under the company patent officer's name. He received no public credit for his historical labor. The family refrained from referencing Dent's work when discussing their history with elite peers or officials, because it was overly technical. Instead, they continued their previous practice of distributing Cyrus McCormick II's historically fictitious 1885 eulogy of their father as well as referencing the findings of judges at prior world's fairs, as they had advertised for decades. While these materials were more palatable to the average person, they were found wanting when compared with the patent records presented by the Deerings and other industrial opponents.[14]

The Deerings seized the initiative in the harvester industry's ongoing history tug-of-war at the Paris Exposition in 1900. With great prescience the Deering Company successfully lobbied the officials of the Parisian exposition in March 1898 through "subtle and forceful methods" to grant them the exclusive right to present a retrospective exhibit on harvesting machinery at the world's fair two years later. Predictably, their exhibit marginalized the McCormick narrative and emphasized the large number of inventors and machines that had contributed to the progress of harvesting technology. The McCormicks vociferously contended that "the attitude of making the [Deering] exhibit has been rather one of advertising than making an impartial historical exhibit." The McCormicks attempted to repeal the Deerings' exclusive right to build such an exhibit and, failing that, they sought to curb the Deerings' historical impact at Paris through all manner of historical protest and counterpresentation.[15]

On the ropes for the third time in seven years, the McCormick family reimagined their ongoing history-as-advertising branding strategy. They sought to fortify their own history with historical research, while demanding that the "perversion of the truth" presented by their opponents be held to the same standard. Even though the mudslinging between their companies was intense, the conversation among the families was cordial. James Deering offered to halt their historical warfare if the McCormicks agreed to the same. Rather than fold up their brand and identity, the McCormicks hedged toward mutually restraining overly broad historical claims to those that could be rigorously supported by evidence. As Harold McCormick admitted to his brother Stanley, "[In the past] we have made defences [*sic*] which . . . stretched the literal interpretation of the records." Moving forward, Harold suggested "both should agree to adhere absolutely to facts, to facts alone." He felt, as did his siblings and mother, that they were on the right side of history and that sufficient evidence could be unearthed that would support their narrative as fact.[16]

The family chartered the McCormick Biographical Association during that summer to find the evidence that would both redeem their company's brand and fortify their private sense of identity. The membership of the association was made up of Cyrus McCormick's widow, Nettie, and four children: Cyrus Jr., Anita Blaine, Harold, and Stanley. In the words of the charter, the association was created "to provide for continuing the work (already begun) of compiling and preserving in convenient form, and of publishing (in such ways and so far as may seem desirable) the life history of Cyrus H. McCormick, Sr.; in order, also to provide for the erection of a monument to his memory." They agreed to provide $25,000 toward a monument and a renewable fund of $5,000 to pay historical laborers.[17]

With a keen sense of purpose and an incorporated entity to pursue it, the family experimented with employees across the professional historical spectrum, searching for laborers who might secure their past. At a relatively early date in the historical profession's tenure, the McCormicks' experiences with this group of professionals reveal historians' struggle for middle-class security, as well as indicating the fluidity of both the guild and objectivity. In a culture where the past was deemed self-evident to everyone, historical laborers faced an uphill battle to prove that their expertise amounted to a professional service that warranted white-collar wages.

In 1900 the association employed at least seven historical laborers. They paid one full-time trained historian, Salem Pattison, and a freelance researcher, Louis Dent, to do historical research and analysis. They were assisted by at least two of the family's secretaries in organizing the collection into a library and by their company's senior patent lawyer, Robert Parkinson, who advised on the finer mechanical points of the reaper's evolution. The association also subsidized two retired inventors from defunct firms, Henry F. Mann and J. D. Easter, to write personal histories that undermined the Deering historical narrative. The association's historical laborers were directed from above by the family in a fairly disorganized manner, frequently answering to Anita, Cyrus II, Harold, and Stanley, as well as the company's patent officer, Rodney Swift. Their short-term objective was to provide specific historical ammunition to Stanley McCormick, who oversaw the company's campaign for the past in Paris. They were also tasked with challenging the "perversions of truth" presented at other museums or in books. In this regard they were just as likely to censure history presented by their competitors or familial rivals on the Leander side of the family as they were to chastise an unassuming museum administrator. For example, in 1907 they waged a campaign to revise an exhibit on the reaper at the Kensington Museum in London—an unlikely product of cognizant historical manipulation.[18]

Salem Pattison, the association's first academically trained historian, was given a $2,000, one-year contract in January 1900. Pattison received his master's degree in history from Cornell University in 1891 but had put his history degree to work as the president of Hastings College in Nebraska beginning in 1896. The McCormick family had been benefactors of the college as early as 1883, continuing their philanthropic support of Presbyterian education, as their father had done since the sectional crisis of the 1850s. This connection brought Pattison and the McCormicks together when the educator left the college in search of a better position.[19]

Pattison diligently fulfilled the family's initial demands, providing ample historical evidence for the ongoing historical showdown in Paris. Pattison located, organized, and sent a large amount of historical documentation to the exposition, including historical advertisements, newspaper clippings, patent records, court testimonies, manuscripts, and mechanical diagrams. An express shipping manifest five pages long from June 1900 serves as a bibliography of just some of the materials he put together. Over the summer the family also had him "fact-check" the claims of the Deering exhibit as well as vet their opposition's supposed evidence. His first major task was writing a history of the "McCormick Patent Extension Case of 1848." The patent-extension case was the major judicial showdown between Obed Hussey and Cyrus McCormick during their lifetimes and offered a wealth of testimony from the patriarch regarding his 1831 invention.[20]

Like most emerging corporate professionals during the Progressive Era, Salem Pattison was intent on demonstrating his value through building his employing institution. He created a bureaucratic structure within the association, assuming a supervisory capacity as the point of communication with the family interests as well as directing the actions of the association's two secretaries and Louis Dent. Pattison pursued a collections policy for the association beyond the McCormicks' single-minded interest in settling the contested history of the reaper. Pattison outlined a scope of research that would "be a complete revelation of the deeper meaning of your father's life." The archive, created in Nettie McCormick's basement, would include Cyrus McCormick's "ideas on religion, politics, business and social affairs" through locating and preserving evidence from his own life as well as those of his contemporaries. Such a collection, he advised the McCormicks, would be "worth infinitely more than any other." With such grand plans he lobbied for more clerical laborers and research assistants within the historical enterprise. Exhibiting professional congeniality, Pattison networked with other historical laborers in hopes of locating additional resources to support the enterprise and his ambitions. Through this process other aspiring historians reached out to Pattison and offered their services to the McCormick Biographical Association.[21]

Pattison strove to demonstrate his utility to the McCormicks' interests. He drew attention to his initiative and professional acumen through frequent detailed reports, hoping to establish himself as an asset worthy of a higher salary. Aware that his colleagues' interests were parallel to his own, Pattison sang his co-workers praises in his correspondence with the McCormicks and requested that they receive higher pay as well. He appreciated the unique professional opportunity that the McCormicks' historical agenda presented and sought to shape it into something more.[22]

In this pursuit Pattison brought his historical imagination to the McCormicks' service. Leveraging their desires for his own benefit, Pattison offered historical awareness and perspective beyond the family's own grandiose conception of their father's past. Demonstrating his understanding of public knowledge production, Pattison recommended that focusing on "school histories will . . . lay the basis for general and popular recognition of his invention by the masses more than anything." Beyond means of knowledge distribution, he also tantalized the family with a broader interpretation of their patriarch's legacy. Pattison asserted that "the invention of the reaper by him has been the most potent influence in banishing the fear of famine from all lands." Within this glorious reimagining of the past, Pattison revised McCormick's Civil War record from a Confederate sympathizer to a Union hero. While he was not the one responsible for fabricating Stanton's quote, he was the first to argue that McCormick's reaper "enable[d] the country to spare a great army for putting down the Rebellion."[23]

Pattison's decision to rewrite McCormick's Civil War record with questionable conclusions must be understood in light of his quest for a middle-class living. Pattison, like many other professionals and historians during this era, was less concerned with dilemmas of historical "objectivity" and more interested in securing the higher wages befitting an educated professional worker. Underscoring this point, Pattison did work as a historian for the McCormicks and eventually as a professor but also spent substantial time as an administrator at universities and insurance companies. His bottom line was gaining the trappings of professional status, but not necessarily within his trained vocation as a historian.[24]

In September 1900 he attempted to leverage the value he had created for himself into a higher salary. He frankly admitted to the McCormicks that his historical labor alone was not personally rewarding: "I find the constant every day work on the old correspondence very hard trying work." He then informed them that he required no less than $4,000 annually to stay on with the association and that, if they did not accede to his request, he would leave their employ for a higher-paying job at an insurance company in Indiana. Despite all that he had done for the family's historical enterprise, they balked at doubling his salary, believing that "he is setting too high a value upon his work." Pattison followed through with his threat, leaving for Indiana at the end of October. He committed to finish out his one-year contract with the McCormicks from his home office after work.[25]

Taking the long view of the negotiation, upon leaving and intermittently in the closing months of 1900, Pattison stressed to the family the importance of replacing him with a professional historian who could be trusted to continue building their collection. Referring to himself in thinly guised language, Pattison stated that the work demanded "a man of historical instinct and thorough training as well as the strictest moral integrity." He implied that only he could be trusted with the confidential organization and indexing of their father's sensitive personal manuscripts. Reminding them that he was not beyond their reach, Pattison stated he "had a strong desire to continue the work but my own financial needs and the prospect of an enlarged income . . . decided me to make the change." As the year and his contract neared conclusion, he made a final calculated move. Pattison informed the family that he did not find his position in Indiana "congenial" and offered to come back to the association. Playing on the McCormicks' anxieties, he shrewdly reminded them that if they did not take him back at an increased salary, he "thought of making application for a position with Deerings, who . . . had two openings that they wanted me to consider." The McCormicks hired back him at $4,000 annually and seemed to have had no ill-will about the proceedings.[26]

The results of Pattison's negotiating tactics provide insight into historians' search for professional status and a middle-class income. When his approach is compared with that of other professionals in that era or afterward, it seems typical. He had a specific expertise and demonstrated the value of that expertise through serving and building his employer's institution. Pattison and the McCormicks disagreed about what his services were worth, so he decided to see what the free-labor market would yield. In a labor market with uniquely high demand for experts on reaper history, Pattison achieved his goal by threatening to serve the company's chief opposition. After the amalgamation of McCormick and Deering with the creation of International Harvester in 1902, however, he was no longer be able to maintain his higher wage because the competition for his labor became restrained.

The episode also reveals that the McCormicks were aware of the fragility of the past. The McCormicks believed that historical evidence and "facts" were the key to redeeming their father's legacy but also knew that historical labor could swing the pendulum of history away from their favor. While historians in academia pursued that "noble dream" of objective study, trained historians outside of the ivory tower's confines, like Salem Pattison, could not afford such a luxury. Pattison was determined to demonstrate the concrete value of his services to his employers, hoping to secure a middle-class lifestyle. His willingness to play fast and loose with the past seems fitting when considering that within the McCormick Company the trained historian had to compete against lawyers, advertisers, journalists, and others for historical authority.

When the family formed their biographical association, they had a short-term need to refute the Deerings' counterhistory at the Paris Exposition. Before long, however, that need dissipated, as the competitors merged to become International Harvester and agreed to drop their historical dispute. Without Pattison's efforts it is unlikely that the McCormicks would have continued their biographical association or employed their historical laborers. He successfully offered a grander interpretation of their father's past, implemented a bold collections policy to secure new materials, and created a bureaucratic labor system to execute that policy and organize a library. He argued that once such a collection was built, it would be the solid foundation for an authoritative life history of Cyrus McCormick. Perhaps most important, in August 1900 Pattison located an outlet for the McCormicks' yearnings to see a monument erected to their father that might ensure that he receive the public recognition he deserved for generations to come. He proposed that the McCormicks set their sights on the recently created Hall of Fame for Great Americans at New York University as the best institution to preserve their patriarch's legacy. Pattison was able to prolong the family's interest in employing historical laborers by fashioning their abstract goals for a collection, a biography, and a monument into a concrete plan of action. Pattison ultimately left the McCormicks' employ on his own terms in 1903. He had "completed the work" that he had laid out for the association in 1900 and traded up for a better-paying job at yet another insurance company in Indiana.[27]

New York University's Hall of Fame for Great Americans was conceived in 1900 after the university received a large endowment from Jay Gould's heir, Helen Gould. Like the McCormicks, Helen Gould was intent on rescuing her deceased father's reputation. Searching for philanthropic support and eager to prove the usefulness of his institution to wealthy benefactors, the university's chancellor, Henry MacCracken, imagined building a Hall of Fame to secure Helen Gould's support for a new university library. He promised that creating a monument that recognized businessmen alongside inventors, politicians, and artists would provide a fitting memorial venue to restore her father's legacy in the public mind. The heir donated $1,150,000 to erect the library and the adjacent Hall of Fame for Great Americans.[28]

The concept of the Hall of Fame was to have a jury elect 50 "Great Americans" in 1900. Then 5 inductees were to be added every five years until the year 2000, bringing the total of Great Americans to 150. Each honored person would have a statue, bust, or portrait presented in the hall. This plan was delayed when jurists made only 29 selections on the first vote. Mass elections were then held again in 1905 and 1910 to fulfill the number of Great Americans they sought. The one hundred jurists were societal elite and academics from across the country, including President Theodore Roosevelt. The Hall of Fame was a classical colonnade structure built in University Heights on the original campus of New York University. It was opened on Memorial Day of 1901 and held elections until it went defunct in 1976.[29]

To some degree, the Hall of Fame was the perfect encapsulation of new Progressive Era ideas about history, which matched the McCormick family's needs. It emphasized the emerging historical synthesis of progress, empire, commerce, and industry as the new hub of national tradition and unified identity, which was fomenting in conjunction with racist Lost Cause amnesia regarding the Civil War. It honored a new history of material national improvement while erasing uncomfortable memories of sectionalism, slavery, and racism that had defined the nation for its first eighty-nine years and led to eight hundred thousand American deaths. Moreover, the Hall of Fame represented a decidedly elitist mode of memorialization, simplistically prioritizing the celebration of individual heroes while ignoring the contributions of the larger population in a democratic society of "equals." Perhaps most typical of the era, the Hall of Fame's historically Great Americans were not selected by the masses but rather by select men of status, learning, wealth, and privilege who were believed to be best equipped to make discerning choices on posterity's behalf.

Judged by elite white men to honor dead elite white men, the Hall of Fame offered the McCormick Biographical Association the perfect venue for honoring their patriarch's legacy, and in 1900 they immediately commenced a campaign to have him inducted. If successful, they would legitimize their patriarch's legacy as the inventor of the reaper and vanquish their industrial rivals' and antagonistic cousins' claims to the past. With Pattison's guidance the family shifted its focus from producing works that argued the genesis of the reaper to histories that lionized the life of Cyrus McCormick and his contributions to U.S. history. Over the next ten years, the family made many attempts to influence the Hall of Fame electors. Their lobbying efforts came to a climax in a public relations blitz that was part of their 1909 centennial celebration of McCormick's birth. As part of this effort, the McCormick Biographical Association commissioned two authors to write biographies of the family patriarch and distributed thousands of copies. They also wrote countless newspaper articles featuring excerpts from the books. Included in these histories was Pattison's revision of the Civil War. This monumental effort in knowledge production is the origin of the misinterpretation of Stanton's tribute to McCormick and the reason for its ubiquity throughout the historiography of the Civil War and the nineteenth century.

Once aware of the Hall of Fame, the McCormick Biographical Association began gathering information about the election process and the jurists to formulate a strategy to secure Cyrus Sr.'s election. Their efforts commenced in August of that year, and the election was held in October, so it was too late to launch a grand campaign while the family was still entrenched in Paris. Pattison did most of the initial reconnaissance. The first jurist Pattison contacted was Dr. David Schaff of the Lane Theological Seminary in Cincinnati.[30]

The cornerstone of the argument Pattison presented to Schaff was McCormick's contributions to the Civil War. On August 18, 1900, Pattison wrote to Schaff, "I fully believe that his invention made possible the freedom of 4,000,000 of slaves in the [1860s]." Pattison's letter revealed the new angle the family was taking. Pattison went on to comment that this contribution had been overlooked, but he presciently predicted "that later historians will put a great emphasis upon this fact." This was the seed of their later endeavors.[31]

No other correspondences appear in the McCormick Biographical Association files at the McCormick–International Harvester Collection in Madison, Wisconsin, in reference to the 1900 Hall of Fame elections. However, given Pattison's enthusiasm for demonstrating his usefulness, it is likely that he contacted other jurists from the list given to him by Schaff. When the votes were cast in mid-October, Cyrus McCormick Sr. received twenty-six votes.[32]

The campaign for the 1905 election began in 1904, with letters from Harold McCormick to Dr. William Faunce, another Hall of Fame voter. In these letters Faunce recommended that the family find a credible biographer to write a book plainly stating the case for Cyrus Sr. as a Great American. However, the biography would need to be presented to the jurists in an unassuming manner that would not appear as a shameless plea. Harold inquired about how others had lobbied for an election and mentioned, "We contemplate collaborating a statement of some kind to present in a dignified manner to the judges. Who should make this and how the treatise should be handled, we are uncertain of." Faunce encouraged Harold to have such a biography written but cautioned that "anything like an attempt to pledge the committee to vote one way or the other . . . would only harm." Harold responded that they would begin an effort to find "somebody who, we could feel would, be qualified to write an interesting statement of the facts in an attractive manner."[33]

The McCormick Biographical Association consulted with other Hall of Fame jurors sympathetic to their cause in search of an author and tried to craft a strategy for natural distribution that would not offend the judges. Woodrow Wilson, a native Virginian and then president of Princeton, met with Cyrus II on the matter and also prompted him to have a biographical sketch written and proposed "not [to] confine the sending of this booklet to the judges of the Hall of Fame, but would send it also to scientists, and editorial writers, issuing perhaps fifteen hundred of them. In this way it would be evidenced that it was not aimed at any one set of men, but was information of a proper character for any who wished to have it." This strategy of mass distribution to make the presentation of the material to the judges seem coincidental became an integral part of the family's strategy for the next several decades.[34]

The McCormick Biographical Association had come into contact with several potential biographers between 1900 and 1905 from across the spectrum of historical laborers. Some had learned about their historical ambitions from McCormick Biographical Association or company employees while rubbing shoulders with them in libraries or elsewhere. Others were directly solicited by the family. This talent pool of potential biographers included an advertiser, a journalist, two lawyers of varying pedigree (one of whom might be considered an early historical consultant), a museum administrator, and several academics. This wide range of laborers offered their services at different prices depending on how established their profession was within the corporate order. On the high end the McCormicks paid the company patent lawyer, Robert Parkinson, to write a history of the McCormick reaper in legalistic detail, keeping him on a $7,500 retainer. On the low end journalists offered to do the work for as little as $100 a month. Moonlighting academics bid only $500 for the entire project, most likely because of the emerging profession's unfamiliarity with the value of their historical labor outside of the university.[35]

The first historical laborer to solicit his services as a biographer was the farm-implement journalist Robert L. Ardrey in 1901. Ardrey had already written a history of the farm-implement business in 1894 for the National Association of Agricultural Implement and Vehicle Manufacturers. Financed by McCormick's competitors, his book attributed the invention of the reaper to a wider cohort of inventors in the 1820s and 1830s, including both Hussey and McCormick. As part of his project, and reflecting the flexibility of his scholarly mores, he offered to revise his previous book, which "did Mr. McCormick an injustice."[36]

Ardrey outlined a biography of Cyrus McCormick that ostensibly restated decades of the McCormick Harvesting Machine Company's "established 1831" advertising narrative. Reflecting the family's technological surplus-value ideology, he stated that "McCormick's inventors has contributed to the progress of the world" and that, before his grand mechanical innovation, "the farmer . . . was a stranger to wealth." He proposed to "dress up all these bare facts, and bring them out in a brilliant style of writing, with enough color to make them readable." He offered to do the work if advanced $100 a month for his historical labor, plus expenses. Ardrey promised that if he was given six months to work on the book, the finished product "would be a standard authority throughout the world on American inventions in this industry." Playing to the family's desires, he vowed that such a book would be a valuable reference for experts, agricultural colleges, and experiment stations and would be purchased by "every library in the country." The McCormicks were not interested in Ardrey as the authoritative biographer of their father; however, they took the opportunity to root out dissenting narratives, paying him to rewrite his previous book.[37]

Another historical laborer, an opportunistic lawyer turned government clerk and author named Frank Flower, provided the family with a much more enticing proposal in 1903. Flower was particularly attuned to the McCormicks' specific interests and needs. He had come into contact with Salem Pattison during one of Pattison's research trips to Washington DC and had mined the McCormicks' historian for much information about his employer's agenda. In his proposal he promised to write a well-researched four-hundred-page biography and also to "unearth" any reaper made by McCormick or any other in 1839 and 1840 (the year McCormick first offered his machines for sale in Virginia). Finally, he promised the family that he could secure "the McCormick portrait on our currency" for little expense, except wining and dining the right "public men." He assured them that he could do all of this for $3,000. He noted that such a monetary "grub stake" was necessary. No other author would undertake the project without funding, because there is "no public taste for industrial literature." Aware of the importance of history to the McCormicks' identity, he told them that "members of the family . . . who desire to see him (and themselves with him) given his proper place and honor in history" must finance the work themselves.[38]

Flower framed himself less as a historian and more as an able operator with connections. He stressed the importance of his geographic location in in Washington DC as the "location to accomplish all three of the things mentioned." He further emphasized himself as the man for the job: "I know the public men and records; I know the Patent Office; I know the Libraries in which all printed documents rest, and I am familiar with the people and sections in which the search must be made for the old reapers." Demonstrating the resources at his disposal, Flower detailed his involvement with a cohort of freelance researchers at the Library of Congress, who might be called historical consultants. Working on a for-hire basis, he and apparently about fifty other "learned men" provided research services on "historical, statistical, industrial and biographical subjects." The historical laborers worked together, each one "turning over to all others any fact he finds of value to them."[39]

Providing the family with a savory morsel of evidence as an example of his services, Flower ended his proposition with a reference to Edwin McMasters Stanton's high regard for McCormick's contributions to Union victory. Flower had doctored Stanton's "the reaper is to the North . . ." quote to improve his own appeal to a potential client. He later placed the quote in his biography of Stanton, the first location where it appeared in print. Importantly, the fabrication and its publication provided the family with the needed "facts" to support Pattison's revision of Cyrus McCormick's Civil War record. The McCormicks did not hire Flower to write the biography but did pay him to do research.[40]

For their Hall of Fame campaign, the McCormicks were intent on hiring a biographer "whose name would carry conviction and a weight of dignity" to persuade the Hall of Fame's gentlemen jurists. Reflecting both confidence in the work that had been done by Salem Pattison and simultaneously a disregard for the academic historian's expertise, Stanley McCormick wrote his family in 1905: "No one . . . can bring any very new lights upon the subject. His [the historian's] name at the foot of the paper is the greatest benefit he can furnish! Therefore I think the character of the paper can be formulated while or before we finally engage the man." The family apparently followed the policy set forth by Stanley and sought a historian who could turn around an article-length biography in a mere six weeks. By 1905 Salem Pattison was no longer a full-time employee because he had completed his grand vision for the collection and moved on to a different job. But he remained available to the McCormicks for side work that they deemed required a historian's mind. In his absence the family had their association's longtime secretary, Frances Smith, put together the materials for the publication.[41]

Cyrus II and Harold spearheaded the shotgun search for a historian, utilizing their personal connections and status as societal elites to locate candidates. Reflecting their grand ambition, they contacted the famous British author and poet Robert Bridges. After Bridges rejected them they solicited the services of two of the most prominent historians in the country: James Franklin Jameson and John Bach McMasters. Jameson was the foremost leader of the academic professionalization movement, while McMasters was the last great and untrained "gentleman amateur." Each supported the McCormicks' project but declined the commission because, as Hall of Fame jurors, they felt it was a conflict of interest. Following a suggestion from the dean of the University of Chicago, Harry Judson, the family then set out to convince Frederick Jackson Turner, the great historian of the U.S. West, to be their biographer.[42]

Cyrus II visited Turner in Madison on March 18, 1905. Initially, he convinced Turner to take the commission through providing ample financial, personnel, and manuscript resource support for the project. The family believed Turner was the ideal candidate for job and would "fulfill it with good taste and . . . enthusiasm," because he "is making a life study of the development of the western part of this county, particularly with regards to agricultural development." They had long advertised their company's geographic location in Chicago and its close association with the economic and agricultural success of the Midwest. Surely they believed that solidifying the relationship between the reaper and the nation's breadbasket through historical inquiry and publication would be profitable to their historical quest and larger reputation. Two days later, however, Turner reneged on his contract. In a letter Turner stated that, after going through the family's historical material, he believed "to your father belongs the credit of the invention of the reaper as a practical machine, which revolutionized the economic history of the Middle West and consequently the Nation." Unfortunately, Turner went on to explain that such a study "should only be undertaken with leisure and entirely apart from any consideration but a desire to know the truth." When he agreed to the contract, he did not "realize the fact . . . that the conditions necessarily involved in writing the paper would give room for criticism of my motives." He could not undertake the commission because it posed a dilemma of objectivity.[43]

Turner was the only historian to ever raise the question of professional ethics to the family directly. His position can be attributed to several possibilities, not least of which was his prominent position in the academic historical guild and his own relative job security. Alternatively, his moral dilemma may also have been a cover for his seeming inability to write research papers on a deadline. Either way, he freely proposed to pass the project along to Reuben Gold Thwaites, the director of the State Historical Society of Wisconsin, who he doubted would have the same quandaries of conscience. Turner's "urging" was instrumental in convincing Thwaites to take the job.[44]

Despite having only a master's degree from Yale, Thwaites was considered a peer of doctored academic professionals. He had devoted his career to building the State Historical Society into a premier historical research institution and published 168 edited manuscript volumes as well as fifteen works of original research. He also had strong connections with Turner, the University of Wisconsin history faculty, and other "Prairie Historians" who labored to demonstrate the Midwest's importance to the historical development of the nation. With Thwaites's solid academic reputation, a clear interest in midwestern history, and a "strong sentiment" of the reaper's "great importance," the McCormicks were "satisfied that he could do the work well."[45]

After one meeting on March 27, 1905, Thwaites agreed to write an article-length biography of Cyrus McCormick. The family paid him $500 and provided him with a large volume of their historical propaganda, including Parkinson's article on the patent history of the reaper, the articles written by Swift and Dent in 1897, Ardrey's revised history of the farm-implement industry, and Cyrus II's 1885 eulogy to his father, "Memorial to Cyrus McCormick," among several others. They also delivered a selection of the biographical association's indexed manuscript materials that had been pulled together by their historical laborers in the opening years of the decade. Robert Parkinson, Salem Pattison (on a short-term leave from his job in Indiana), a stenographer, and a research assistant also journeyed to Madison to help Thwaites with the project.[46]

As an academically credible historian, Thwaites did not question the McCormicks' motives. He was satisfied that everything was accurate because of the sheer volume of evidence the family provided, the expert quality of the assistance he received, and the strong recommendation from Turner to take on the project. Surely, the gravitas of the McCormicks as an economically elite family furnishing him with a commission also contributed to solidifying his resolve and abating suspicion. In a mere three weeks, Thwaites completed a twenty-three-page article, an ideal length for Hall of Fame jurists to digest. The finished product was substantively ghostwritten by the biographical association, and the family found it to be a "dignified and valuable contribution to the literature on the subject."[47]

Seemingly, Thwaites's only research contribution was discovering a history of the reaper written by Margaret Schaffner, a graduate student at the University of Iowa. In a sexist tone typical of the male-dominated historical profession during the Progressive Era, Thwaites reported to the McCormicks that Schaffner was a "rambling . . . rather eccentric person" and that her scholarship was influenced by the "misinformation received by [John F.] Steward," recognizing the more contentious history of the reaper. Perhaps protecting his own credibility on the topic and certainly promoting the McCormicks' interests, Thwaites then committed an unnecessarily cruel act of scholarly assassination. He utilized his strong connections in the historical profession to discredit Schaffner's work and make sure that it was not published by the Carnegie Institute. Pattison agreed with Thwaites that "it would be a great mistake for her article to go to press" and stated on behalf of the McCormicks that "it is kind of you to take up the matter."[48]

It is in Thwaites's manuscript that Stanton's quote first became inserted into the historiography of Cyrus McCormick's life. Undoubtedly the McCormick Biographical Association had placed Frank

Flower's fabrication of the quote in Thwaites's hands. In his version Stanton's quote read, "'The reaper is to the North,' he said, 'what slavery is to the South. By taking the places of regiments of young men in the Western harvest fields, it releases them to do battle for the Union at the front, and at the same time keeps up the bread supply for the nation and the nation's armies. Thus without McCormick's invention I fear the North could not win and the Union would be dismembered.'" In his article there is no citation for Stanton's quote. Thwaites's version lacked what little information was available to contextualize the quote. He did not go as far as calling Stanton the secretary of war, but he certainly did not reference Stanton's involvement in representing McCormick during the 1861 patent-extension case.[49]

Thwaites's biographical article, "Cyrus Hall McCormick and the Reaper," would not be published for almost four years. While Thwaites was writing the biographical sketch, most of the family was discussing how best to distribute the biography to the jurors. They met with several of their lawyers, including Robert Parkinson, Cyrus Bentley, and John Wilson, but other historical laborers were excluded from the discussion. Their lawyers suggested not distributing Thwaites's essay, "in view of the fact that no natural occasion can now be found for a treatise of this kind, or sending it out." Parkinson feared that distributing the biography the wrong way would "involve more peril than promise of success." After much debate the family agreed that it was probably better to wait "rather than to subject ourselves to serious criticism for doing the thing itself the wrong way." They were searching for a natural occasion to distribute the article and filed away Thwaites's work for future use.[50]

The Hall of Fame vote came and went in 1905 without Cyrus Sr.'s election. While the McCormick Biographical Association had been busy scheming, they had chosen not to act. Their "natural occasion" would arrive in 1909 as an opportunity to celebrate the centennial anniversary of Cyrus McCormick's birth. The family would turn to an advertising professional, Herbert Casson, to write a more attractive full-length biography and orchestrate a grand public relations campaign in hopes of persuading the Hall of Fame judges.

Herbert Casson had come into contact with the family through his dealings with the International Harvester Company as a public relations adviser. He had been paid by the company in 1907 to prepare a glorified history of the harvester industry and the new corporation. His work, *Romance of the Reaper*, was widely distributed to newspapers and by company sales agents in hopes to promote the "good trust" image conceived by George Perkins, the company's chair. Perkins hoped that portraying the company as the "good trust" would convince the Bureau of Corporations to encourage the Department of Justice not to pursue antitrust proceedings. He had cultivated a similar image for the U.S. Steel Corporation and in that campaign had paid Casson to write a similar history of the steel industry, *The Romance of Steel*. In both endeavors Casson worked to establish that the great millionaires of industry were not parasites but rather bootstrapping entrepreneurs whose enterprise was a boon to the nation. Casson had clearly come across the work of the McCormick Biographical Association, as he included Stanton's quote in his publication for the International Harvester Company. Crucially important and reflecting the historical contentions among the corporation's ownership by both the Deerings and the McCormicks, Casson's book credited the invention of the reaper to a wider cohort of inventors rather than solely to Cyrus McCormick.[51]

In June 1908 the family renewed their campaign for the Hall of Fame, and Smith contacted Herbert Casson about orchestrating a public relations campaign. Following up on Smith's recommendation, after a brief meeting Cyrus II hired Casson to undertake the project. Casson became the historical laborer most prized and highly rewarded by the McCormicks, earning around $5,000, because he packaged history within a public relations campaign to fulfill their ambitions. His professional expertise managing several similar projects for their company and others had given him the requisite credibility to oversee their affairs publicly. The family would not give an academically trained historian this sort of power over their affairs until 1929.[52]

The family seized on their patriarch's centennial birthday as an "appropriate occasion" to write articles for magazines, publish a full biography, and submit letters to the editors of numerous newspapers. Harold stated their intentions clearly in a letter to Frances Smith: "It seems to me this year is a great opportunity for us to have these articles spread all over the country in such a way that they will come to the eyes and ears of the men who are going to vote in the next Hall of Fame. . . . Such a program would call to their attention in a legitimate way . . . the merit of the invention and the inventor." Herbert Casson engineered a scheme that would fulfill both their need for a biography and their interest in producing a mass of newspaper articles that would reach the Hall of Fame voters. He would write a series of six articles that would be widely circulated to newspapers and then published as a book. Cyrus II liked the plan, writing in a memorandum to the other members of the biographical association, "This work should be begun at once." Casson's 184-page biography was completed and ready for publication by late 1908. The association also had Thwaites publish his article in the *Proceedings* of the State Historical Society of Wisconsin in late 1908.[53]

The centennial birthday of Cyrus McCormick in 1909 saw an epic public relations scheme carried out by the McCormick Biographical Association in an effort to shift the public mind and specifically the thoughts of the Hall of Fame election committee toward the family's prerogative. Under Casson's tutelage they printed and distributed 1,500 copies of Thwaites's article to historians, libraries, universities, newspapers, and notably forty-two of the Hall of Fame judges who they felt were most likely to read the document in a positive light. They also purchased and distributed a staggering 10,000 copies of Casson's biography, *Cyrus Hall McCormick: His Life and Work*. Frances Smith proposed a strategy for distribution of 9,000 copies. It is unclear where the last 1,000 went, but 6,000 copies were to be sent to "Public Libraries, Institutional Libraries and Educators"; 1,000 for "representative men in the Association of Commerce," which was a Chicago-based business association; 1,000 copies for the press; 300 copies for family and friends; and an additional 200 for stock on hand. She also proposed that 500 be sent to professors of history and economics, because "these are the men who write the histories of our country." They believed putting the biography in the hands of historians was an investment for the future. Their investment came to fruition as Cyrus McCormick was included in many history books afterward. The McCormick Biographical Association also sent out an additional 1,000 copies of Casson's *Romance of the Reaper* to the press.[54]

This blitz saturated the literary world with the family's version of history and specifically Stanton's quote. Judging from the response in the press, the McCormick Biographical Association's effort appears to have reached far more than simply the individual recipients of their books. The association furnished many newspapers with articles featuring Stanton's quote as well. The McCormicks' version of history was featured in popular national publications such as *Harper's Weekly*, the *Wall Street Journal*, and the *Saturday Evening Post*, among many other national magazines and newspapers.[55]

The centennial campaign went beyond literature, including celebratory events and addresses at the Chicago Association of Commerce and several universities. The centennial was observed mostly by institutions that had been endowed by the McCormick family. For instance, the McCormick Theological Seminary in Chicago and Washington and Lee University in Virginia (which the family endowed with $75,000 in the spring of 1909) held celebrations. McCormick was also commemorated as the inaugural inductee into the Farmers Hall of Fame at the University of Illinois in Champaign. Coincidentally, the Farmers Hall of Fame came into existence that same October and held their inaugural induction ceremony honoring Cyrus in December.[56]

Ironically and perhaps comically, relatives successfully sabotaged the McCormick Biographical Association's bid to have Cyrus inducted into the Hall of Fame in 1910. While the McCormick Biographical Association was well aware of their relatives' alternative version of the past, they had remained silent on the historical debate since the 1889 buyout. Gouged by their relatives' arrogant public relations campaign, the cousins Robert Hall McCormick II and James Shields nominated Robert Hall McCormick as the inventor of the reaper. They also independently published their own history, *Robert McCormick, Inventor*, which they directly distributed to all the electors. After the elections were held in October, a gloating Robert Hall McCormick II revealed the disruptive plot to his totally surprised and unaware cousin, Cyrus II. After describing his nomination of their mutual grandfather and the publication of his book, Robert Hall remarked that he would "take great pleasure in sending you one," as he prepared to distribute the work more widely. In the Hall of Fame polling, Cyrus McCormick garnered only sixteen votes, while Robert McCormick received seven. In spite of all their lobbying, plotting, and paying for professional resources, the McCormick Biographical Association's plans had been spoiled by their own kin. For the next twenty-five years, Cyrus McCormick's heirs continued to campaign for the Hall of Fame and were endlessly worried about their cousins' nefarious tampering and power to derail their historical objectives.[57]

The McCormick Biographical Association had indelibly marked the historical record in 1909. After the failed Hall of Fame election bid, the family feud among cousins rose to the surface, and Cyrus's family would redouble its efforts, continuing to finance historical laborers for the next forty years to quell their own family's rebellion. The unaware scholarly bystanders of this conflict were won over by the McCormick Biographical Association's ubiquitous propaganda and often repeated its version of the past. Through them the McCormick family's heritage of invention and other associated fabrications would spread to monographs and textbooks and finally into public memory.

Moving forward, the McCormick Biographical Association continued to produce its versions of history, including Stanton's quote.

Within these works the family's historians continued to consciously craft misleading interpretations of Cyrus's Civil War era activities. Cyrus Hall McCormick III's *Century of the Reaper* is a good example of just such a work, which featured Stanton's quote and a blatantly misleading narrative of the Civil War. Furthermore, this perspective and Stanton's quote would be present in many of the corporate histories of International Harvester, which they helped create. Along with the 1931 public relations history referenced at the beginning of this chapter, the quote would to be used in "History and Development of International Harvester," published in 1976.[58]

The family also sought to influence the history produced by others. Prior to 1930 their historians sent out copies of Casson's two books and Thwaites's article to anyone who inquired about the history of McCormick. In 1928 they would again engage an academic historian, William T. Hutchinson, to write a two-volume authoritative biography of their father. The association's laborers also actively prepared entries for encyclopedias and sought out museums to present their version of history, including the Museum of Science and Industry in Chicago and the Smithsonian National Museum of American History in Washington DC.[59]

As a result of the McCormick family's historical laborers, Stanton's quote and their heritage would become ever-present in the historiography of Cyrus McCormick, the Civil War, and the nineteenth century. Within two years of the biographical association's public relations blitz in 1909, the quote would be used in its first Civil War history book. All context for the quote was lost, and it was attributed to "the Secretary of War." Arthur M. Schlesinger Sr. used the quote in his *Political and Social History of the United States*, as would many others on the topic of broader U.S. history. Stanton's quote became substantially shorter, generally only including the last portion: "without McCormick's invention I feel the North could not win and that the Union would be dismembered."[60]

The works that the McCormick Biographical Association produced would seep into mainstream historiography and contaminate the histories of the Civil War and nineteenth-century United States. Stanton's quote is evidence of this. The fabrication has been repeated often, perpetually confirming the image of Cyrus McCormick as a patriotic and important supporter of the Union cause. The quote would end up being used by just about any historian that wanted to make a claim that their topic contributed to Union victory, if they could connect their interests to the reaper or McCormick. Chicago historians would use the quote as evidence of their city's contribution to the war efforts. Historians of agriculture and the Midwest would do the same. Strangely, the quote is even used by Virginia historians as evidence of the greatness of the state's people.[61]

Crucially important to the McCormicks' historical enterprise were the laborers that the family paid to fulfill their ambitions. The full spectrum of historical laborers who interacted with the McCormicks indicates the range of professionals that attempted to claim the past as their area of expertise. The spectrum included those academically trained, alongside lawyers, advertisers, journalists, and freelance consultants. These historians may seem to be professional worlds apart, but most of them mutually agreed to interpret the past flexibly to prove their value in the corporate order and secure financial remuneration. While Frederick Jackson Turner seems nothing like Frank Flower, the mercenary research by Flower was published under the byline of Turner's credible colleague Reuben Gold Thwaites. The academically trained Salem Pattison bears a striking resemblance to the advertising professional Herbert Casson. Both succeeded in getting paid because they offered a concrete plan of action to meet their employer's historical needs. Moreover, the research services and legalistic briefs of the trained lawyers Louis Dent and Robert Parkinson seem very similar to the labor of the academically trained historian. Academic historians would not secure authority within the McCormicks' historical enterprise until 1929. In the meantime the McCormicks would continue to hold lawyers and advertisers above their own academic historians as the historical professionals of merit.

4

Realigning History with the Rising Corporate Order

In mid-August 1913 residents of Glenwood and surrounding Mills County in Iowa flocked to the chautauqua tent on the east edge of town for a week of lectures, debates, musical performances, and motion pictures. Every summer since 1904 the Midland Chautauqua Circuit had made a stop in Glenwood, erecting a massive canvas tent and arranging a program of interesting, uplifting, and educational talent for each day and evening of its stay. Praised by Theodore Roosevelt as "the most American thing in America," circuit chautauqua companies toured the Midwest, engaging rural Americans in the cultural, social, civic, and spiritual debates of the Progressive Era. Like most midwesterners, Mills County residents eagerly anticipated and treasured the annual chautauqua as the event of the season. It was not uncommon for attendees to save and cherish programs from each annual gathering and discuss what they had seen and heard in the tent year-round. Local boosters promoted the event for months preceding the arrival of the circuit, hanging banners, decorating storefronts, and widely publicizing the occasion in local papers. In Glenwood adults readily paid $2 for a season ticket in advance to see the whole bill of enlightening presentations and an additional $1 for each of their children to enjoy the festivities as well. Once the chautauqua opened, local entrepreneurs sold food on-site to feed the more than two thousand people that packed into the tent each day. Merchants closed for the week, farmers left their fields, and out-of-towners stayed with local friends and family or camped in the canvas village adjacent to the big top so that they would not miss a moment of the presentations.[1]

Spanning from August 9 to August 16, the Midland Chautauqua Circuit offered an educational and morally enriching variety show of over thirty acts on the platform. Glenwood's 1913 bill included fourteen choral and instrumental concerts, seven motion-picture shows, an impersonator, a debate on military armament and foreign tensions in Europe, and seven lectures. Directed at intent audiences, the lectures generally focused on Christian morality, ranging in topics from advice for youth in the workplace to the importance of strong parenting for the future of the nation and a sermon on the perils of socialism for the independent Christian.[2]

Among the lectures two addresses focused on the nation's economic order—a popular topic. Americans, and farmers in particular, were anxious about and hostile toward big businesses at a time when economic power was increasingly concentrated in the hands of fewer and fewer corporations. Many saw the corporate merger movement of 1895–1904 as further proof that the farmer's independence and the nation's sacred democracy were in jeopardy. Chautauqua performers commonly spoke to these issues and invigorated populist antitrust sentiments. L. F. Lybarger filled this role on the second night of the Glenwood chautauqua, lambasting railroads and robber barons for "gobbling up the country" and the wealth of the common man. At the conclusion of his lecture, "Land, Labor and Wealth," Lybarger repeated a common Progressive Era call to arms, praying that the government intervene to rescue the nation, lest the country's children be condemned to a life of poverty at the hands of trusts. In juxtaposition to Lybarger's tirade, Frank Stockdale offered a harmonious rendering of the nation's interests, titled "The Dawn of Plenty."[3]

As the closing lecture of the week, Frank Stockdale took center stage and for an hour regaled the audience with a history of the world "as a record of man's struggle for bread." Assisted by illustrations, motion pictures, and dramatic lighting effects, Stockdale argued that, prior to the nineteenth century, 97 percent of humanity struggled merely to provide bread to feed themselves because they lacked the appropriate tools to harvest grain efficiently. For over fifty centuries progress stood still, while farmers were enslaved by tyrants who stole the fruits of their labor. Crucially, Stockdale explained that this condition of drudgery and deprivation ceased in 1831, when Cyrus McCormick invented the reaper. He illustrated that the reaper and its successive improvements freed Americans to leave the farm and pursue the progress that made the nation great, while other "lesser races" were still enslaved by the tools of the ancients. Stockdale preached that in the reaper's wake cities sprang up, Americans pushed westward, railroads followed across the continent, industry boomed, commerce matured, universities opened, and technological ingenuity was unleashed, creating a modern civilization of abundance. He opined that modern industrialization, urbanization, and corporatization were not at odds with agrarians. Rather, the farmer's "common sense" and embrace of "up-to-date methods" allowed him to profit as a partner and crucial contributor to the new economic order. The grain the farmer raised enabled civilization and progress to flourish.[4]

The audience sat in rapt silence throughout Stockdale's performance and was wowed by his accompanying multimedia imagery. The editor of the *Glenwood Opinion* believed that Stockdale's show alone was worth the price of the season's admission. He raved that "The Dawn of Plenty" was "meritorious for its instruction and education," placing the week's preceding lecturers "far in the shade." Billed as the "Mirthful Orator," Stockdale was a polished and engaging public speaker. He had taken "The Dawn of Plenty" to lyceum halls the previous winter. During the summer of 1913, Stockdale executed it at scores of chautauqua across the Midwest, including three other times that same week for audiences in Illinois, Iowa, and Nebraska.[5] Unpublicized and unbeknownst to all these onlookers, and indeed the editor of the *Glenwood Opinion*, Frank Stockdale worked for the International Harvester Company. The rural masses filling the chautauqua benches had paid to witness a public relations spectacle prepared by the despised "harvester trust."

As a growing monopolistic power in the United States' farm-implement industry, the International Harvester Company was beset during the Progressive Era by antitrust antagonism and real legal threats since its creation in 1902. The trust's illegal competitive practices, deplorable treatment of workers, and outright bribery of public officials made it the target of rural animosity, labor strikes, muckrakers, middle-class concerns, political stumping, and, eventually, government inquiry and regulation. Rising from this swirling cacophony of protest, in 1912 the U.S. Department of Justice brought suit against the harvester trust to dissolve the corporation.

As antitrust pressure against the company mounted and the real threat of destruction emerged, the company developed an evolving and increasingly sophisticated public relations campaign to convince Americans that it was a "good trust." This initiative began in 1907 with new corporate welfare programs for its workers and then a 1909 overhaul of advertising material and branding efforts. By 1912 it included an Agricultural Extension Department to demonstrate the corporation's goodwill toward farmers and a public education campaign under the auspices of its own Service Bureau. At the height of antitrust antagonism, the Service Bureau saturated the nation with a wealth of veiled propaganda in the form of educational lectures and materials for schoolchildren. These "indirect advertisements" reimagined and realigned traditional understandings of the past to demonstrate that the corporation was a cooperative ally of the common man in the present, happily aiding in his pursuit of progress and prosperity. To further legitimize these public relations narratives, the company's ownership also set out to influence the academic historians of the Mississippi Valley Historical Association to ensure that their corporate myths would stay in the public mind for generations to come.[6]

International Harvester was founded in 1902 to eliminate competition across the harvesting industry and to increase profits. One of many such mergers during the era, it quickly earned a reputation as another hated "trust" designed to rob the common man. In an industry previously defined by consumer power and rigorous competition, the corporation unified the five largest harvester manufacturers—McCormick, Deering, Milwaukee, Osborne, and Champion—and immediately gained the power of price making over its customers. The corporation soon faced animosity from a variety of sources, including agrarians, laborers, journalists, and politicians. These forces culminated to instigate government inquiry, regulation, and, eventually, an antitrust suit against the harvester trust in 1912.

Farmers made up the largest group aggrieved by the trust. At its creation International Harvester produced 85 percent of harvesting machines in the country and immediately doubled the real price a farmer paid for the machine. Through manufacturer-exclusive contracts with retailers, the firm expanded its monopoly on harvester machines to build monopolies on other farm implements, like seeders, spreaders, wagons, and harrows. Seemingly overnight, farmers went from being able to skillfully play competitors off of one another and purchasing a harvester for $60 to having no negotiation leverage and paying more than $125 for the same machine. They saw the "monster octopus" ensnaring other implement lines as well and railed against the firm as their "greatest enemy."[7]

The trust posed a grave threat not only to farmers' pocketbook but also to their identity and way of life. Into the twentieth century many agrarians believed that they were Thomas Jefferson's yeoman farmers—morally protecting democracy through mastering the land, paternally providing for their families, contributing to their communities, and remaining independently unencumbered by outside interests or obligations. This "agrarian fundamentalism" provided the basis for a masculine preindustrial national ideal. Corporations like International Harvester undermined this gender ideal because they contributed to making farmers powerlessly dependent on outside market forces and distant arbitrary decisions that could not be negotiated or challenged. Increasingly in debt and reliant on commodity prices that were never high enough, farmers had to take on more debt to buy more machinery and land or quit the farm. Moreover, their paternal authority was diminished, as they were less able to provide for their family, and their children either had to earn wages elsewhere to support the family or left the farm in pursuit of urban opportunities. As neighbors encountered these forces and choices simultaneously, farmers were anxious that their former way of life would disappear along with their children and neighbors. The harvester trust was the most recent and egregious example of the corporate order's threat to farmers' livelihood and masculinity. Resentful and outraged, they looked to politicians to regulate the morass and restore the democratic order.[8]

The corporation's reputation in the city was not much better. Early after its creation International Harvester was the target of Chicago muckrakers in publications such as *Collier's* and the *Day Book*, among many others, who exposed the company's exploitation of its workers and administrative chicanery to middle-class urban readers. These journalists revealed the real impact of the trust's low wages, dangerous working conditions in factories, disregard for employee welfare, and scandalous relationship with the city's tax board, igniting the ire of urban progressives. In conjunction the corporation also faced five waves of labor strikes, from 1903 to 1919. Workers went on strike for better wages and conditions and shorter hours, attracting still more negative publicity and the interests of "trust-busting" reform politicians.[9]

The harvester trust's undesirable image in both the country and the city, as well as its real monopolistic control of the industry, invited state and federal government intervention on behalf of the American people. The corporation had faced intense political and legal scrutiny in a number of western states, including Arkansas, Illinois, Indiana, Iowa, Kentucky, Minnesota, Missouri, Nebraska, North Dakota, Ohio, Tennessee, and Texas. Most of these states passed antitrust laws and imposed fines on the corporation in the few years following its creation. In the most extreme cases, International Harvester was ousted from doing business within Missouri in 1910 and Kentucky in 1911. At the behest of western senators, the Bureau of Corporations initiated an investigation of the trust in 1907. In 1912 President William Howard Taft instructed the Department of Justice to commence its antitrust prosecution of International Harvester, after Roosevelt had previously stayed the suit pending the ongoing bureau investigation. Lasting from 1912 to 1918, the federal suit against International Harvester pursued enforcement of the Sherman Anti-Trust Act of 1890 and the dissolution of the trust.[10]

With the company facing myriad challenges to its reputation and existence from 1907 to 1918, management desperately struggled to improve the corporation's public image through public relations efforts. The company created welfare programs, profit sharing, and industrial relations committees in hopes of assuaging labor animosity and currying favor with reformers and politicians. In the countryside advertisements and educational programs, focused on cultivating a benevolent image of the corporation, were the core of the company's public relations strategy for placating hostility and promoting sales. Attracting attention from later historians, the 1912 creation of the Agricultural Extension Department brought scientific best-practices education to farmers across the nation to assist them in their pursuit of prosperity. The company also created a Service Bureau in 1910, which, though largely unnoticed, offered educational materials to the rural masses that culturally sanctioned the corporation's position in American society. The Service Bureau was engaged in historical production, teaching farmers and their children that business and the common farmer were partners, mutually benefiting each other while walking hand in hand to advance the progress of civilization.[11]

International Harvester began overhauling its advertising to recast the trust as the farmer's cooperative ally in 1909. Under the direction of M. R. D. Owings, the Advertising Department dramatically renovated its promotional materials and expanded its offerings. The department began to publish a monthly magazine, the *Harvester World*, to inform its workforce and its customers. It also undertook to distribute an annual almanac to 3.5 million farmers, serving them as a "constant reference" that was "free of miscellaneous advertising, but incidentally advertising our line and the Company." They also improved the company's catalogs so that they were no longer "big, cheaply printed, small type affairs . . . in which the biggest thing is the price." Rather, the catalogs became "books of information," educating both agents and the farmer about the best methods and modern tools for attaining prosperity on the farm.[12]

This advertising overhaul was accompanied by a rebranding initiative to make the company synonymous with prosperity. In its inaugural October 1909 issue of the *Harvester World*, the department unveiled a new company logo as well as a mascot. The mascot they imagined was a "genial little Farm-Sprite" named "Prospy" (short for "Prosperity"). Indicating the Advertising Department's awareness of public antitrust sentiment, Prospy's first printed words were "business is or should be and will be cooperation—not robbery." Committed to the concepts of "prosperity" and "cooperation" as a more desirable public image, all of the company's advertising materials became educational in nature and included Prospy's likeness.[13]

The message of the new brand is best conveyed in Prospy's feature booklet, *Glimpses of Thrift-Land*. In this illustrated booklet, Prospy demonstrates to the backward "Farmer Brown" that "the ideal farmer on an ideal farm . . . saves time and expense and preserves himself to enjoy in his old age his rapidly growing wealth by using the peerless I.H.C. farm machines and implements." The story opens with an exasperated Farmer Brown cutting hay by hand. Prospy appears and introduces himself to the flabbergasted farmer as a "Son of the Soil" and a "Genius of Farm Thrift," before taking him on a journey to "thrift land." In the course of their adventures together through "thrift land," Prospy shows Farmer Brown the entire line of International Harvester machines (clearly identified with the new IHC trademark) and educates an amazed Farmer Brown in modern farming methods that will ensure the success of his crops. Reflecting the company's desired public image, Prospy also stresses that the company exists solely to help the farmer succeed, through educating him in scientific farming methods and giving him access to cutting-edge implements. Functioning as an allegory for the company's new brand, Prospy points "the unprogressive farmer to 'Thrift-Land'" and, fittingly, prosperity.[14]

As a curious invention of the Advertising Department, Prospy's image and thrifty wisdom recommended a new agrarian masculinity (see fig. 9). Prospy was a freakish amalgamation of "primitivism," International Harvester iconography, and common farm commodities. With an ear of corn for a body; a headdress of alfalfa, oats, and clover; a spear of wheat; a quiver of timothy grass arrows; and a golden IHC trademark shield, he resembled a generic warrior that might be found in the pages of *National Geographic*. Unlike these racial stereotypes, however, he was white, proffered sagacious wisdom about modern farming, and peddled expensive machinery. Prospy was a vision of primitive white masculinity that suggested the compatibility of the prosperous independent farmer and the emerging corporate order. This gendered message, and indeed Prospy, were ubiquitous in International Harvester's sales and service materials as a cultural hedge against agrarian fears of corporate enslavement.[15]

The Service Bureau was another facet of the Prospy-advertising revolution and rebranding effort in 1910. The Advertising Department hired knowledgeable, formally educated employees who specialized in key areas of interest, like mechanics and horticulture, to make catalogs more educational. The department included useful and practical farming content alongside sales text designed to demonstrate the company's thoughtful engagement with the farmer's interests. In tandem the Service Bureau was formed to garner greater public trust by carrying out this educational mission outside of sales and advertising purposes. Department manager Owings noted that the new bureau allowed the company "to place with the schools, agricultural colleges, institutes, on cars, boats, boards of trade, commercial organizations,

9. *Prospy*, advertising poster, 1909. Beginning in 1909, the new International Harvester Company mascot was emblazoned on a wide variety of the corporation's public relations materials. Prospy instructed farmers on the path to securing "prosperity." A "genial sprite," the mascot was constructed of farm commodities, and his shield was the corporation's new trademark monogram. Wisconsin Historical Society, WHI-4625.

and through our own organization, literature that is highly appreciated and accepted as educational without the tincture of advertising, but which indirectly advertises the Company in advance educational work." In the manager's mind the bureau offered double value by reframing the public image of the company and subtly cultivating demand for International Harvester products through its seemingly benevolent initiatives.[16]

Reflecting the self-serving interests of the company's supposed benevolent enterprise, the Service Bureau and Advertising Department were practically one entity. According to the Service Bureau manager Owings, advertising and service were so "closely allied . . . that it would be difficult to tell where one begins and the others leaves off." Frequently content and artwork developed for one of the branches was freely utilized by the other. They remained necessarily intertwined, because in "back of service ever stands the shadow of advertising," so much so that the two branches occupied the same office space. Owings and his staff were careful to conceal this relationship from the public.[17]

Cyrus McCormick II overtly stated the public relations objectives of the Service Bureau when he expanded it to include a new Extension Department in 1912. In a circular denying the veracity of the federal antitrust case and promoting the new department, McCormick argued that his corporation was compatible with traditional American values and communities. Addressing popular anxieties, he was certain that International Harvester could demonstrate that it was "inspired by the same high ideals which so often characterize the management of a private business." He noted that the company served the farmer's interests through developing, building, and selling modern machinery. Beyond this most basic business function, he also underlined that the corporation benevolently assisted the masses through its Service Bureau initiatives. The bureau was "giving a definite and valuable service to the country at large." It was committed to "spreading the doctrine of more intelligent farming" and carried "directly to the farm house the discoveries and results of the work" in agricultural science.

To further meet the "great need" for public education, McCormick announced that he had hired Perry G. Holden, the agronomist and famous extension worker from Iowa State University, to enlarge the bureau's work by creating an Extension Department for the company. He also suggested that these benevolent expenditures on the farmer's education were possible only because of the business's massive scale.[18]

Many International Harvester publications emphasized the upstanding character of the corporation by pointing to its Service Bureau. In contrast to rural fears of corporate infringement, these publications and messages consistently stressed that the corporation was a positive social force. An Extension Department publication stated that "the International Harvester Company, as a citizen of the nation, feels the responsibility of its obligations to the people." Such "obligations of citizenship" were met through the bureau's mission "to simplify and to modernize scientific agriculture and to carry the most efficient methods to the homes of the people." Another pamphlet suggested that the corporation was on the frontlines of a war on famine and want. Aware that Americans would not naively accept such public relations messages on faith alone, most publications explained that the corporation's success was reliant on the farmer's prosperity. Educating the farmer ensured his own progress and the company's profits.[19]

While Perry Holden and the Extension Department offered adult education, publishing booklets and offering demonstrations and lectures that informed the farmer's methods, another branch of the Service Bureau was dedicated entirely to the farmer's cultural indoctrination. According to Edwin Lincoln Barker, the architect of the corporation's cultural promotion efforts, his work was nothing short of propaganda tailored to "molding public opinion and putting the right thoughts into the minds" of the masses. These men engaged in dubious historical labor—creating booklets, "dramalogues," motion pictures, and lantern-slide lectures that justified the corporation's existence through celebratory narratives of the past. Their teleological tales wove together the interests of the farmer, the corporation, and the nation into a unified fable of progress, prosperity, and civilization. They emphasized that, prior to the creation of International Harvester's philanthropic departments, the corporation and its predecessors provided service indirectly to the farmer and society. Resurrecting the McCormick Harvesting Machine Company's former historical brand, their case in point was that McCormick's "invention of the reaper . . . founded agricultural greatness and the Company." From 1831 forward American civilization progressed and prospered.[20]

Indicating the less-than-scholarly tenor of this pursuit, Edwin Lincoln Barker, the man responsible for the historical branch of the Service Bureau, was a veteran of the theater and entertainment industry. Born in 1868, Barker had made his career as a humorist, monologist, playwright, and impersonator in Chicago during the 1890s. In the first decade of the 1900s, he co-owned the Bush Temple Theater and booked variety-show performers and orators. Building on this background in the emerging field of educational show business, Barker became very involved in the professionalization of lyceums and chautauquas. In 1904 he opened and operated the Midwest's premier trade journal for traveling circuit professionals, the *Lyceumite*. His Chicago office was the hub of the new industry. Bustling with activity, managers and performers hustled in and out. They sought jobs, publicized their circuits, asked for information about good chautauqua towns, practiced their performances, and wrung their hands over railroad maps trying to figure out the logistics of their traveling educational extravaganzas. As an orator himself, a manager, and the man at the center of the professional network, Barker knew everything about, and everyone in, the midwestern lyceum and circuit-chautauqua industry.[21]

During the first three decades of the twentieth century, circuit chautauquas were a celebrated institution in rural America. The commercialized progeny of the stationary chautauqua assemblies and akin to lyceum lectures, the traveling circuits brought a full week of morally, intellectually, and culturally uplifting presentations to rural communities across the nation. Hungry for inspiration, leisure, and affirmation, chautauqua audiences witnessed a variety of educational and cultural presentations, including orations, special programming for children, and musical groups. Addressing rural anxieties about citizenship, race, gender, urbanization, corporatization, foreign affairs, politics, government, and Christian morality, performances in the big tent connected the countryside with the larger world. Progressive Era politicians and reformers such as William Jennings Bryan, Robert Lafollette, Ida Tarbell, and Eugene Debs frequented the same circuit stages as minstrel shows, gospel choirs, string quartets, exotic foreign acts, and comedians. Millions of rural Americans attended these educational variety shows, because the performers on the platform and the audience in the seats briefly actualized an ideal vision of rural modernity. In juxtaposition to their anxieties, that cherished vision reassured audiences that their farms, their communities, and their values were righteous, pervasive, and vital to the strength of the nation.[22]

International Harvester hired Edwin Barker to lead its Service Bureau and present public relations materials to rural audiences. Considered an "exceptionally fine writer," Barker brought chautauqua-style didactics and themes to the company's publications and later to its public presentations. Barker blended rural-centric tropes with a simplistic sense of American exceptionalism and the corporation's gendered branding messages to craft a set of corporate propaganda tools and messages from scratch. Within Barker's literary creations the power and prosperity of civilization flowed from the farmer's mastery of machines and scientific agricultural knowledge rather than his principled Jeffersonian independence. In his renderings the virtuous modern farmer was assisted by misunderstood businesses to acquire wealth and feed the world. While Barker acknowledged social and economic discontent, he assured farmers that the concerns of the modern age were natural growing pains of progress and most certainly were negligible in comparison to the hardships of their distant and more recent ancestors. Time would iron out any wrinkles, as it always had, and soon all of society would be contently on the path upward. To underline these points Barker relied on teleological anecdotes and histories that revolved around McCormick's 1831 invention of the reaper as the key moment when progress commenced and the farmer was liberated from primitive drudgery. Historyesque narratives had been almost entirely absent from the company's promotional materials from 1902 to 1910, but Barker quickly made it the corporation's principal cultural asset.

Over his five years in the Service Bureau, Barker's influence and responsibility gradually advanced. He began by assisting the Advertising Department in livening up copy, collaborating on scientific farming booklets as Service Bureau publications, and contributing articles to *Harvester World*. He also fabricated unassuming school histories that instilled a logic of progress into children and offered lectures in limited numbers. After the antitrust suit was filed in 1912, the Service Bureau was greatly enlarged, and Barker was given a staff that included an artist, a film editor, three lecturers, three motion-picture operators, and several assistants. With more resources at his command and greater imperative, Barker imagined a grand chautauqua-circuit campaign to influence public opinion through hundreds of multimedia-assisted oratory spectacles.[23]

Barker's first work laying out the corporation's public relations history was *The Story of Bread*. Written in 1911, the twenty-nine-page booklet recounts the transformative influence of the reaper on the world. The story dramatically emphasizes the machine's conclusive impact on the age-old struggle for bread and the farmer's importance to modernity. Inviting the reader to fathom the era before the current "Age of Plenty," Barker opens the story: "For fifty centuries the world stood still, waiting to be fed," a condition that continued until "no farther back than your great-grandfather and mine." A full 97 percent of these ancestors of humanity fought to avoid starvation, "for there was no bread to be had, for there was no flour, for there was no wheat, for there were no large fields planted, for there were no quick ways of gathering the harvest." After sixteen pages expounding on the centuries of humankind's deprivation and the comparative abundance in the modern age, Cyrus McCormick's 1831 invention of the reaper appears as the great turning point in human history. The reaper's efficiency "released two-thirds of the population" to pursue vocations beyond the farm because it ended starvation by making bread cheap and abundant.[24]

From the invention of the reaper onward, *The Story of Bread* argues humanity was on the path of progress toward modernity. In a wonderfully overstated passage on the importance of the invention of the mechanized reaper, Barker explains, "The wheels of industry were set in motion, modern business was born, and commerce reached its arms around the world. American civilization pushed westward at the rate of thirty miles a year, and older nations awoke to greatness[.] Railroads came, cities were builded, and inventions multiplied. Every tall building is a monument to cheap bread." The invention and the agrarians who adopted it were responsible for populating the wilderness of the West, the expansion of railroads, the formation of factories, the rising of skyscrapers, the commerce of cities, the founding of universities and agriculture schools, the creation of jobs, and many other trappings of modernity. In this conception agrarian independence was not at odds with the new modern order, as was commonly feared. Rather, Barker cast mechanized farmers as the crucial heroes of civilization who fed the world and allowed progress to flourish.[25]

Predictably, Cyrus McCormick was lionized as a great inventor-businessman to be revered as the farmer's paternal benefactor and role model. He was peer to all the great inventors, intellectuals, and businessmen, including Galileo, Charles Darwin, Thomas Edison, Robert Fulton, James J. Hill, and John D. Rockefeller. With ingenuity and forthright moral character, he had kept "plugging away" until he had invented a working reaper and successfully marketed it to the masses, ensuring that "no longer is the farmer a drudge." He had "the wonderful foresight (or was it inspiration?)" to build his business in Chicago amid the wild prairies, "the center of where wheat fields were to be" in the future. His reaper single-handedly ended slavery during the Civil War and, in words that alluded to the Declaration of Independence, "removed the hobble from man's right to the pursuit of happiness." The reaper was the great machine of democracy and farmer liberation. Its inventor was in turn the ultimate harbinger of progress.[26]

Reflecting the corporation's more immediate political, legal, and social woes, *The Story of Bread* historically reframed corporate capitalism and class conflict. Barker stressed that the current complaints of modern capitalism paled in comparison to the class stratification and hardships before the reaper. For centuries "great wealth sat in the high places," in the hands of the few "round and fat." Meanwhile, the toiling farmer "furrowed his brow, bent his back, and crumbled away before his time, all in an effort to scratch from the earth a few grains of wheat with which to keep the spark of life flickering in his starved and shivering body." Beyond starvation, even in the more recent prereaper history, people labored "in the hot harvest field for sixteen hours a day at a wage of three cents an hour." Comparatively, Barker noted that modern workers on the farm, in the office, and in the factory had far shorter days, earning much higher wages.[27]

Despite that *The Story of Bread* clearly paid tribute to the farmer, the booklet's focus on bread reflected a substantial shift in the historyesque advertising of the harvester industry. As described in chapter 2, advertising materials from the 1880s and 1890s emphasized producerism, celebrating myriad forms of labor as the source of all wealth and value in the world, as a common thread drawing farmers and so-called captains of industry together. Moreover, within the wider culture, the producerist ethos was felt to be a core tenant of virtuous, self-sustaining, and independent national citizenship, particularly in the rural United States. *The Story of Bread* twisted this cultural ideal, suggesting that productive labor was important only because it was in the service of ever-expanding availability and consumption of bread—

which enabled the mushrooming of other modern goods and services. As one artifact reflecting a sea change in advertising literature and shifting values more generally, *The Story of Bread* contributed to smothering traditional notions of producer citizenship and suggested the consumption of modern goods and lifestyles as a new benchmark for American identity.

The narrative also offered a progressive vision of U.S. history that conveniently forgot national divisions that had defined the country during the past century. Rather than emphasizing regional differences between the North and South or geographic cultural difference between the romantic rural ethos of the countryside and the corrupt morals of the city, *The Story of Bread* suggested that Americans were a single people. Everyone was unified by their pursuit of progress and an ever-improving standard of living. Barker inferred that corporations in general and International Harvester in particular were the crucial glue that bound everyone in this order together, organizing and guaranteeing progress and prosperity for all.

Within this new progressive framework of history, *The Story of Bread* supposed that International Harvester was a persecuted martyr ahead of its time, unrecognized for its crucial ingenuity and importance. Historically, past leaders were "assassinated" and intellectuals were "beheaded" or "burned," but "as proof of how civilization has advanced, today we merely sick onto them penny humorists and muckrakers." Though International Harvester had suffered continuous bad press and legal challenges, in the future the nation would think better of the company in light of how it "has benefitted the world." Barker reminded readers that "business men of every description" were not the enemies of the farmer but rather cooperative allies, sincerely concerned "with the welfare of the farm"—again reflecting the new unified rendering of society as it pursued progress.[28]

As a concise statement of the corporation's contributions to humanity and the narrative behind its "Prosperity" brand, *The Story of Bread* was adopted as reference material for executive speeches throughout the antitrust proceedings of the 1910s. It showed the company's commitment to "eliminate the centuries of drudgery on the farm," its "great part . . . in the world's advancement," and the resulting "tremendous progress of the American farmer," signified by the farmers' "confidence in our willingness to treat them as co-partners." Any speech and publication by the company or its owners on the topic of the antitrust suit ostensibly restated ideas from *The Story of Bread*. In a 1912 speech typical of this type and reprinted in *Harvester World*, Harold McCormick summarized *The Story of Bread* before concluding that this history demonstrated International Harvester's focus on "the general welfare and progress of . . . the farm."[29]

Barker also wrote other histories that followed the same teleological arch patterned in *The Story of Bread*. *The Creeds of Great Business Men* told the stories of thriving businessmen who were enabled by farmers and McCormick's invention to serve the common good. In line with the impulse behind the Hall of Fame for Great Americans and a Progressive Era sense of history, *The Creeds of Great Business Men* reduced history to literally the actions of "Great Business Men" and relegated the masses of farmers to a passive role as followers. *The Story of Twine* follows the historical development and production of the innocuous material that uplifted Mexican laborers, employed factory workers, and allowed U.S. farmers to be still more productive. Among several others these publications suggested that corporations were the active ally of farmers and leading the way toward improving the nation and the world as partners with the public.

The Service Bureau distributed millions of copies of these booklets annually. The sales force gave them to farmers, commercial clubs, and newspaper editors, among many others. For his part Barker particularly focused on getting the books in the hands of schoolchildren and into agricultural universities and libraries. In February 1912 the bureau sent copies of *The Story of Bread* to every state education superintendent. They also reported that several states had provided the bureau with a complete list of county superintendents to solicit and had prepared lesson plans "for the use of their teachers in presenting 'the Story of Bread' to pupils." Along these same lines the bureau prepared "the Development of Agriculture" lantern-slide lecture for teachers to deliver in tandem with the reading materials. The bureau also sponsored spelling bee competitions for schools that used a bureau-provided vocabulary list in 1912 and created a cash-prize essay competition for students to answer the prompt "What Cheap Bread has Done for the World" in 1913. The company trumpeted the bureau's success, proclaiming that thousands of schools and colleges were using the booklets "as supplemental reading to the delight" of students.[30]

Through creating materials for classrooms, the Service Bureau was contributing to the rural educational reform movement. A contentious undertaking instigated by urban progressives and politicians to the chagrin of rural residents, school reform focused on consolidating schools into expensive modern facilities, professionalizing teachers, creating higher educational standards, and providing better content for pupils. As part of the Country Life movement to civilize rural society and modernize its industry, the reorganization of schools was met with hostility from agrarians because of its expense and its cultural warfare on rural traditions. As obvious supporters of such an undertaking in the name of their own profits, the Service Bureau's contributions were readily accepted by school administrators and teachers to help fill the content void in an era when educational funding was still minimal. The bureau's literary combinations of civilized progress and mechanized farming matched the cultural values that the reformers sought to instill. Moreover, the bureau's decision to focus on children allowed it to indirectly advertise the benefits of the corporation to parents and ensured that in the future it would be "regarded as a broad, liberal, human-betterment organization." These educational efforts supposedly illustrated the corporation's commitment to public service, while advancing its self-serving image as a historical promoter of progress and prosperity.[31]

With the commencement of the federal antitrust suit in 1912, International Harvester increased the Service Bureau's annual budget to $1 million so that public relations efforts could be expanded. While part of this money went to create the Extension Department, the rest was available to Barker. Utilizing his background in oratory and circuit management, Barker used this financial influx to produce a high-quality lecture campaign presented in chautauqua tents and lyceum halls by three teams of Service Bureau employees. Barker placed his lectures on summer chautauqua circuits and utilized the corporation's sales organization to locate suitable winter venues. The lectures, like the one offered by Frank Stockdale in 1913 described at the beginning of this chapter, were also booked at schools, agricultural colleges, churches, YMCAs, commercial clubs, farmers' institutes, teachers' organizations, theaters, and a variety of other locations across the agricultural sections of the Midwest and the far West. Exercising audience awareness, the orators revealed their corporate connections only to those more likely to be amicable toward the company as "progressive minded" citizens, like business associations and agricultural colleges.[32]

The new lectures were dramatic enactments of the bureau's booklets. Initially Barker adapted *The Story of Bread* into a script called "The Dawn of Plenty" in 1911, but it was offered only a few times as traditional platform orations. By 1914 he added "The Dawn of Commerce," a discussion of the modern economy, and "The Dawn of Power," a history of mechanization, to the bureau's offerings. Billed as an "industrialogue" series, the Three Dawns were multimedia sensations that included colored lantern-slide illustrations, motion pictures, and theatrical lighting to dramatically enhance the traditional chautauqua-style performances. Engaged as companion events, the industrialogues demonstrated "why big business is necessary" to the "great industrial and commercial age in which we live."[33]

As a series, the Three Dawns were histories of civilization, saturated with racialized and gendered cultural messages that reflected the corporation's public relations ambitions and projected "modern" ideals onto the audience. The series was intended to convince farmers of their mutually beneficial relationship with corporations and modernity. To accomplish this goal these narratives transformed the established ideal of the independent and self-sustaining farmer, into the Advertising Department's vision of the prosperous and mechanized master of the land that "Prospy" suggested. The shift in masculine archetypes necessarily altered the farmer's supposed relationship with manufacturers and indeed the rest of the progressive order. Barker's metamorphosis of agrarian masculinity rested on interpreting the farmer's tools and property "as the signposts of civilization."[34]

With such an emphasis "The Dawn of Plenty," "The Dawn of Power," and "The Dawn of Commerce" ascribed cultural value to farm tools, industrial machines, and consumer goods, respectively. The first two recounted chronologies of invention as material marches from ancient times to modern civilization. As the concluding lecture, "The Dawn of Commerce" expounded on the cooperation between the farmer and the manufacturer that had resulted in the proliferation of trade and the accumulation of material wealth. Within this framework the lecturer still paid homage to the independent farmer, who "conquered nature," provided for his family, and enabled progress, but it was evident that his masculine authority was built on shifting ground.[35]

The lectures were also saturated with bigoted notions of race, which were common place in Progressive Era America. Striking the hammer of anxiety on the audience's consciousness, the performances constantly compared the civilized tools of modern, enlightened white farmers with the primitive implements of foreign, "savage" races. Assisted by the new technology of film, the lecturers assessed images of white farmers riding tractors and binders, driving combines, or shipping large crop commodities on trains against clips of brown farmers crouching to cut wheat by hand, sending small surpluses by boat, and grinding flour with stones. The narrators explained that American farmers had been assisted by technological ingenuity to become prosperous while the "foreigners"—Indians, Koreans, Chinese, and Egyptians—were kept in "ignorance and poverty" because they continued to use the tools of ancient times. They offered further mocking asides about the brown farmers' lowly huts, their lack of shoes, and their "dinky methods of agriculture." Providing overarching meaning, the orator noted that in the tools "we see the difference between a nation that goes backward and a nation that goes forward."[36]

Importantly, the lectures demonstrated that the difference between the civilized and the primitive was not exclusively racial but was also yoked to masculinity. A farmer was manly if he had the most modern tools available, and he was primitive if he fell short of that standard. Sowing seeds of anxiety, these racial comparisons implied that materiality was crucial to "white" status. Directly conveying these messages, the orators related the civilized farmer with his rundown neighbor. The civilized farmer had well-maintained buildings, ubiquitous machinery, diversified crops, a herd of livestock, and a mansion filled with "modern improvements and conveniences." Meanwhile, his rundown neighbor had slipshod fences, fields covered in filth, a barn going to ruin, and a hole in the roof of his house. This farmer was unprogressive and unmechanized. Like the "foreigner," his surroundings signified his mockable "poverty." The lectures had replaced the old image of the independent and self-sufficient farmer with a new prosperous and progressive man who not only provided for his family but could supply them with the consumer trappings of middle-class life. He had freed his wife from the drudgery of home manufacture and could take his leisure. They had connected the masculinity of middle-class consumption that had been created by advertisers in the consumer-goods industry and offered modern machinery as the farmer's pathway to that ideal.[37]

With such a cultural imperative placed on modern farm implements and consumer goods, the lectures reoriented the ideal farmer's relationship with the industrial order. While all of Barker's work was oriented toward rescuing International Harvester's public image during the federal antitrust suit, none was more direct and overstated than "The Dawn of Commerce," which stressed the interconnected and mutually beneficial relationships among agriculture, commerce, labor, and capital as they walked "shoulder to shoulder" in pursuit of prosperity. While prosperity sprang from the farms, mines, and forests of the land, engines of commerce transformed those resources and increased their value through manufacturing and distribution that moved the supply to new points of demand. In this iteration all parties generated wealth through their labor as "producers," converting raw materials into valuable commodities and goods. Through numerous historical and imaginary anecdotes charting the flow of consumer dollars, the orator demonstrated how the fortunes of all rose and fell together.[38]

In particular, "The Dawn of Commerce" was concerned with demonstrating that corporations were a vital and legitimate part of the system. Corporations were simply larger businesses that promoted commercial efficiency and prosperity through organizing "raw materials, mechanical skill, advertising, salesmanship . . . for the profit of all, including the farmer who feeds us." "Big organizations" like International Harvester, U.S. Steel, and the United Shoe Machinery Company, among others, were necessary "to blaze trails into the markets of the world," spreading the "light of civilization" into the "darkest corners of the earth" and securing greater prosperity at home. The lecture also defended corporations as democratically owned entities and argued that the highly compensated executive was necessary to ensure the company's profits and productivity that made Americans "the best paid worker[s] in the world."[39]

Within this celebratory framework critics of big business and corporations were cast as enemies of the entire economic system. "Agitators" maligned Wall Street and big business for their own benefit at the expense of prosperity. The orator coached the audience "not to let the agitator sour you with discontent" but to remember that "you and business are partners!" Along the same lines the lecturer emphasized that "a strike is a small war," created by labors' disregarded of capital's benevolent act of feeding and clothing them. As an enemy of commerce, "strikes waste time and money," and "both sides lose." The dramalogue also went out of its way to address those who have "the artistic temperament" and complain about commercialization. Rebutting such armchair critics, the orator reminded the audience that "if the world were less commercial, the artistic would be less artistic. Commerce discovered us—commerce civilized us—commerce improved us—and commerce supports us." The narrative's most important point, however, was that "every time an American Company is dissolved or held up to scorn . . . it makes it harder to get foreign trade," to the injury of farmers and workers. Despite this antagonism, "alone, unaided and often obstructed, the trusts have built up our commerce" to the benefit of all and "are still fighting that we may have a better world in which to live and work." In much the same way as their other press releases and publications, "The Dawn of Plenty," suggested the International Harvester was no less than a trailblazing martyr, bringing about modern changes ahead of its time.[40]

In promoting these "industrialogues" to potential hosts and sponsors, the Service Bureau stressed that they were "free from advertising" and billed them as "big, vital, educational, entertaining lecture[s]." While the lectures were void of International Harvester's brand or specific farm implements, they clearly "promote[d] sales by indirect publicity." The gendered messages of the lectures cultivated desire for products through generating cultural anxieties about material wealth. They also restored the corporation's reputation. The Advertising Department, Service Bureau, and the *Harvester World* constantly urged regional sales agents to book performances and provided sample marketing strategies and materials to support these efforts. Agents were sent a wealth of unbranded promotional goods, including postcards, posters, press copy, four-page circulars, and small flyers to "keep the lecture constantly before" the potential audience. They also recommended reserving the most prominent local venues, selling tickets in advance, issuing coupons in the newspaper, and making announcements in schools the days before the event. Reflecting the thought process behind their other school-outreach efforts, the Advertising Department noted that if schoolchildren "can be sent home two or three times a week talking about the lecture, it is sure to have its influence" on their parents. The content of these materials implied that only the backwards and unmanly who were not "interested in progress and prosperity" would miss the event.[41]

The Service Bureau industrialogues were a sensational success. Barnstorming about the country, lecture teams presented daily in chautauqua tents and lyceum halls from 1912 to 1915. According to the bureau, they reached hundreds of thousands of people. With admission rates ranging from ten to twenty-five cents for adults and a discounted rate for school pupils, *Harvester World* regularly reported that single lectures grossed proceeds up to $100 for audiences in the hundreds—generating profits that sustained the bureau's invisible propaganda campaign. Most of these audiences were totally unaware of the corporation's involvement with the lectures because they were planned and advertised through institutional third parties, like chautauqua circuits or local commercial clubs.[42]

Aside from these traditional rural institutional venues, the industrialogues were also carried to land-grant universities and became part of university-extension efforts. As early as 1912, Barker built a close relationship with the agricultural professors at the University of Illinois at Urbana-Champaign so that the lectures were regularly presented to students. The University of Illinois also invited Service Bureau orators to headline at their annual farmers' institute on campus and included the bureau in their other outreach efforts. In 1913 Barker solidified a partnership with the University of Wisconsin's Extension Department. The department offered the lectures on campus in Madison and undertook to book and promote them throughout the state. *Harvester World* noted that universities in other states were doing the same.[43]

Widely accepted as educational, Barker's massive propaganda campaign did generate some criticism both inside the corporation and in some corners of the wider world. Outside of the business some muckrakers recognized the Service Bureau and the Extension Department as no more than self-interested campaigns to "teach the farmer how to make more money for" International Harvester by buoying demand. Inside the company such critiques struck a chord with at least the former educator, Perry Holden, who was quickly disenchanted with the close relationship between the Service Bureau and the Advertising Department. Sincerely believing in the corporation's philanthropic duty and rhetoric, he was disgusted with Barker's underhanded labor. Igniting internal corporate conflict, he wholly separated the scientific educational efforts from the Service Bureau and the Advertising Department to his own Extension Department in 1913. At that point the bureau existed solely as International Harvester's engine of cultural propaganda.[44]

Furthermore, the bureau's ubiquitous romantic histories of corporate contributions to civilization spurred a least one dissenting historical narrative. In 1912 the descendants of Obed Hussey again called into question the veracity of the corporation's claims that Cyrus McCormick invented the reaper. The volume they published, *Obed Hussey, Who, of All Inventors, Made Bread Cheap*, was a direct challenge to *The Story of Bread*. This publication was not widely distributed and thus could not compete with the volume of the Service Bureau's efforts for public attention. It did, however, prompt anxiety within the McCormick family, who both owned the company and treasured their patriarch's past as sacred. They began to search for means to muzzle historical discord in tandem with their company's powerful propaganda campaigns.[45]

International Harvester did not employ any academic or trained historians to participate in the Service Bureau's historical productions, nor did any academics advise the corporation's legal team, which rigorously argued to Bureau of Corporations investigators and Department of Justice lawyers that understanding the corporation's origins "required a knowledge of the history." From the perspective of the corporation and the McCormick family, lawyers, entertainers, and advertisers could carry out historical production and labor on behalf of their interests as ably as anyone. Their messages about the past were easily conveyed to the general public through the sheer volume of materials that the corporation produced without the need of trained historians.[46]

While International Harvester produced oceans of historical propaganda, the family continued to be concerned about the potential damage of dissenting historical narratives to the public image of both their company and themselves. They had discovered in the past that bulk distribution alone was not enough to verify historical legitimacy in the face of conflicting narratives. In the 1890s their historical brand had been scuttled by John F. Steward and the Deering Company through dissenting historical advertising. In 1910 members of their estranged family foiled their plans to have their patriarch honored in the Hall of Fame for Great Americans. The appearance of yet another oppositional history in 1912 presented by the descendants of Obed Hussey gave them pause. They worried that this counterhistory or a renewed campaign by their cousins might injure their company in the midst of the federal antitrust trial or prove detrimental to their Hall of Fame ambitions.

While they had resolved their conflict with Deering and Steward through the merger in 1902, they had yet to figure out how to silence the pasts presented by private citizens. In the early 1910s the family began to turn to emerging historical professionals, whose supposed "disinterested" and "scientific" training made the findings of their historical labor irrefutable. They hoped that securing widespread professorial certification would legitimize their heritage as fact beyond reproach. After a bit of trial and error, by 1914 the family settled on the Mississippi Valley Historical Association as the best instrument for fulfilling its objectives and protecting the corporation's heritage.

The McCormicks took a circuitous route to this plan of action. After 1910, when their cousins Robert Hall McCormick II and James Shields had spoiled their Hall of Fame bid, the McCormicks tried to dissuade them of their "false" understanding of the past. Their relatives refused to abandon their claims and maintained they were entitled to a sizeable portion of the reaper fortune. The cousins held that the heirs of

Cyrus McCormick could expect vociferous protest to their Hall of Fame ambitions until they recognized Robert Hall McCormick as the principal inventor of the reaper. Rejecting a historical concession that would damage their corporation's public image and their familial sense of identity, the McCormick Biographical Association devised a bizarre plan that combined legalistic procedure, historical evidence, and academic historians to end their interfamily conflict. They proposed to have both sides present their case and evidence to a "historical tribunal" of three of the "foremost American historical scholars" to settle the dispute once and for all.[47]

The "tribunal" concept was hatched by Cyrus Bentley, the family's longtime lawyer, hired in early 1911 to manage the McCormick Biographical Association. Paid a handsome $10,000 annually, Bentley's salary reflected the high professional standing of lawyers at this time, and his legal background informed his approach to the family's specific historical dispute. Within the tribunal concept Bentley prepared a legalistic-style brief that argued both sides of the question. Prior to Bentley's intervention the family had focused only on demonstrating that Cyrus McCormick invented the reaper. Bentley believed it was equally important "to show the essential falsity of the Testimony for Robert [McCormick]," through demonstrating that these "untruths" originated in the "hatred," "unscrupulous and malignant" motivations, and "degraded moral standards" of the opposing relatives. Reflecting his legalistic mentality, Bentley set out to support this undertaking by surveying public memory of the first reaper trial in Virginia. Eighty years removed from 1831, his goal was to collect legal-style depositions of residents who had heard about the invention from the now-deceased older generation. Focusing on collecting Virginian's oral traditions about the reaper's invention, Bentley totally neglected searching for extant historical documents.[48]

Within his purview as the manager of the McCormick Biographical Association, Bentley was also responsible for vetting materials created by the Service Bureau. In this capacity Bentley made sure that

Barker was not overreaching what historical evidence could support and "avoid[ing] actions which might precipitate further controversy" with their relatives. While Bentley did exercise editorial authority over the Service Bureau, he did not prevent the sprouting of new challenges from unexpected sources. In 1912 the publication of *Obed Hussey, Who, of All Inventors, Made Bread Cheap* made it apparent that the family needed to develop a new strategy to censor historical dissent.[49]

Bentley's efforts ultimately amounted to very little. While the family theoretically favored his aggressive approach and his "historical tribunal" scheme, they found the "violent language" of his finished work to be undignified. Cyrus II rewrote everything that Bentley produced for readers outside of the immediate family. Moreover, their cousins refused to participate in the charade, and so Bentley's historical brief had no clear purpose. The family kept the lawyer on the payroll to manage their historical endeavors, and for the next fifteen years he continued to revise his history brief as a book, in case the family needed it as a tool of last resort. The family valued Bentley's commitment to their historical problems but believed that they probably needed a more impartial representative to tactfully pursue their interests.[50]

By coincidence the McCormicks arrived at a new historical strategy through nurturing a relationship with the Mississippi Valley Historical Association. As a collector of historical materials outside of his family's private historical association, Cyrus McCormick II frequented rare manuscript auctions. At an auction in the fall of 1913, he outbid historian Clarence W. Alvord, from the University of Illinois at Urbana-Champaign, for an eighteenth-century register of the Illinois-Wabash Land Company. Afterward Alvord approached McCormick about making the manuscript available to historians because of its incredible historical value. Impressed with the historian's knowledge of frontier Illinois, McCormick agreed to make fifty photogravures of the manuscript for leading universities and invited Alvord to write an introduction for the volume.[51]

As a trained historian specializing in midwestern history, Clarence Alvord was a leading member of the fledgling Mississippi Valley Historical Association (MVHA). Founded in 1907, the association was meant to promote greater interest and collaboration in the history of the U.S. heartland. Seeking to fulfill the implied vision of Frederick Jackson Turner's frontier thesis, it believed greater emphasis should be placed on the Mississippi Valley as the core of the nation's power. This emphasis attracted many other midwestern organizations and scholars to their ranks, as the association blossomed from regional seeds of resentment for the established American Historical Association's East Coast bias.[52]

In early 1912 Alvord initiated the MVHA movement to publish its own journal, the *Mississippi Valley Historical Review*. As an instrument that would legitimize the professional endeavors of midwestern historians, the journal would be "devoted to western history . . . be of creditable character and edited by the men that are doing scientific work in the field." A feasibility study revealed that most members supported Alvord's endeavor and thought that the American Historical Association neglected midwestern history and historians. While there was an immediate windfall of interested historical contributors to the *Review*, the project required financial support. Before publication could commence, they needed to secure a three-year guarantor fund, amounting to $1,500 annually, to underwrite the *Review*. Dreaming of "some person of means and leisure" to support the *Review*, the MVHA's secretary Clarence Paine and Alvord "work[ed] like the devil" broadly soliciting potential benefactors but could not muster the requisite funds.[53]

With the withering *Review* in mind, in February 1914 Alvord met with Cyrus McCormick II to discuss the publication of the Illinois-Wabash Land Company manuscript. He also hoped to "interest him in the project" of underwriting the *Review*. After a brief conversation McCormick supported the objectives of the enterprise and was "perfectly willing to give the money." He contributed $200 as a donation for the association to allocate freely rather than as part of the guarantee fund. While Alvord had been struggling to secure funds from other penny-pinching "cranks," McCormick's liberal patronage was a welcome relief for which the MVHA held him in high regard. Privately, Alvord and Paine praised McCormick's generosity: "That is the way that kind of fellows do business."[54]

McCormick seized on the opportunity in hopes of making the professional historians of the Midwest an asset to his family and corporation's interests. Thinking through the problems that history battles posed to his corporation's public relations strategy and his family's own historical ambitions, McCormick recognized Alvord and the *Review* as potential allies. Before sending his first $200 contribution to the *Review*, McCormick disclosed to Alvord the "intimate" details of his family's historical disputes. He also revealed the efforts of his family's historical association and intention to publish a historical biography of their father. The unwritten implication was that McCormick was trusting Alvord and the *Review* to participate in protecting his father's reputation as the inventor of the reaper. Alvord readily accepted these "minor conditions." Working to stay in McCormick's good graces, Alvord secured the benefactor's annual contributions to the *Review* for seventeen years and also lobbied to be chosen as the family's biographer.[55]

Alvord's agreement to serve McCormick's interests should be considered in light of his professional and cultural context. Until the disenchanting experience of World War II, most academics considered themselves to be professional intellectuals within the new corporate order rather than discontents of modernization. They were usually uncritical of established bases of power and wealth. Historians during the Progressive Era generally perceived their task as charting the material progress of civilization—a new history in which all of society benefited from the modernizing influence of technological innovation, corporations, and industry. Moreover, Alvord did not perceive his commitment as unethical, because McCormick's request was to help defend an idea that was an accepted part of public memory. No different from any other American, Alvord in particular and historians in general were unconscious consumers of advertised historical narratives that had been widely promoted by companies, like the McCormicks', for decades. Alvord likely already believed that Cyrus McCormick invented the reaper in 1831, because the nation had been saturated with advertisements carrying that idea since the 1870s. In his mind McCormick was most likely asking him to defend "facts" from malicious elements, an idea entirely congruent with his identity as a historian during the Progressive Era.[56]

Cyrus McCormick II was eager to fund the *Review*, not only because it provided a professional asset to overturn historical opposition but also because it was directly concerned with increasing the historical profile of the Midwest. McCormick and his family and company had been working toward a parallel objective with specific regard to their patriarch for decades. After their February meeting Alvord presented McCormick with a promotional circular for the *Review*, which summarized its historical focus. The circular illustrated the overlapping interests of the journal and McCormick's own intentions. The *Review* was created to promote "recognition of the part played by the Mississippi Valley in the development of the United States. . . . In its pages will appear discussion of all phases of the westward march of American civilization from the time the first Spaniards visited the coasts of the Gulf of Mexico to the present time when a new civilization has resulted." Within such a scholarly movement, McCormick recognized there was space for his father's inventive genius and dramatic impact on the region. Indeed, the *Review*'s purported fixation on the "westward march of American civilization" was reminiscent of his company's advertising since the 1880s as well as its more recent public relations campaigns. While McCormick had been excited about the academic movement in frontier studies since meeting Frederick Jackson Turner in 1905, Alvord and the MVHA offered him an opportunity to broadly support this specific branch of the historical profession. If western and frontier history rose to prominence, it would buoy his own claims to the past.[57]

McCormick's support immediately provided a boon to Alvord's fundraising efforts with Chicago's elite, politicians, and cultural institutions. Following McCormick's lead, the *Review* gained financial backing from Julius Rosenwald of Sears, Roebuck; Joy Morton of Morton Salt; Henry J. Patten (the Chicago "Grain King" of trading); future vice president Charles Dawes; and future Illinois governor Frank O. Lowden. They supported the *Review* because, like McCormick, they too were interested in raising the profile of the region. Since the nineteenth century Chicago's rich had financed cultural institutions and endeavors. Philanthropically creating and supporting institutions such as the Civic Opera, the Art Institute, the Field Museum, and the 1893 world's fair, they aspired to create a cultural reputation for the city that both softened and mirrored its recognized industrial significance. Supporting the *Review* and historians' intent on demonstrating the importance of the Midwest was another way to lend gravitas to their success as midwestern moguls.[58]

Reflecting the newfound trust that the McCormicks had in the historical profession, the family also tapped the MVHA in 1915 to assist them in finding a trained historian to work for their recently renamed McCormick Historical Association. Bringing his needs to Alvord, Cyrus II was directed to send his inquiry to a variety of established MVHA historians, in an effort to recruit their graduate students for the job. Cyrus McCormick sent one such request to Dana C. Munro at the University of Wisconsin. Munro conferred with Guy Stanton Ford at the University of Minnesota, and both agreed that Herbert Anthony Kellar was a strong fit for the position. Kellar had been one of Munro's advisees at Madison and in 1915 was an adjunct colleague of Ford's in Minneapolis. Following these recommendations, Kellar was hired by the McCormicks to catalog and round out their archival collection. Importantly, he was also to function as a "representative" for the family's interests within professional historical organizations.

Arriving in August 1915, Kellar remained with the family for the next forty years and expanded the scope of their work and influence on academic history through his prolific participation in their professional associations.[59]

The federal antitrust case against International Harvester carried on until 1918, when the Department of Justice settled with the corporation. The department agreed to allow the company to keep its important Deering and McCormick holdings, but it was required to sell off all of its other corporate acquisitions to reestablish competition in the harvester industry. While it was a loss for the owners of International Harvester, it was far better than a total dissolution of the business and reflected the public's softening perception of corporations—which had played an important role in driving the country's victory during World War I. While Barker's branch of the Service Bureau disbanded in 1915, the company continued to use historical propaganda and advertising during the trying period of popular and legal antagonism. Barker left International Harvester to start his own lecture and film company but continued to perform the industrialogues, using the large network of contacts he had created across the country. International Harvester regional sales agencies continued to book Barker for local lectures, and he also offered his services to help other companies develop similar campaigns. The corporation also distributed the public relations materials he had created well into the 1920s, and more direct historical advertising remained a staple of their marketing efforts in perpetuity.[60]

Barker's production of public relations histories from 1910 to 1915 and beyond were accepted by the general public as legitimate and educational. The wide distribution of the booklets, the Advertising Department's canned press blitzes, and the utilization of new motion-picture technology generated public interest in, and acceptance of, these narratives. The success of the enterprise can be attributed to both utilizing agrarian-centric tropes and inserting the industrialogues into the era's popular public education institutions of the chautauqua circuit and lyceum hall. Indeed, the industrialogues were so convincing and popular in these venues that other circuit performers began to present them outside of the corporation's control, including at least one who presented "The Dawn of Plenty" as an endorsement of socialism. The venture was further legitimized under the auspices of formal educational institutions, which adopted the materials for use in both public schools and universities. Within a year of *The Story of Bread*'s publication, Cyrus H. McCormick and his reaper became commonplace in U.S. history textbooks, where previously they were rarely mentioned.[61]

After the close of the antitrust case, the corporation continued to use the invention of the reaper for its advertising campaigns but scaled back its historical-educational propaganda. Meanwhile, the McCormicks' historical initiatives came to rest on academic historians. The family had successfully broadcast and utilized its heritage to sanctify the corporation during the antitrust moment, but they needed trained historical professionals to legitimize that heritage as history. For the next two decades, the family promoted the field of academic historical inquiry as a vehicle to advance its patriarch's reputation and fortify the corporate brand. The McCormicks also secured allies and Herbert Anthony Kellar to allow them to monitor and influence the historical profession from within. Over time their investment would pay dividends, and their father's legacy would become further entrenched in the canon of U.S. history.

5

Herbert Anthony Kellar and the Quest for Professional Authority

The last week of April 1932, Herbert Kellar journeyed from his office at the McCormick Agricultural Library in Chicago to the Smithsonian Institution in Washington DC to discuss the museum's exhibition of reaper models. Since 1930 the Smithsonian had displayed several replicas of a reaper with labels that attributed the invention to Robert Hall McCormick. Kellar's employers were alerted to the deplorable situation almost immediately by a clipping service, which also reported the donation of the models by the descendants of Leander J. McCormick. In light of the upcoming Hall of Fame election and the Harvester Company's yearlong Reaper Centennial festivities planned for 1931, Cyrus McCormick's progeny thought better of drawing attention to their family controversy.[1]

Unaware of the McCormicks' decision, International Harvester's Advertising Department attempted to donate a replica of Cyrus McCormick's 1831 reaper to the Smithsonian in 1931. With Kellar's assistance the company created several hundred historically accurate replicas to distribute to International Harvester sales agencies across the nation as promotional pieces for the Reaper Centennial celebration. Taking further initiative, the Advertising Department began distributing the models to museums. Upon learning of these plans, Cyrus McCormick II and his brother Harold intervened. They halted the company's donation to the Smithsonian before the proceedings had gone too far or stirred up any unwanted trouble. Given that the company had already cultivated a relationship with the national institution, however, the brothers further instructed the advertising manager to send a formal protest about the Robert McCormick display in January 1932. Later that spring Kellar was sent by the family to handle the situation.[2]

When Kellar journeyed to the Smithsonian in 1932, he first called his longtime friend and Smithsonian curator of agriculture, Frederick Lewton, to help him resolve the situation. Kellar had known Lewton for at least twelve years, as active members of the Agricultural History Society (AHS). Most notably, both were seated on the AHS National Agricultural Museum Committee, which aspired to fulfill the committee's title. In 1921 this committee successfully lobbied the Smithsonian National Museum to create a Division of Agricultural History that would collect farming artifacts for an eventual national museum of agriculture, and Lewton was appointed to lead the small agricultural division. By 1932 he had collected around one thousand objects, including the models in question.[3]

When Kellar arrived, Lewton provided him with a wealth of information regarding the reaper display's donation by Leander McCormick-Goodharts's family (the grandson of Leander J. McCormick). The situation was delicate because the politically connected and wealthy McCormick-Goodhart family financially supported the Smithsonian's astronomy programs. They donated the models and the label text directly to the head of the Smithsonian, Dr. Charles Abbott, in 1930, which he readily accepted on account of the family's philanthropic assistance. Lewton protested the "suspicious exhibit" as soon as he learned about it, but Abbott ignored him. He further noted that the McCormick-Goodharts regularly brought guests to visit the exhibit, including Norbert Lyons, an author who intended to refute the "spurious claims for Cyrus."[4]

Kellar found all this information very instructive. He was well aware of the McCormick cousins' historical tampering throughout the tenure of his employment with the McCormick Historical Association. Their "distasteful" acts had intensified more recently in response to the company's centennial celebration. The cousins had created similar delicate and embarrassing situations at the museum of the Chicago Historical

Society as well as the University of Virginia. Additionally, Kellar had actually met and ejected Lyons from the McCormick Agricultural Library not a week before his meeting with Lewton. In the library Lyons, lacking in scholarly credentials, was suspiciously interested in the reaper controversy. At the time Kellar did not know who Lyons worked for, but now Lewton had closed that circle for him.[5]

Lewton further explained that the formal complaint by the Harvester Company in early 1932 gave him the opportunity to again present his case against the exhibit. He showed Abbott the relevant patent documentation and demonstrated that the exhibit was erroneous because it attributed the invention to Robert, rather than Cyrus, as the patents indicated. Abbott partially acceded, and they removed the offending labels but left up the models. Unprompted by Kellar, Lewton planned to make a further case to Abbott that the models should be removed as well. On April 28 he wrote Kellar, requesting additional documentation, and to his surprise Kellar (already en route to DC) arrived the next day with a suitcase of manuscripts.[6]

Over the next several days, the two historians poured over the documents and presented their argument to Abbott, who had recently faced similar "first invention" controversies regarding the airplane. The museum was involved in an ongoing lawsuit over inaccurate labels on a radial engine exhibit. On the one hand Abbott was worried that offending the McCormick-Goodharts "might result in great harm to the Institution." On the other he was afraid that leaving the exhibit intact would result in a lawsuit against the museum by the McCormick Historical Association. Faced with the evidence, Lewton's support, and these dire alternatives, Abbott gave in to Kellar's request. He agreed to remove the Robert McCormick models and adopted a policy of strictly displaying inventions with official patent documentation. He also approved Kellar and Lewton's plan to display models of Cyrus McCormick's patented inventions from 1834, but not the unpatented 1831 version.[7]

As a trained historian, Lewton acted to protect the history of the reaper that Herbert Kellar had labored to establish in historical circles for the previous seventeen years. In handling the situation, Kellar commented to his employers that Lewton's "heart was full of the subject" and that he had done everything in his power to rectify the injustice to Cyrus McCormick at the Smithsonian. Lewton continued the campaign until 1934, when the Smithsonian finally placed a label on Cyrus's 1834 machine that emphasized its origins in 1831 as the first functional reaper. The episode was a perfect example of Kellar's invaluable service to the McCormick Historical Association and the high esteem he had earned for the family's legacy in the historical profession. Herbert Kellar had become the family's man inside the profession, and his influence helped push other historians to recognize Cyrus McCormick as the inventor of the reaper.[8]

When Cyrus II and his siblings hired their archivist in 1915, they could not have imagined that he would become such an influential asset to their historical crusade. He was initially charged only with organizing historical manuscripts for a future biography of Cyrus McCormick and acting as a historical watchdog for the family. Over the next two decades, however, Kellar expanded his responsibilities while competing for historical authority with his supervisor and the family's lawyer, Cyrus Bentley. Crucially, he needed to demonstrate that historical expertise was more than simply "proving" the facts of the past and that it could be applied along broader lines for greater ends.

Early in his career Kellar demonstrated his value to the family through actively participating in the historical profession. He skillfully fed the family's desire for scholarly sanctification of their heritage and impacted public memory in the process. Kellar reveled in building the family's historical library and promoted its reputation in scholarly circles. Concurrently, he participated in historical organizations such as the Mississippi Valley Historical Association (MVHA) and the AHS and assisted in their drives to expand the profession's purview. By the 1930s Kellar was considered a leader in the professional world, and his activities had gained academic acceptance for his employer's prized heritage and the Harvester Company's brand as historical fact.

While Kellar's endeavors within the profession were effective over time, the benefits of his labor were too slow in coming for Cyrus Bentley, who was concerned that the family's investment in Kellar's activities and the larger profession would never pay off. Moreover, he worried that giving Kellar more authority within the family's affairs would diminish his own usefulness to their historical projects. As the family's longtime trusted adviser, Bentley preserved his own authority within the McCormick Historical Association at Kellar's expense through denigrating his contributions and erecting barriers to Kellar's professional ambitions.

Ultimately, Kellar was able to work around Bentley's sandbagging to secure professional autonomy when he made the collection and his training an asset to International Harvester. His welcome involvement with the company's Advertising Department in preparing materials for the 1931 centennial celebration of the invention of the reaper clearly improved the historical content of the company's publicity and reached the general public. Harvester Company officials sang his praises directly to Cyrus II and Harold McCormick. This third-party validation of Kellar's professional value freed him from Bentley's draconian grip and earned him considerable influence and higher wages with the McCormick family.

Unlike the family's previous historian, Salem Pattison, who was more committed to middle-class wages than scholarly work, Herbert Kellar was personally invested in the historical profession. Seeking to expand the influence of his profession, Kellar was part of a professional cadre of midwestern "prairie historians." This group intended to raise the profile of midwestern history while making the discipline a useful resource for government decision making and American life. As progressive-minded intellectuals, these historians wanted to use their historical training to inform and resolve the issues of the modern age. Unlike his colleagues employed in academia or at state historical societies, Kellar was unique in that he participated as a historian for an elite family. While he was involved in many of the movement's public initiatives, however, he had great difficulty establishing that these projects were beneficial to his employers. Through trial and error he discovered that he could continue to advance his career as a historian and serve the family's interests by bringing historical expertise to bear on their company. As a prairie historian, his key contribution was as a pioneer of the corporate archive. Predating the founding of the "first" such archive at Firestone in the late 1930s, Kellar demonstrated the value of historical expertise to the corporate order in his work for International Harvester almost a decade earlier.[9]

Prior to Kellar's arrival in August 1915, the McCormick Historical Association was managed by Cyrus Bentley, who had been the family's primary legal counselor since the turn of century, when he had been heavily involved in negotiating the International Harvester merger with the Deerings. In the years that followed, he had offered financial counsel for the family's estate, advised during the antitrust proceedings, managed Stanley McCormick's long-term psychological medical care, offered his opinion on the Hall of Fame campaigns, and acted as the family's general counsel on a variety of other issues.[10]

Intimately familiar with the family and their historical problems, Bentley, when hired to lead the McCormick Biographical Association in 1911, took the appointment as a crucial opportunity to demonstrate his commitment to the family. Engaged to manage the family's historical conflict with their cousins, their Hall of Fame initiatives, and their plans for an authoritative biography, Bentley took an overly combative and legalistic approach that reflected his close personal association with the family's interests. By 1915 Cyrus II and Harold began to doubt if Bentley was capable of being an effective public advocate for the "true history" of the reaper because of his absolutist and antagonistic approach. While they leaned toward more subtle tactics, Bentley seemed incapable of putting aside his legal instinct and personal mission to win unconditional victory for their patriarch's legacy.

When the McCormick Historical Association began its search for a librarian in 1915, these differing perspectives created division among the close-knit group of family members and the trusted counselor about the function of that employee. Spearheading their efforts, Bentley initiated the hunt for an assistant who would support his professional labor. Anticipating a short-term hire of a year or less, he wanted someone to catalog the collection to streamline his own legalistic writing on the reaper controversy and to fact-check the accuracy of his finished work. Unsatisfied with Bentley's work but unwilling to part with their lawyer and friend, Cyrus McCormick II hoped to steer the association into the hands of trained historians. After his interactions with Clarence Alvord the previous year, he was convinced that a historical expert might broaden their horizons and act as a representative to preserve the history of the reaper within the historical profession. Following this inclination, he suggested that Bentley tap into the network of professional historians that the family had cultivated. Through these channels the family hired Herbert Anthony Kellar.[11]

Bentley's and Kellar's differing professional identities and training created a conflict of authority within the McCormick Historical Association between the lawyer and the historian that lasted for the next fifteen years. To Bentley's mind the scope of their project was limited to unequivocally proving that Cyrus invented the reaper, regardless of its larger impact or context. Intent on this legalistic and decidedly antiquarian approach, the older Bentley was unwilling to yield his role as the champion of Cyrus McCormick's legacy and refused to recognize Kellar's historical talents beyond the legal program he had laid out. For his part Kellar strove to use his academic background and the tools of his professional training to establish his own value to the family. He also embraced the positivist notion that public knowledge of historical scholarship could resolve contemporary problems. Consistently obstructed by Bentley, Kellar resiliently formulated new historical strategies to broaden the family's mission by locating the larger impact of the reaper's invention on American civilization and cultivating new avenues for sharing that history for the benefit of the larger society. He hoped such efforts would bolster his professional authority within the McCormick Historical Association.

Prior to his employment with the McCormicks, Kellar had spent his young career intermittently teaching courses and conducting archival surveys after completing his graduate course work. A son of the Midwest, Kellar was born in 1887 in Nebraska but was raised in Illinois. He earned a history degree at the University of Chicago in 1909, before attending four years of graduate school between the University of Wisconsin and Stanford University. Never completing his dissertation, Kellar cobbled together a career as an adjunct, teaching medieval history courses at the University of Texas and the University of Minnesota. To that point his most notable historical accomplishment was completing an inventory in 1915 of the Minnesota Historical Society's collection. When he was taken on by the McCormicks, he was twenty-eight years old. In Chicago he had secured an income of $2,000 annually, on par with the $900 a semester he received for teaching but substantially more stable. He was determined to improve his lot with the elite family through impressing them beyond their expectations.[12]

Kellar was initially confined to Bentley's narrow intentions for his position and the association. Kellar surveyed the extant McCormick collection, which at that point included about 1,600 original publications, ten thousand manuscripts, and ten boxes of facsimiles and transcribed materials from the Library of Congress. These materials documented Cyrus McCormick's invention of the reaper and the associated familial strife. The collection had been compiled since 1900 by Salem Pattison, Louis Dent, and Cyrus Bentley for the family's various biographical, Hall of Fame, and associated advertising efforts. Housed in a room within the mansion of Cyrus H. McCormick's widow, these resources were utilized only for the family's historical efforts. Following Bentley's suggestion, Kellar outlined and commenced a plan for cataloging the collection to highlight content relevant in the Robert-Cyrus McCormick invention controversy, as the lawyer instructed.[13]

In Bentley's imagination Kellar's cataloging was a final step before moving forward with a biography. Betraying his rigid managerial and legalistic approach to the historical enterprise, Bentley's 1915 "outline of work" demonstrated that he believed the association had almost exhausted all relevant avenues of investigation. The only evidence left to collect was "depositions" from both sides of the McCormick family. He then intended to submit his completed historical brief to Leander McCormick's progeny, in hopes of forcing them to back down. Failing that, Bentley planned for the association to proceed with publishing a commissioned history of the reaper that would overwhelm the cousins and the general public with an unimpeachable case that Cyrus McCormick invented the reaper. According to Bentley, the agenda would be accomplished within a single year.[14]

Unlike Bentley, Kellar envisioned a much broader public-oriented agenda. Interacting with the materials and the family sparked his historical imagination far beyond Bentley's objectives. He believed that the collection could be expanded and the family's historical influence could be augmented through a variety of means. The library could easily add agricultural periodicals and early newspapers that discussed the advent of the reaper and placed its adoption into the context of the expansion of the republic. Historical correspondence and manuscripts authored by Virginians outside the immediate family could probably be found, shedding light on the origins of the reaper. Following such a course, Kellar believed that the family's historical dispute could be resolved if the collection was enlarged and opened to outside historians. Supporting wider historical scholarship could provide an important resource to the family. Demonstrating a commitment to congenial intellectual exchange, other historians could help the McCormick Historical Association locate distant source materials, monitor scholarship, and provide new insight on the history of the reaper. Promoting broader scholarly use of the collection would garner good will and further raise the association's profile within the profession. Perhaps most important, wider study of the reaper would support the invention's importance to the progress of U.S. civilization.[15]

Finally, in March 1916, after biding his time Kellar eventually worked around Bentley's managerial control and personally was able to share his vision for the organization with Cyrus McCormick II. By coincidence or contrivance Kellar was invited from his work in the library of Nettie McCormick's mansion to enjoy a cup of tea with her son, Cyrus II, in the parlor. During his eight months of employment for the association, it was probably only the second time that Kellar directly spoke with Cyrus II. After some prodding from the McCormicks, Kellar shared his larger ambitions for their organization. Referencing his recent trip to Washington DC for the American Historical Association (AHA) annual meeting in December, he expounded on the many leads that other historians had shared with him about repositories and collections that might prove useful for the family. Along with these threads of opportunity to expand their collections, he noted that conservation work was needed on some of the existing documents and that better library shelves, cases, and boxes were necessary to preserve the material.[16]

Uninspired by Bentley's approach and long intrigued by the promise of the historical profession, Cyrus McCormick II seized on his employee's suggestions to make his family's collection more substantial, formal, and scholarly. Going beyond Kellar's scope of work, Cyrus II also proposed hiring two research assistants and a personal stenographer and renovating his mother's carriage house behind the mansion into a modern library with a fireproof vault, better housing for documents, and a museum. With a descriptive memorandum from Kellar, he outlined a ten-point plan with sixteen collection "leads to follow" for the next meeting of the McCormick Historical Association, which of course was approved. The family also agreed to pay for Kellar to attend historical conferences in the future and subscribed to the *American Historical Review (AHA)*. Kellar successfully brought his historical training to bear on the organization, securing his job beyond the lone year Bentley had predicted.[17]

Undoubtedly, Kellar's insubordination rankled Bentley's nerves and bruised his ego. Petulantly, Bentley briefly resigned his position but shortly thereafter was persuaded to resume his work by the family. From that point forward Bentley tightly micromanaged Kellar and limited the historian's access to the family. He continually demanded more results, frequently contested Kellar's proposals, and rarely shared those ideas with the McCormicks. He further required detailed weekly, monthly, quarterly, and yearly reports on all the activities within the library. While Kellar was able to easily influence the family in 1916 through direct contact with Cyrus II, gaining support for his later designs would be an uphill battle.[18]

Despite Bentley's later restrictive efforts, gaining family adherence to his program in 1916 gave Kellar wide latitude to operate for many years. The transformation of the carriage house into the McCormick Agricultural Library was not complete until 1919, at which time the staff was also enlarged. In the meantime Kellar commenced his work along the broad lines approved by the McCormicks. He began searching Chicago-area libraries for materials and transcribing relevant items for the collection. He sent correspondence across the nation to other librarians and historians requesting information and relevant documents. He also used his trips to meetings of the Mississippi Valley Historical Association and the American Historical Association to hunt for more sources as well as raise the professional profile of agricultural history and the McCormick Agricultural Library.

In reports on his activities, he explained that his goal was to make the collection "notable" and "create for the Association a [historical] standing of its own." The key was not only to compile a complete record on the origins of Cyrus McCormick's reaper but "to increase it to cover the material on agricultural or industrial history of the west." If his "ideal" was attained and promoted, Kellar had no doubt the collection would attract historians from across the country. He emphasized that the library would provide a solid foundation for a biography of Cyrus McCormick, which remained the focus of the enterprise.[19]

After 1916 Herbert Kellar became a fixture in the historical profession as a supportive archivist, knowledgeable interlocutor, and well-endowed patron rather than an active writer of history. He was ubiquitous at major historical conferences for the rest of his life and was energetically involved in organizational functions. Within this context he assumed dual roles as both an employee and a fellow intellectual among his peers. The McCormicks financially supported his participation in the guild so that he could advance their interests as a professional among professionals. At the same time, Kellar exercised personal agency, lobbying the McCormicks for additional support for scholarly enterprises.

Issuing detailed summaries of his activities at annual conferences, Kellar was determined to show that his attendance at these functions was an asset to the McCormick Historical Association. In his earliest reports on the meetings of the Mississippi Valley Historical Association and the American Historical Association, he listed dozens of historians who expressed interest in the family's historical endeavor and further documented the manuscript leads they provided. A typical report, on the 1916 MVHA meeting in Nashville, Kellar named the twenty-three historians whom he had conversed with about his work. He also provided eight pages of painstaking details on known manuscript collections ranging over ten states that could be potential resources for the McCormicks' efforts. This ongoing professional reconnaissance was the basis for Kellar's later manuscript hunts and library searches. Indeed, his reliable presence at meetings and his enthusiastic promotion of the family's library and their patriarch's reputation make it unlikely that any professionally engaged historian was unaware of the McCormicks' historical agenda.[20]

Kellar also used conferences as an opportunity to monitor scholarship that directly concerned the history of the reaper and Cyrus H.

McCormick. Indicating that the family and their company's previous effort already had a significant impact, he drew the family's attention to historians who had already recognized the historical importance of their patriarch. As an early example, after the 1917 AHA meeting in Philadelphia, Kellar praised Louis Schmidt's paper "A Study of the Influence of Wheat and Cotton on Anglo-American Relations during the Civil War" for giving "due credit . . . to agricultural machinery, with the emphasis upon the reaper." In 1919 Kellar sent copies of Schmidt's foundational "The Economic History of American Agriculture as a Field for Study" to all the members of the McCormick family, because it prominently discussed McCormick's contributions to Union victory. Later he would draw attention to the scholars whom he had directly influenced and whose work advanced the family's cherished heritage.[21]

In instances when Kellar discovered scholars who damaged McCormick's reputation or ignored his contributions, he openly criticized the work and recorded his attempts to rectify the situation. In a particularly noteworthy episode, Kellar intervened in a Carnegie Foundation–supported history of northern agriculture by Percy Bidwell and John Falconer almost a decade before it was published. In 1916 he visited Madison to discuss the work with the director of the project, agricultural economist Henry C. Taylor. Allowed to see a draft, Kellar was "surprised at the inadequacy and superficiality of the chapter on agricultural implements," which, among many faults, did not mention McCormick. Leveling harsh criticism on the various omissions, he proceeded to suggest a wide array of source material that might improve the work. Taylor was receptive to Kellar's feedback and agreed to include McCormick in the chapter.[22]

The archivist's affiliation with an elite family quickly garnered the attention of his colleagues. In particular, the leadership of the Mississippi Valley Historical Association, with whom he was already acquainted, ushered him into their inner circle. The cohort of Clarence Alvord, Solon Buck, Milo Quaife, Harlow Lindley, Otto Schmidt, and Benjamin Shambaugh was very supportive of Kellar's work. They offered him suggestions, eagerly engaged him in conversation about the family's ambitions, and encouraged him to present papers and publish articles about the McCormick Historical Association. With such enthusiastic support Kellar rose to professional prominence rapidly. In 1919 he was the chair of the program committee for MVHA's annual conference in St. Louis. By 1923 he was appointed the chair of MVHA's Committee on Historical Cooperation, charged with creating a centralized system for sharing information about historical archives. He was also welcomed as a member of editorial board for the *Mississippi Valley Historical Review*.[23]

Reflecting self-interest, this group and others utilized Kellar as an access point to his elite employers. As a congenial colleague with his own aspirations for the profession, Kellar generally sent their requests up the chain to Cyrus Bentley, but it is unclear if they ever reached the family. In 1917 Buck encouraged Kellar to create fellowships for graduate student researchers. The following year a group of midwestern state historical society directors hoped to gain McCormick financing for a researcher in Washington DC to collect relevant documents for their collective benefit. For several years William E. Dodd at the University of Chicago lobbied the McCormicks to buy a massive collection of manuscripts from Virginia so that he could make use of them closer to home. James Franklin Jameson successfully secured funds from Cyrus McCormick II for the AHA. The MVHA regularly solicited Cyrus McCormick II to double his annual contribution to the publication. Clarence Alvord was particularly close with Kellar and was keen on becoming Cyrus McCormick's commissioned biographer. From 1916 through 1925 Kellar frequently dropped hints in his reports about Alvord's interest in the project and his ability as a man of "historical imagination."[24]

Kellar's prominent position, networking, and promotional efforts almost immediately led to other historians using the library for their own research. William T. Trimble, an early champion of agricultural history as a field of study, was the first professional historian to use the family's collection, in late December 1916. Despite Kellar's glowing recommendation of Trimble character's and scholarship, the McCormicks were leery of allowing an outsider to use their jealously guarded collection. Trimble was granted access only after being interviewed by Cyrus McCormick II on Christmas morning in his mother's home and with Kellar's close supervision. A parade of historians over the next thirty-five years, including Ulrich B. Phillips, Avery Craven, Bessie Louise Pierce, Leo Rogin, and Paul Gates, were allowed entry with much less scrutiny. Until the collection moved to Madison in 1951, Kellar was the gatekeeper, and scholarly access was granted at his discretion. Once Nettie McCormick's carriage house was renovated as the McCormick library in 1919, Kellar promoted its growing archive in the pages of historical journals and in conference presentations.[25]

Kellar was able to open the archive for scholarly use by successfully arguing that developing a larger historiographical context was paramount to the McCormicks' historical ambitions. Reflecting professional awareness, Kellar pointed out that the collection itself was "raw material," which would prove impossible for a single biographer to master. Moreover, in a scholarly vacuum any potential biography would garner little intellectual notice. If however, other historians wrote monographs on topics that touched on McCormick and the reaper using the collection, a later biographer's efforts would be more intellectually relevant.[26]

Kellar recognized that the newly emerging field of agricultural history was crucial to securing Cyrus McCormick's legacy. In 1917 Kellar reported that World War I was generating historical interest in the production of food and the influence of agriculture on the development of the country. He emphasized that "the importance of such a situation in its relation to Mr. C. H. McCormick is manifest." Following his own interests and acting on the family's behalf, Kellar inserted himself into the professional movement and soon became a leader within it. He worked to guide the infant field by coordinating scholarly activities "to consciously control the lines of development, in accordance with the high standards of scholarship" and the McCormicks' interests.[27]

Throughout the 1920s Kellar was primarily affiliated with the Agricultural History Society. The society was founded in 1919 under the auspices of the U.S. Department of Agriculture (USDA) and with support from the AHA. Kellar joined the organization several months after its founding and was an integral "moving spirit." Because he was aware that they needed to not only advance their scholarship but share it with the wider public, his first formal proposal to the AHS in 1919 was to create a national museum of agriculture "to portray the development of harvesting machinery." A formal committee to accomplish this task was created in 1921, led by Frederick Lewton, who began collecting materials for the museum at the Smithsonian Institution. Kellar became vice president of the AHS from 1921 to 1922 and president from 1922 to 1924. As president, he imparted his vision as a profession builder, creating the first AHS committees for membership, publications, programs, agricultural surveys, archives, and fields of research. He was then the secretary-treasurer from 1924 to 1927. Kellar was also the guiding force behind the establishment of *Agricultural History* in 1927 and served on its board of editors for the rest of his life.[28]

In 1930 Kellar explained to Cyrus McCormick II that the purpose of his job and all of his professional activities was to "control . . . information published about Mr. C. H. McCormick." His network of contacts in the profession kept him apprised of ongoing projects relevant to Cyrus McCormick. The reputation of the library alone attracted intellectuals and other writers to his doorstep. In contact with these authors, he could steer them in the right direction and "caution" them about using misleading and nefarious materials. Moreover, his standing in the field solicited many invitations for lectures and gave him power to affect appointments of professionals at other historical institutions. The director of the Museum of Science and Industry in Chicago allowed Kellar to handpick its curator of agriculture. Selecting a friend from the University of Illinois, Kellar ensured that the museum would present a favorable exhibit on Cyrus McCormick and the reaper. His reputation in the profession was paying dividends on the McCormicks' historical investment.[29]

Although Kellar certainly curated and promoted the family's collection to shape the scholarly reputation of Cyrus McCormick, it is unfair to solely characterize him as a historical mercenary. Kellar, and indeed most of his colleagues, probably already believed that Cyrus McCormick invented the reaper in 1831, because of the family and their company's previous public relations, advertising, and historical endeavors. Indeed, the narratives of progress that International Harvester had distributed during the early 1910s that trumpeted Cyrus McCormick's contributions to civilization probably sat particularly well with the prairie historians of the Midwest. Having migrated from life on the farm to pursue high-minded work in urban academia, many of these historians probably felt that the International Harvester's Service Bureau tales of mutually reinforcing urban and rural progress reflected their own experience. Moreover, they viewed themselves as agents within that movement and perceived their profession as a potentially powerful force for progressive good in the larger nation.[30]

Reflecting their progressive mindset and professional ambition, agricultural historians in particular had faith that their work could be instrumental in resolving rural, social, and economic problems. Built on a partnership between the USDA and the AHA, the Agricultural History Society focused on using historical research and methodology to inform government agricultural policy. They believed that their historical expertise could provide "the light of experience" to inform decisions about volatile commodity markets, tariffs, crops, pests, soil conditions, and other issues. In this context and well aware of the McCormicks' ability to further their agenda, they welcomed Kellar as a valuable contributor and resource. It is telling that in 1923, during the first annual meeting that he presided over the AHS as president, his colleagues suggested that he ask the McCormicks for a $100,000 endowment to fortify their organization.[31]

Within the AHS Kellar was vehement about the value of history to the larger nation and the profession's obligations to share their expertise with the general public. He frequently urged his academic colleagues to be less esoteric in their research and more cognizant of their duty to people outside of their profession. Similarly, he pressed the agricultural scientists within the AHS and USDA to be open-minded to academic ideas and more courageous in actively lobbying policy reform rather than passively providing solicited information to politicians. On all fronts he stressed the need to develop tools to share historical knowledge with the general public through schools, manuscript collecting, local historical societies, and agricultural extension offices.[32]

At the heart of his historical efforts, Kellar held a dynamic theory of agricultural history. He believed agricultural, social, economic, and political problems in the present and throughout time stemmed from a sort of generational amnesia inherent in the orality of passing farming traditions. Simply stated, farmers taught their sons in light of their own experiences but failed to impart wisdom that they had learned from their own fathers, resulting in "curious recurrence of mistakes every other generation." In his estimation, then, contemporary agricultural problems were fundamentally historical in nature because they were rooted in flawed systems of vernacular education about the past. This theory of agricultural history accounted for farmers' fluctuating relationship with progressive methods and beliefs.[33]

Kellar's theory presented an obvious opportunity for agricultural historians to demonstrate the concrete value of their expertise. The profession could resolve contemporary rural problems through better public education. Kellar's intellectual configuration and mission for the profession was completely compatible with the McCormicks' own desires to increase sales of their modern farm equipment among sometimes resistant agrarians. If farmers had a better knowledge of the past, they would be more willing to embrace the materiality of progress. In these instances Kellar's sincere beliefs about the value of his work and his profession are apparent, even though it also reflects his culturally "modern" view of rural life.[34]

Not simply the McCormicks' "hired gun," Kellar attempted to garner greater financial support from the McCormick family to advance this practical historical agenda and the interests of agricultural history. Making frequent requests of varying size, Kellar typically obscured his own desires behind the McCormicks' yearning to "settle the question of the invention of the reaper." For example, in 1922 Kellar laid out a particularly ambitious twenty-year strategic plan, proposing to triple the family's historical expenditures to financially and intellectually fortify agricultural history. Kellar explained that such expenditures were necessary to build a context for their father's biography. If this was done, Kellar noted, "the McCormick family can expect a return of their investment about equal to what they are willing to do for the public good. If they are broad minded enough to encourage the study of agricultural history . . . they will not only be performing a great service for American History but will at the same time materially aid in the acceptance of the truth with regard to the reaper." Pandering to the McCormicks' interests, he also couched his proposal in terms of its value for the "public good," served by agricultural historians. His proposal included salaries for three full-time historians as well as a support staff of stenographers, librarians, and secretaries to handle the administration of the library.[35]

This proposal and many others were stymied by Cyrus Bentley. In response to Kellar's fourteen-page proposition in 1922, he told the archivist that his plan was untenable and would "prove surprising" to the family on account of the expense. As an efficiency-minded and spiteful middle manager, Bentley supplied the family only with a single-page synopsis of the plan, which emphasized the bottom-line budget and omitted Kellar's carefully articulated arguments. Afterward Kellar became increasingly resistant to Bentley's management. In direct confrontation he bluntly told the lawyer that he could not appreciate the historical prerogative, "in the light of your legal training." With his program for professionalization consistently dashed and his access to the family limited, Kellar increasingly turned to manuscript collecting as a more direct avenue to demonstrate his value and advance the interests of his profession.[36]

On a damp and cold spring afternoon in 1926, Herbert Kellar, Ulrich B. Phillips—the era's most important historian of the South—and Rion McKissick rattled along the dirt roads of Augusta County, Virginia, in a Model T Ford. When the day began, they originally intended to find George Armentrout, an aging local who had mentioned to Kellar in 1919 that he had a collection of old papers. Chasing this lead, they discovered that Mr. Armentrout had recently passed away. As a stroke of good fortune, however, they found his sister, who agreed to take them to his abandoned house, where she believed there were several bags of papers in the attic.[37]

After a cold and bumpy ride in the open-cab Ford, they pulled up to a creek. To their dismay Ms. Armentrout announced that they would have to leave the car and cross a treacherous swinging bridge to reach the house. McKissick, a University of South Carolina professor, "rashly" charged ahead and promptly fell off the rickety bridge into the deepest part of the creek. After fishing out their waterlogged friend, the group continued on to the boarded-up house. Ms. Armentrout struck a fire to warm them and then went to the attic in search of the papers. She returned with a huge cotton-picking sack of old documents. The first manuscript Kellar pulled out was dated 1795. Recognizing the potential value, Kellar asked if there were any more, and Ms. Armentrout told them that there were four other bags just like it. Experienced in the art of manuscript speculating, Kellar then coolly offered her $5 a bag, sight unseen. She agreed. With great difficulty they then hauled the precious cargo back across the hazardous bridge and tied them to the roof and the running boards of the Model T. "Looking like a moving hay stack," the party drove back to Ms. Armentrout's farm.[38]

Eventually reaching the train station, they had to send the sacks by freight to their hotel in Lexington. Tasked with assessing their uncommon package, the station agent refused to take them, because bags of letters were not listed in his book of fares. After some haggling and threatening to bring the musty sacks into the passenger car, the troop of historians convinced the agent to send them as "corn shucks." Later that night and for the next several days, they poured over the contents of the bags in a hotel room at the Dutch Inn in Lexington. As they sorted through the collection, they gradually discovered that the Armentrout haul of twelve thousand items was a bonanza for all three: Phillips found items on slavery, McKissick had papers on South Carolina, and Kellar had his own pile of agricultural documents and several letters by C. H. McCormick. The last document in the bags, however, was easily the most impressive. Reaching to the bottom of the final sack, Kellar pulled out a land-survey receipt for a plot "in the Dark and Bloody Ground," signed by Daniel Boone.[39]

In historical circles the tale quickly became known as the "corn shucks" story. It was just one of a veritable library of yarns that Kellar spun at conferences and cocktail parties about his adventures on the hunt. Beginning in 1919 and with increasing frequency after 1922, Kellar journeyed to the valley of Virginia for weeks and sometimes months at a time in search of manuscripts regarding Cyrus McCormick and early nineteenth-century agriculture. A legendary collector, Kellar was famous for his ability to "charm documents out of the attics of patrician mansions and humble farm houses" and arrive just before "the match was struck to bonfires of family papers." He then preserved them in the McCormick Agricultural Library or sold them to other historical repositories. Nicknamed the "boll weevil," Kellar thoroughly surveyed and plundered old papers out of western Virginia, leaving "slim pickings" in his wake.[40]

Kellar's collecting activities in Virginia and elsewhere were liberally supported by the McCormick Historical Association. Kellar argued that securing evanescent and documentary materials that were privately held, relevant to their project, and at risk of destruction should be a top priority. Finding these sources would "complete" their collection on Cyrus McCormick's life and prove paramount to ensuring the scholarly quality of the future biography. Lending additional urgency to the situation, Kellar discovered that the McCormick-Goodharts were actively working to prevent the McCormick Historical Association from acquiring such papers from their mutual friends in Virginia. Finding himself engaged in a historical arms race, Kellar pressed the family to "act quickly." Alarmed by their cousins' impropriety and accepting Kellar's rationale, the McCormicks agreed to finance his annual manuscript hunts, providing him with letters of introduction to their various contacts in the region and buying all the trunks, bags, and boxes of old papers that he believed were worthwhile.[41]

While collecting manuscripts to fill the McCormick Agricultural Library, Kellar was also advancing his own historical agenda. Most obviously, he was preserving a larger mass of materials for historians to study. In this regard not only was he searching for materials relevant to McCormick, but in the mold of his fellow "New Historians," he also took a broader view to enable future scholars to write more instructive and complete social histories. He compiled a collection that touched on the social, agricultural, and economic realities of McCormick's contemporaries in Virginia rather than only empirical details of the invention. When he came across collections irrelevant to the McCormicks, he either alerted other repositories or bought and sold them himself. He also invited universities to create special collections and advised them on their organizations.[42]

Well-informed about collections throughout the Midwest, South, and East, Kellar soon became a promoter of centralized surveying and cataloging efforts to help his fellow scholars locate materials. Along these lines he viewed the activity of manuscript collecting as a vital avenue for garnering greater public interest in history. Barnstorming the countryside for old documents excited local historical interest. He believed that it invited Americans to participate in preserving their own papers and founding local historical societies, while attracting popular engagement with historical scholarship. Indicative of his vision and ambitions for the profession, his interest would trickle upward from the local to the national level, generating additional demand for scholarship and support for the historical guild as a whole.[43]

Not simply a magic trick like "pulling a rabbit out of a hat," as his colleagues joked, Kellar's success in collecting was largely the product of networking and diligent note-taking. He kept meticulous track of the people with whom Cyrus McCormick associated, which he discovered while indexing the library's collections. Tracing these historical actors, he attempted to contact their descendants to see if they had extant papers. Kellar also made use of his professional colleagues who were familiar with Virginia and might know of privately held collections there or elsewhere. His most productive tactic, however, was to modestly discuss his historical projects with total strangers while he was on the trail. Kellar's reports on his trips to Virginia are littered with serendipitous encounters in hotels, on trains, and at random farmhouses with interested locals who freely shared their own papers or directed him to their friends.[44]

Through these means Kellar eventually created an informal partnership with a local surgeon and stamp collector in Lynchburg, Virginia: Dr. Don Preston Peters. Continuously on the hunt for his own artifacts and locally situated, Peters forwarded his on-the-ground discoveries to Kellar in Chicago. Using this information, Kellar began remote negotiations with distant Virginians and, in many instances, bought papers by proxy through Peters, which he then held or forwarded. As they became fast friends, Kellar, and sometimes Ulrich Phillips (a collector in his own right), stayed with Peters's family on trips to Virginia. The group then spent weeks roving the countryside together in search of manuscript treasures. In exchange the historians gave Peters stamps from the collections they procured and used their network of historical colleagues to help locate stamps farther afield.[45]

Engaged in these active collecting efforts, Kellar built the McCormick Agricultural Library into a substantial archive. Kellar advanced the family's collection from tens of thousands of items related to their patriarch to a million and a half items that supported a historical context for Cyrus McCormick's life and demonstrated his influence on the nation. He reassured the family that their library "is as complete a collection about any one man as can be found in America." The McCormicks came to own the largest archive of materials related to western Virginia in the country and substantial resources on the wheat-producing states of the interior. Kellar's broader collections policy and promotional efforts made it a magnet for historians doing research on the South, the Midwest, and agriculture more generally. At the end of his life, it was recognized by his peers as "the best collection of colonial and nineteenth-century agricultural materials in the country."[46]

For a relatively brief period, from mid-1926 to 1930, Bentley disrupted Kellar's archival agenda and restrained the McCormick Historical Association's support of his efforts. In a somewhat humorous episode in 1926, Kellar seemed to invite financial sanctions and limits on his professional freedom by intentionally aggravating Bentley. That spring Kellar informed Bentley that he was taking a two-week personal vacation to go manuscript collecting with Ulrich B. Phillips and would secure incidental McCormick materials that he found along the way. In a rare moment of good will, Bentley suggested that the McCormicks pay for his time and expenses, encouraging Kellar to "finish up your unfinished work in Virginia." Kellar took advantage of Bentley's generosity, staying in Virginia for three months and accumulating over $750 in expenses.[47]

With no set deadline, Bentley began urging Kellar to return after several weeks and was increasingly infuriated by Kellar's evasiveness. Bentley's responses to Kellar's biweekly reports made it obvious that the archivist was getting underneath his skin. In late May Bentley wrote, "How far do you think we should make an effort to collect letters . . . ? Have you any limit . . . in your mind?" Kellar's windy responses about the value of such activities to their larger project seems to have been a passive-aggressive "no." After Kellar's return he presented Bentley with a detailed report and suggested still more collections for the family to acquire. Responding unequivocally, Bentley wrote, "I will only say that we will buy no more collections."[48]

In Bentley's estimation the entire trip was a waste of time, and Kellar's historical approach was unnecessarily "extravagant." Kellar had spent a lot of time and money to locate collections and materials of "negligible importance" to the biography or the reaper controversy. Moreover, finding the materials was just the beginning of the expense. Kellar would then need to pour over "this haystack of correspondence" to find the "needle of reference to the machine," which might result in hardly a sentence in the larger biography. He stated both his frustration with Kellar's ever-expanding agenda and a likely historical truth: "Probably more time has been spent to collect material in this case than in the case of any single biography which has ever been published." Kellar's collecting enterprise had become a distraction from his primary task of outlining and organizing material for that biography. Bentley reported back to the McCormicks that it had become necessary to exert greater "control" over Kellar's work rather than "allow him to follow his own bent." Without the family's consent or awareness, Bentley unilaterally defunded Kellar's collecting efforts and any future trips.[49]

Despite being cut off from the family's travel funds, Kellar continued his personal and professional pursuit of archive building, moonlighting in manuscript speculation and dealing. Beginning in 1925 and accounting for his extended journey to Virginia in 1926, Kellar partnered with Ulrich Phillips and Don Peters to discover, purchase, and sell old manuscripts. After 1926 and into the 1930s, Kellar took up these adventures on his personal vacations and managed their partnership from Chicago through telegrams and mail. Correspondence among Phillips, Peters, and Kellar are filled with details of their exploits, ranging from manuscript leads to haggling with owners, discovering the fruits of their speculation, and eventually selling their hauls to other repositories. Working around Bentley's embargo, he raided the library's discretionary petty-cash funds, so he could continue to secure McCormick documents for the library. Bentley eventually became wise to this ruse and closed the loophole, renewing the fund on a monthly basis rather than "as needed." Kellar also processed his own collections, purchased as a speculation. While on the McCormick Library clock, he prepared inventories for potential buyers and carried out his clandestine business correspondence. Because Kellar was camouflaged in his ubiquitous indexing, cataloging, and processing of old documents owned by the library, Bentley was unable to detect his deception.[50]

The trio almost exclusively sold their wares to research universities and libraries rather than private collectors. Drumming up interest in their holdings, they solicited librarians, historians, and administrators at institutions such as the University of Michigan, the University of Illinois, the Business Historical Society, the American Antiquarian Society, Duke University, Washington and Lee University, the University of Virginia, and the USDA. While they had success selling their collections fairly broadly in small lots, their best success was selling the "Massie Papers" to the University of Texas in 1927 for $1,600. They purchased this collection in Virginia for $275 during their 1926 spree. Their collections were not solely an entrepreneurial enterprise; they conscientiously sold them to research institutions to advance historical scholarship and their particular interests in southern history. On several occasions Kellar actively encouraged the University of Virginia and Washington and Lee University to establish special collections and offered assistance to help them organize their new archives. He argued that such efforts would promote a higher quality of southern history scholarship and prevent northern libraries and private collectors from stealing away Virginia's historical manuscripts.[51]

By the mid-1920s Kellar's library and active reconnaissance, as well as his manuscript dealings, made him the guru of archives and collections in the historical profession. He was famous for his willingness to share information about archives he had visited and help connect historians with collections. Moreover, his applied experience collecting and organizing the McCormick collection made him an expert on archival management, and he was sought by other institutions interested in undertaking similar efforts. Recognizing his unique and valuable skill set, the MVHA made him the chair of its Historical Co-operation Committee in 1923 (later renamed the Historical Manuscripts Committee). Much later, in 1939, the AHA followed suit and appointed him to lead their Committee on Historical Source Materials.

While Herbert Kellar was most interested in archive and profession building, the majority of his time was spent in the McCormick Agricultural Library preparing materials for the biography of Cyrus McCormick. Initially, Kellar had been responsible for a wider spectrum of library activities, including facilitating its use by outside scholars, responding to family research inquiries, performing genealogical studies, fulfilling occasional company requests, and cataloging collections as well as writing for external publications. Gradually, this list of responsibilities was delegated to an ever-growing staff so that he could focus on preparing materials for the biography.[52]

As the family's foremost priority since 1900, the authoritative biography, in their minds, was the key to protecting their father's past and securing his enshrinement in the Hall of Fame for Great Americans at New York University. A scholarly biography was seen as the essential means to accomplishing this goal in a dignified manner. Failing to have Cyrus McCormick elected in 1915 and 1920, they did not even attempt a campaign in 1925 because they did not yet have the biography in hand as their desired tool of influence.[53]

Bentley and the McCormick Historical Association had the same multifaceted strategy for completing the biography. As already demonstrated, they believed that building a complete collection of materials on their patriarch's life was crucial to the enterprise and agreed with Kellar on at least a philosophical level that encouraging scholarly use of that collection would be beneficial. Furthermore, they had Kellar prepare a historically informed, incredibly detailed outline for the future authoritative biography, supported by an extensive note-card index of the evidence. Within this strategy Bentley also used these materials as evidence to support his own legalistic brief. With all these carefully manicured materials prepared, they could simply hand them over to a commissioned historian to write the biography they envisioned. The historian would provide only his name and writing style rather than his historical imagination.[54]

Given the importance of the historian's reputation and prose to the project, their search for a biographer was intensive. Their quest began in 1919. Illustrative of their unconventional approach, they began their quest by flipping through a booklet about the "New Historians" in Columbia University's Chronicles of America Series. They jotted notes in the margins and circled scholars that seemed the most desirable, as if buying furniture in a Sears, Roebuck catalog. They then consulted with James Franklin Jameson, Clarence Alvord, and Dana Munro to get their thoughts on these candidates. Writing numerous "Pros and Cons" memorandums, they assessed and compared historians, including Frederick Jackson Turner, John Bach McMasters, Ellis Oberholzer, Carl Becker, Clarence Alvord, Frederic Paxson, and Arthur Cole, as well as many others. Their assessments were not engaged with scholarship but instead chiefly interested in superficial questions of character. McMasters was undesirable because "he is . . . crotchety"; in the wake of anti-German sentiment sparked by World War I, Oberholzer's "name would be an insuperable obstacle"; and Turner was an "interminable procrastinator." Cyrus McCormick II noted from his personal experience that Alvord had "excellent qualifications," but after correspondence with Jameson the notes on Alvord were changed, and he was "not . . . up to our standards." This research eventually led to a succession of interviews during the early 1920s with Arthur Cole, Frederic Paxson, and William E. Dodd, but all were found wanting.[55]

To his chagrin Kellar was kept outside of the candidate search. In 1922 he attempted to assume authority over the process. At the MVHA meeting that year, he discussed the biographical project with several historians, outlining the family's ambitions for the project. After generating some interest, he wrote a report on his work to Bentley, recommending Clarence Alvord, Carl Becker, Milo Quaife, and himself as qualified candidates for the job. In response Bentley sharply reprimanded him for holding conversations with possible biographers without the McCormicks' consent and demanded "that you do not speak to anybody else." Indignantly, Kellar noted the irony of being excluded from Bentley's search, "in view of [my] familiarity with Mr. C H McCormick's life, knowledge of the historical field of America, and acquaintance with members of the profession." Despite his protests, Kellar predictably remained excluded from the biographer search.[56]

After becoming intensively involved in the search from 1919 to 1922, the McCormick Historical Association delegated the job to Bentley. In this capacity Bentley did almost nothing, because he intended to be selected as the biographer by default. In 1927 Cyrus McCormick II discovered that Bentley had neglected the search. He confronted Bentley about his disregard for the family's important priority, wondering aloud why the family paid him anything at all. Bentley's job was preserved only because Anita and Harold quickly chided Cyrus II for his malicious treatment of their longtime counselor and shamed their brother into keeping Bentley on the payroll. Despite Bentley's continued employment, McCormick and his brother took control of the biographer search and, in short order, commissioned William T. Hutchinson, who came on the recommendation of William E. Dodd of the University of Chicago. The latter was a southern-born Democrat, whose writings on southern history and Woodrow Wilson, a fellow Virginian and McCormick II's Princeton classmate, all made him compatible with the McCormick family's outlook. Hutchinson had just received his doctorate from the University of Chicago, and Dodd was looking out for one of his graduate students. Ironically, this culminating decision after decades of preparation was made for the sake of expedience, regardless of the fact that Hutchinson had no reputation to speak of and Cyrus II found Dodd's biography of his friend Woodrow Wilson to be lackluster. They selected Hutchinson because he was available, and they needed the job done in time for the next Hall of Fame vote in 1930.[57]

William E. Dodd took the opportunity to lobby the family for financial support with some success. Initially, he asked the McCormicks for a $200,000 endowment for the University of Chicago's History Department. After that ploy was rejected, he informed the family that the department chair, Andrew McLaughlin, was going to retire, leaving him with a larger workload and less time to assist Hutchinson. Dodd suggested that the family sweeten McLaughlin's salary by $1,500 to keep him on the job, which the family obliged. Following that escapade, Dodd went to their wallets again, explaining that he would leave the University of Chicago for a better-paying job at Cornell, unless the family subsidized his salary for the next five years. In an odd turn of events, the family actually wrote a check for $25,000 and directly presented it to Dodd. Embarrassed by the outward corruptive appearance of this transaction and indicating the changing professional ethos, Dodd gave the check back and explained that he would arrange it as a gift to the History Department. Dodd never followed up on this plan, and the check sat in the McCormick Estate Office for many years. The series of events between McCormick and Dodd suggests the degree to which the historian was able to leverage his position and the family's anxieties to secure greater financial support. It also indicates the lengths that the family would go to secure the biography.[58]

Hutchinson began research for the project in June 1927. In collaboration the family and their various historians decided to divide Hutchinson's project into two chronological volumes pivoting at 1858—just before the Civil War. The family agreed not to interfere with Hutchinson's writing but retained the right to leave the finished manuscript unpublished if they found it unfavorable. The McCormicks were confident, however, that Dodd would guide Hutchinson toward honoring their father's legacy. The McCormick Historical Association paid the biographer a salary of $3,500 annually. Hutchinson was given free access to the McCormick Agricultural Library and Kellar's outlines and notes. He was also thoroughly briefed by Cyrus Bentley on the reaper controversy and the forcible argument against the "Robert legend."[59]

When the first volume was complete and published in late 1930, the family was satisfied that Hutchinson had unequivocally demonstrated that Cyrus McCormick invented the reaper in 1831. Unfortunately, however, it was released too late for the 1930 Hall of Fame election. Hutchinson's "beautifully written" *Cyrus Hall McCormick: Seed-Time* presented a full and contextualized history of the reaper magnate from his humble origins on a Virginia plantation to the dawn of the Civil War. The family distributed this first volume and its 1935 companion, *Cyrus Hall McCormick: Harvest*, to historians, libraries, and notable dignitaries across the country as the primary proof that their patriarch had invented the reaper. The carefully curated two-volume biography was the product of more than thirty years of collection building by the family and still stands today as the authoritative account on the origins of the reaper, its supposed inventor, and the harvester industry.

On the issue of the reaper controversy, Hutchinson included a full chapter detailing the interfamily conflict that systematically countered the points of the "Robert legend" as a wholesale fabrication. This crucial point rested on Leander and William's testimony in mid-nineteenth-century patent trials. In these instances both brothers testified that Cyrus had invented the reaper in 1831. Uncritical of these sources, Hutchinson ignored that Cyrus's brothers made these statements to protect their mutual company's market supremacy and intellectual property. As co-owners of the family business, their self-interested testimony was compatible with the alternative story that Robert invented the reaper and entrusted it to Cyrus to manage for the family's collective interests. During the antebellum era Cyrus was financially taking care of all of his immediate relatives, as he had supposedly promised his father. If they had testified that Cyrus did not invent the reaper, it would have jeopardized their entire clan's economic well-being. With the patent testimony as "proof" that Cyrus's brothers were lying about Robert inventing the reaper, Hutchinson utilized a wealth of archived correspondence to show that the cousins' antagonistically advanced this "myth" to extort wealth from the heirs.[60]

To the family's dismay in 1928 Hutchinson insisted on handling the original materials himself and coming to his own conclusions. His refusal cast aside years of Kellar's work carefully preparing notes to support his detailed outline for the monumental project. In that moment Kellar seemed to serve no function for the McCormick Historical Association. Noticing the lull in the archivist's work by the end of 1928, Bentley recommended they let Kellar go, stating to the family that the archivist's "usefulness is drawing to a close." Cognizant of his vulnerable position, Kellar saved his job by making himself more available to International Harvester Company in 1928, as it began planning the 1931 centennial celebration of the reaper.[61]

Oddly, International Harvester's preparations for the hundredth anniversary of the invention of the reaper began independently of the McCormick family in 1927. In April of that year, a copywriter in the Advertising Department, Sanford B. White, boldly suggested to the company's vice president, Cyrus McCormick III, that the company create a film about Cyrus McCormick's reaper and carry out a nationwide celebration of the invention for the centennial. White's idea fit well within the company's entrenched nostalgic advertising campaigns; however, he was most likely encouraged by the new emphasis placed on history in the advertising profession. Historical advertising was again in vogue during the mid-1920s. He further noted that the Baltimore and Ohio Railroad's own centennial celebration in 1927, which included exhibits, pageants, speeches, souvenirs, advertising, and huge public picnics, could provide the company with ideas about how best to honor the occasion. Predictably, McCormick III, the company, the

Advertising Department, and the rest of the family quickly endorsed the scheme.[62]

The Advertising Department laid out an ambitious itinerary for the centennial festivities by the spring of 1928. The yearlong fete would include a film, a permanent McCormick reaper monument, celebrations at regional offices around the world, radio broadcasts, and striking advertising features in all of the nation's newspapers. They would also hand out free centennial medallions, stamps, calendars, books, and special editions of *Harvester World* to people across the country. Reminiscent of Edwin Barker's *Story of Bread*, these activities would lead the public "to regard the centenary of the birth of the new agriculture—of the farmer's emancipation from the slavery of hand labor, and of the world's emancipation from the perils of famine." Presenting this campaign to the company's executive committee, marketing executive E. S. Simpson explained that the campaign would be expensive but would "produce a great volume of publicity of a kind unpurchasable at any price and unobtainable in any other way." He stressed that "no other . . . Company . . . has such a historical background . . . universally recognized as the source of the industry and of a world-wide economic revolution."[63]

To fulfill its monumental aspirations, the Advertising Department turned to Herbert Kellar to give their activities the weight of historical authenticity. Prior to 1927 the company had intermittently used the McCormick Agricultural Library as a resource for their legal and advertising needs. Holding all of McCormick Harvesting Machine Company's pre-1902 legal, patent, advertising, and sales records, the library served an obvious, if underutilized, corporate function as its informal archives. With renewed professional weight placed on historical advertising, however, the collection and its historian-archivist became increasingly valuable. For his part Kellar jumped at the opportunity to provide a concrete service to the McCormicks' enterprise at a moment when his job was hanging in the balance. In his capacity as the company's historical adviser among advertising professionals, Kellar was finally respected as a historical authority and given autonomy.[64]

Kellar's point of entry into the advertising work was the company's film production, *The Romance of the Reaper*, named after Herbert Casson's 1908 history of the corporation. The idea was to film a historical reenactment of the evolution of harvesting machinery with emphasis on Cyrus McCormick's invention and trial of the reaper in 1831. The company planned on shooting the film at Walnut Grove, Virginia, the family plantation where Cyrus allegedly invented the reaper. As a historical adviser, Kellar began incrementally by providing the effort with information about the actual geographic location where the reaper was invented and the condition of the relevant historical buildings. With Kellar delivering detailed, fruitful, and interesting information, the director of the Advertising Department instructed his staff to make greater use of him.[65]

The historian was soon involved in every facet of the production. Already thoroughly acquainted with the story of the reaper's inception and patent documentation, Kellar did more research to become thoroughly versed on the specific conditions of the landscape and the geography. He also became an expert in the relevant craft methods and material cultures of the nineteenth century to make the film appear historically authentic. Bringing all this knowledge to bear, he revised the script, chose the harvest fields to plant in 1928, picked camera sight lines, revised the script with the family, helped company mechanics to recreate historical machines, and selected the props and costumes. No detail was left unnoticed, as he considered everything from top hats to narrative syntax.[66]

During this process Cyrus Bentley peevishly attempted to wrest control of the McCormick Historical Association's participation in the company's movie. He successfully convinced the family that he should be their primary liaison with the company on matters of the film and the centennial celebration. Kellar's authoritative role in the project was preserved only by the company's preference for his energy and historical expertise over the lawyer's balky pace. At the behest of the Advertising Department, the company president, Alexander Legge, lobbied the family to reconsider. Legge tactfully notified the family that the company did not wish to "impose" on Bentley's time but favored Kellar as a better fit for their needs. Harold McCormick agreed. In his estimation Kellar had taken the initiative and was "already on the ground with representatives of the Harvester Company." Not to take anything away from Bentley, Harold stated that in his experience "Kellar is the most effective continuous contact man in detail work." Cyrus McCormick II heartily consented, and Kellar became the official historical adviser for not only the film but all of the company's centennial planning.[67]

With International Harvester's endorsement Kellar was able to co-opt Bentley's authority within the McCormick Historical Association. As the principal historical adviser to the company, he gained increased access to the family as he reported on the company's plans, recorded their input on the corporate heritage campaigns, and shared his personal insights. Bentley's influence waned as it became apparent that his participation was superfluous. Moreover, his assistance was equally unnecessary for Hutchinson's biography. In 1929 it became apparent that the McCormicks maintained Bentley's counsel only as an act of personal courtesy rather than for any actual value to their historical efforts. He remained in this lame-duck position until his death in 1930.

During June and July 1929 International Harvester mechanics and advertising men, a Fox-Case Corporation film crew, hundreds of cast members, and Herbert Kellar descended on Walnut Grove, Virginia. When they reached the site, Kellar was everywhere, fastidiously paying attention to all of the physical details of the film and tweaking the script on-site to achieve the best effect. He took care of costuming the entire cast in proper attire and made sure that all the men were clean shaven per the fashion of the day. Taking tools in his hands, he led the physical reconditioning of the Walnut Grove blacksmith shop into a period piece. With assistance from company mechanics, he removed gutters, telephone poles, light fixtures, and electrical wires; covered cement with clay; put in a footscraper on the front step; placed benches; created curtains; and made a variety of other alterations. He also oversaw the construction of a replica carriage and learned how to drive oxen. After that he tweaked the old and replica machines to work in the fields—rediscovering how to make them cut productively. In all these activities he closely explained his historical process to A. C. Seyfarth and Sanford B. White of the Advertising Department, earning the nickname "Historical Accuracy Kellar" by the time the filming wrapped in mid-July.[68]

When Fox-Case finished editing *The Romance of the Reaper* in 1930, it was a twenty-six-minute synthesis of the Cyrus McCormick family's story of the invention, along with decades of company advertising. The overarching plot was a march of progress from pre-1831 grain-cutting technology to the pinnacle of modern grain-harvesting machinery in the twentieth century, the combine. Heavily informed by Edwin Barker's Service Bureau narratives of the early 1910s, Cyrus McCormick's invention of 1831 was no less than the watershed end of toil and famine, harkening a new age of progress.[69]

Importantly, however, the film emphasized and depicted the moment of invention. *The Romance of the Reaper* showed young McCormick's toil inventing the reaper in 1831, faithfully following the family's longtime tradition of the events and indirectly countering the naysaying of the Leander McCormick family. The film acknowledged that Cyrus's father, Robert Hall, had attempted to invent the machine but could not "unlock the riddle of the reaper" and abandoned the project. While onlookers scoffed and his younger brother, Leander, played childish games, Cyrus McCormick struggled to create the ingenious reaper with only the assistance of his trusty "helper" and "servant," the enslaved Jo Anderson. Eventually, Cyrus took the finished reaper to Steele's Tavern for a test run in front of a crowd of curious friends and locals (including pioneers in a Conestoga wagon headed west). The reaper miraculously worked, and the crowd was amazed, following the machine through the field as it cut grain. Cyrus McCormick had set progress in motion.[70]

While the details of the story were the same as they had been in the 1880s, the visual medium of film imparted more powerful and definite weight to the story through imagery. The fundamental point of contention by Leander's family, that Cyrus had little mechanical instinct, was refuted by scenes of Cyrus working away in the blacksmith shop, hammering and cutting pieces that he fit together to form the machine. Moreover, this narrative was underscored by Kellar's choice of costumes. Cyrus looked every bit the stereotypical manly Jacksonian-era craftsman, with a leather craft apron, rolled-up sleeves, and dirty hands. Alternatively, his brothers, father, and neighbors were all dressed as gentlemen in vests and tailcoats with cravats, white gloves, and top hats, looking too effeminate and incompetent for the arduous work of invention. Among these images one particular detail stands out: Cyrus McCormick building the side-to-side sickle blade in the blacksmith shop. This detail was particularly ahistorical. Documentation in the McCormicks' collection clarified that the sickle blade in 1831 was actually forged by Selah Holbrook, a local smithy, because McCormick lacked the ability to build such an intricate piece of ironwork. The film was another layer of historical fabrication. Through the medium of the film, the family and the corporation made the image of Cyrus McCormick as the inventor more complete than even they had previously claimed (see fig. 10).[71]

Taking many artistic liberties, the movie allowed the company and the family to present a seamless narrative of the past on the silver screen for public consumption. The movie flattened out decades of historical controversy and fabricated new details to make the story of Cyrus McCormick's heroic invention more complete. Herbert Kellar played the important role of making prop, process, and costume decisions that made that narrative more historically believable and compelling. The family was thrilled with the company's finished product and Kellar's prominent role in shaping it.[72]

10. *The Reaper Takes Form*, advertising poster, 1931. The International Harvester Company's many Reaper Centennial celebratory posters borrowed heavily from their film, *The Romance of the Reaper*. Broadly representative of the themes of the film, here a young Cyrus McCormick, clad in shop apron with rolled sleeves, toils away constructing his invention, in front of a variety of passive onlookers. Wisconsin Historical Society, WHI-150034.

Returning from filming in late July 1929, Kellar became involved with International Harvester's larger plans for the centennial celebration on all levels. He supplied images from the archive and historical content for the company's advertising, which ubiquitously included information about Cyrus McCormick's legacy. In this pursuit he even researched and delivered specific historical information for every agency to make use of for their local advertising, including the specific details of who bought and sold the first reapers in each of the different sales territories. Along these lines he wrote a three-volume "source book" on the company's history, which was distributed to schoolteachers and the general public by company salesmen. He also aided Cyrus McCormick III in writing a history of the company, *The Century of the Reaper*. Presenting the company with the 1831 reaper's original design, he assisted in fabricating four hundred replicas to install at all of the company's dealerships and factories, authoring the accompanying interpretive copy. For the company's celebratory banquets and public events, he helped the Advertising Department write a generic speech on the history of the reaper and its impact on civilization. Choosing imagery and phraseology, Kellar participated in designing a commemorative medallion that the company distributed by the millions. By 1931 there was not a single aspect of the centennial that was not covered in Kellar's fingerprints.[73]

Predictably, the Leander McCormick family planned their own countercampaign for the past in 1930. International Harvester was concerned about this potential interference and actually pled with the Cyrus McCormick family not to wage a Hall of Fame effort in 1930. Company officials feared that the vanity project and predictable family fallout might do irreparable damage to their brand. Heeding the company's advice, the family only ensured that their father was on the ballot and took no further promotional steps. Despite their caution, beginning in early 1931 their relatives carried out their own celebrations, distributed medallions honoring Robert McCormick, placed reaper models in museums, and influenced articles in *Com-*

merce and *Fortune* magazines that cast doubt on Cyrus McCormick as the inventor.[74]

When family counterhistories came to light in February 1931, Kellar claimed the mantle of authority and laid out the company's strategic response. He recommended that they simply ignore the cousins and ratchet up the scale of their own celebration, casting a wider net with more advertising, more books, more movie showings, more radio spots, and more press, with the addition of pageants and programs for stage productions in theaters. He noted that such a plan "would have the effect of firmly establishing in the mind of the American people the true fact of the invention of the reaper, in a way they would never forget. . . . It would create a tradition for the future about Cyrus McCormick and the invention of the reaper that would become as truly part of American History as our heritage of Washington and Lincoln. Furthermore any protests or counter-celebrations of the Leander group would be overthrown in the mass of information for Cyrus and eventually drowned out." Offering a clear break from Bentley's plans of officially refuting the cousins, Kellar knew that, regardless of the family's ability to prove that Cyrus McCormick invented the reaper, they could never silence the opposition. Rather, they could diminish those protests in the public mind through sheer volume. With decades of experience as a professional historian, Kellar knew that shaping public memory was a matter of repetition, not litigatory debate.[75]

The company adopted Kellar's strategy, agreeing that washing out the Leander McCormicks in a tide of publicity was the best course of action. The advent of familial dissent and Kellar's response also prompted the McCormick family to initiate its own celebratory preparations apart from International Harvester's. Suspecting that the Leander McCormicks were waging their campaign in Virginia, they plotted their own response in the seat of battle. Following the company's lead, the family appointed Kellar to organize two massive public celebrations at Washington and Lee University in Lexington and Virginia Polytechnic Institute in Blacksburg.[76]

The centennial celebration of 1931 was a yearlong extravaganza of heritage events and publications aimed at reinforcing the company's brand and standing with a variety of audiences. International Harvester held banquets and movie screenings for its employees across the nation in the office, in the field, and in the factory. For the general public a series of articles were printed in the *Saturday Evening Post* as well as other national and local periodicals. Customers received these messages even more forcefully through all of the company's sales literature and commercial exhibits. In rural areas every International Harvester dealership in the nation arranged for public screenings of *The Romance of the Reaper* and sponsored special events for children and adults alike. Virginians were particularly targeted. The family's two McCormick Day celebrations in late summer included pageants, picnics, movie screenings, speeches, and ceremonies, parts of which were broadcast over the radio nationwide. At Washington and Lee University, the family also unveiled a statue of Cyrus McCormick. Every attendee at any of these events was given a bronze medallion to commemorate the occasion.[77]

Attention was also particularly directed to educational and agricultural institutions as the sites for perpetuating the family's history in the future. The company distributed roughly 30,000 copies of Cyrus McCormick III's *Century of the Reaper*; 2,500 copies of Hutchinson's *Cyrus Hall McCormick: Seed-Time*; and untold thousands of its "Centennial Source Book," most of which went to libraries, universities, and grade schools. Along this avenue the company created a 4-H scholarship fund to aid students in learning about modern agricultural practices and presented an endowment to Washington and Lee University in Lexington. It also sent a donation to the American Society of Agricultural Engineers and assisted in creating a pageant and program about Cyrus McCormick for their annual meeting. They further arranged a special screening of *The Romance of the Reaper* for employees of the USDA in Washington. Not losing sight of the importance of museums as repositories of official memory, they presented replicas of the 1831 reaper to the Museum of Science and Industry, the Franklin Institute, and the Minnesota Historical Society, among many other institutions.[78]

By the end of 1931, millions of Americans had been marinated in the celebratory heritage of Cyrus McCormick. In total the family and company spent about $1,250,000 (about $23,000,000 today), excluding the standard advertising budget, to broadcast this message to the nation. As had been advertised for decades, all these promotional endeavors and events stressed the vital importance of Cyrus McCormick's ingenuity to the progress of modern civilization. From the McCormicks' perspective, they hoped that these efforts would solidify their patriarch's legacy in the public imagination and in the pages of history. Meanwhile, International Harvester executives and the Advertising Department utilized the anniversary to bring more attention to their longtime brand, ascribing greater cultural gravity to their company's role in American life.[79]

Recognizing the opportunity to serve both the company's advertising campaigns and the family's concerns about the public memory of their father, Herbert Kellar inserted himself into the proceedings and made himself a central figure in all the celebratory planning and activities. He tightly grasped the occasion to make his historical expertise invaluable to these elite ambitions. Prior to becoming involved with the company's centennial plans and Advertising Department, Kellar had great difficulty demonstrating the concrete value of his historical expertise. While he had been able to advance his salary by expanding the library and influencing the historical profession, by 1924 he had reached a ceiling. Pursuing his own interest in building the historical profession, Kellar was unsuccessful in demonstrating how these activities benefited his employers, despite his belief that they would ultimately yield the family definite results. Cyrus Bentley thwarted his numerous attempts to encourage the McCormicks to tether their association more closely to the historical enterprise, often noting that

Kellar's various schemes were a "waste [of] time." By 1924 Kellar was locked in at an annual salary of $5,000 a year, and Bentley refused his requests for a raise because he believed Kellar was being paid too much for his "unsatisfactory" results and, as recently as 1928, advocated for Kellar's dismissal.[80]

Kellar was able to rescue his job and advance his career only by using his expertise to assist the company's centennial advertising campaigns. In this capacity he could effectively apply his training and historical knowledge to concrete products, like the film. Moreover, as he made his services and his archive more available to the company, employees increasingly took advantage of the historical resources for their corporate purposes. Kellar's contributions were praised by Harvester Company executives and advertisers alike. As a result, Kellar's status within the McCormick Historical Association rose, because he was professionally validated by sources the family felt were credible. Kellar improved his stock by demonstrating the value of his historical expertise to the economic interests of the corporation rather than in the more nebulous scholarly field. While the corporation did not have its own archive until 1971, beginning in the 1920s it utilized the McCormick Agricultural Library's collection to inform contemporary policy, advertising, and legal decisions.

Following the centennial celebrations in 1932, Kellar's efforts in the scholarly community also began to bear tangible fruit for the McCormicks. As he took care of the various situations that their cousins had created at the Smithsonian and other museums, it became apparent to the family that his historical colleagues, like Frederick Lewton, were actively looking out for the McCormick family's interests. They were not only providing Kellar with valuable information but taking professional actions to protect Cyrus McCormick's legacy. As Kellar acted on these leads, he further demonstrated that he could be trusted to look out for the family's interests.

As Herbert Kellar earned the family's trust and respect, in July 1932 the McCormick Historical Association appointed him to be its official "agent." Kellar would be responsible for arranging all their meetings, setting the agendas, keeping them apprised of pressing information, and executing all their decisions. He was also given a raise to $6,000, effectively immediately. As they settled into this new arrangement, it became apparent that the McCormicks were deferential to Kellar's judgment and allowed him to pursue whichever avenues he thought best.[81]

In 1935 the McCormick Historical Association renewed its campaign for the Hall of Fame one final time. Reflecting decades of experience as well as Kellar's more expansive understanding of history, they did not rely solely on the "objectivity" of the past to win over electors. While Kellar was still instrumental in creating and organizing historical materials, they also hired advertising guru Bruce Barton to orchestrate their campaign. Barton conducted market research on the balloted jurists to assess their stance on the reaper's invention. Armed with this information, the family custom-tailored their promotional efforts to each individual voter. Yet, in October 1935, the results of the election came back, and the family had failed to secure a majority by a narrow margin. Of the 120 electors, 55 voted for Cyrus McCormick—just 6 jurists shy of gaining enshrinement in the Hall of Fame. The McCormick Historical Association vowed to continue their efforts and made plans to hire Barton to work on the project for the next five years. Their plot was never carried out, however. Cyrus McCormick II died in 1936 at the age of seventy-seven, and his surviving siblings, Anita and Harold, chose not to pursue the Hall of Fame. Instead, they believed that Kellar's efforts would be enough for their father to eventually be elected on his merits.[82]

In 1949 Anita McCormick Blaine sold the property where the McCormick Agricultural Library stood and appointed Herbert Kellar to locate a new home for its massive collection. Their foremost concern in searching for a new repository was guaranteeing that the collection would be adequately preserved and continue to be used by historians in the future. After an intensive survey and negotiation with upward of thirty interested universities and historical societies over three years, Kellar chose the State Historical Society of Wisconsin in Madison as the new repository for the McCormick archive in 1951. The State Historical Society was chosen because of its close association with the University of Wisconsin. The university's strong history and agriculture departments ensured that the McCormick collection would continue to be used by noteworthy scholars in the future. Moreover, as an addition to a collection already recognized as "the center of the best material on the history of the West," it would become a part of a preeminent archival destination for scholars of the Midwest. Anita Blaine continued to pay Kellar's salary and his expenses until her death in 1954, but even after that time her estate covered his costs.[83]

Having earned professional autonomy as the McCormick Historical Association's "agent" in 1932, Herbert Kellar continued on the family's payroll until his death in 1955, with both intellectual freedom and generous financial support. Predictably, he chose to become more involved in historical organizations and profession building. He believed that historical knowledge and expertise were valuable resources for corporations, farmers, and the general public, but that the profession needed to do a better job demonstrating that value. Reflecting his experience of struggling for historical authority within the McCormick Historical Association, he was determined to drive the discipline toward a higher degree of public engagement that might better justify its professional standing. Supporting this effort, he continually urged his colleagues to provide better historical training for historians assuming jobs outside of academia and took a leading role in the creation of both the Society of American Archivists and the American Association for State and Local History. He felt that these new institutions could address these important topic areas that had been neglected by the American Historical Association and the larger profession. He was also a strong proponent of more historical training within the USDA to bring better historical information to farmers during the Great Depression and was a welcome participant on USDA advisory panels.[84]

Merging his public impulse and his employers' direct interests, Kellar was also a pioneer of the living agricultural museum. In the mid-1930s he used his vast archival resources and the family's wealth to restore the McCormicks' Virginia plantation at Walnut Grove to its 1831 condition. Rebuilding and renovating the farmhouse, barn, corncrib, springhouse, slave quarters, workshop, and gristmill, he believed that the restored historical site was the perfect way to communicate the significance of Cyrus McCormick's life and invention to twentieth-century Americans.[85]

Kellar continued to be the profession's foremost authority on manuscript collecting and archival coordination. He knew that sharing historical documents was crucial to the profession's ability to provide historical insight for the benefit of larger society. He was the head of the AHA and the MVHA committees responsible for centralizing information about archival holdings during the 1920s and 1930s. Carrying this work a step further, he became the director of the Historical Records Survey from 1940 to 1942, coordinating the nationwide archival inventory project after federal funding had been cut from its parent agency, the Works Progress Administration. Around that same time Kellar also became a champion of new microfilm technology, which would allow archives to share materials with historians at great distances and were less burdensome to create than edited volumes.[86]

Kellar was recognized for his work not in crafting historical narrative but in supporting the scholarship of others and boosting the profile of the discipline as a whole. Within the profession, especially among the historians of the Midwest, he was praised as a visionary. Ever present in the historical profession throughout his career, in organizations like the AHA, AHS, the American Association for State and Local History, the Society of American Archivists, Southern Historical Association, the American Council of Learned Societies, and many others, the high mark of his professional achievement was being elected president of the MVHA in 1946. He was further honored posthumously in 1958, when the State Historical Society of Wisconsin published *In*

Support of Clio. An edited volume that included essays by nine of his peers, *In Support of Clio* touched on the importance of endeavors that supported historical scholarship for which Kellar was best known, including manuscript collections, professional associations, archives, and historical restorations. Perhaps most fittingly, the volume included an essay on the importance of wealthy foundations, like that of the Carnegie Corporation, the Rockefeller Foundation, the Rosenwald Fund, and the McCormick Historical Association, in financing the work of academics. Kellar's colleagues recognized that the McCormick family was responsible for underwriting his energetic participation in the profession and were cognizant that other wealthy philanthropists provided similar support.[87]

Coincidentally, in 1955, the same year that Kellar died, Norbert Lyons published *The McCormick Reaper Legend*. With a preface by Robert McCormick III, the book gave the glory for inventing the reaper to Robert McCormick and called out the McCormick Historical Association, and Herbert Kellar specifically, for consciously fabricating history to fit their economic and corporate interests. He even revealed that the family's previous historical laborers, Louis Dent and Salem Pattison, did not believe that Cyrus McCormick invented the reaper but participated in the project only in exchange for pay. Reflecting the influence of Cyrus McCormick's heirs and Herbert Kellar on the historical profession, however, the book was barely noticed. Receiving only one academic critique, in the pages of *Business History Review*, the reviewer dismissed Lyons's book because "the work may not be considered objective, scientific or impartial." It was too little, too late. One book was not enough to overturn decades of McCormick family historical activities. The heirs' and their company's heritage—that Cyrus McCormick invented the reaper in 1831—continued to proliferate unabated in U.S. history textbooks and in the American imagination.[88]

Conclusion

Herbert Kellar began an address to the American Library Association in June 1938, "The mere fact of the physical existence of a manuscript collection is mute evidence of the activities . . . of an individual or a group. . . . Behind the development of practically every important group of manuscript collections, there is a story." While he was referring to the story of how a collection is processed and organized, certainly his experience suggested that there is also a story behind why any collection is assembled as well. *Harvesting History* tells one such story.[1]

Accumulated from decades of heritage initiatives, the McCormick collection is the byproduct of battles for the past with competitors and relatives, corporate-branding efforts to assuage popular unrest and anxieties, and a protracted crusade to win Cyrus McCormick's election into the Hall of Fame for Great Americans. Regardless of particular and incidental outcomes of these activities, the corpus and impact of their work reflected both the corporatized transformation of capitalism and a broader cultural campaign to naturalize the rise of massive businesses in the American imagination as an inevitable outcome of history and progress. Such corporate cultural reimagining was necessary to lessen popular anxieties about the assault on national values, tradition, and identity represented by the massive size of modern trusts. Within the reconfiguration Cyrus McCormick and his supposed invention became a fixture in the newly crafted canon of corporatized United States history.

Though the McCormicks fell short of their particular hopes to enshrine their father's invention in the Hall of Fame, the significant collection they assembled to support that effort unexpectedly became a longer lasting and more effective vehicle for accomplishing their underlying goals. The collection became the primary support of the family's authoritative biography of their father and the reaper but also dialectically verified decades of historical advertising and public relations materials. These promotional, archival, and historical initiatives are what solidified their patriarch's invention as fact. Operating as a sort of historical capital, the collection continues to churn out cultural dividends, attracting historians to study its contents, in effect ensuring that Cyrus McCormick, and his company and family, continued to be historically relevant for generations.

At the heart of their collection and this book is the fiction that Cyrus McCormick invented the reaper in 1831. The roots of this piece of trivia touch on a story larger than the McCormicks' interests and illuminate oft-disguised forces at work in the creation of the historical canon. By considering how a single corporate myth became fixed as fact, the story offers a window into the relationship between professionalizing historical labor and the rising corporate order during the Gilded Age and Progressive Era. In a period of social and economic transformation, concerns about credibility were central to both interests, and in exchange each could bestow legitimacy on the other. Remade through this transaction, the nature of historical inquiry was adapted to suit the modern industrial age and, to some extent, the purposes of its corporations, "trust lords," and "captains of industry."

For the McCormicks and their various enterprises, the myth of the reaper's origins legitimized their power and their farm-implement empire. In a basic sense their use of the past was no different from European kings charting their royal lineage to legitimate their ascendancy to the throne. Within the United States' evolving society of strangers, this sort of genealogical posturing was increasingly widespread and useful to businesses expanding their market reach regionally and eventually nationally. A deeper past could convince skeptical customers that a salesman was aboveboard and not a "fly by night" charlatan scheming to bilk them out of their money. A company's longevity and storied accomplishments created an air of its standing, summoning the past to qualify its present in the anonymous national marketplace among customers and financiers. In an era before credit ratings quantified the past as a risk evaluation for the present and future, long-term reputation mattered and to some degree could be fabricated using the tools of heritage, myth, and advertising.

Toward that end the McCormicks adapted the meaning of the 1831 invention to fit shifting measures of importance within the modernizing industrial order. In that process they actively manipulated public memory as they rewrote the meaning of invention and producerism to fit their purposes. Cyrus McCormick Jr. etched his father's "invention" onto popular imaginings of history and progress that had been around since at least the age of Andrew Jackson to create a recognized story of American triumph. In his hands Cyrus Sr.'s 1831 invention became a fabled exemplar of the individualism, ingenuity, effort, and competitive spirit believed to be the core of the country's democratically driven westward expansion and pursuit of progress. Akin to Horatio Alger's rags-to-riches tales, the McCormick Harvesting Machine Company's past, as told by family members, salesmen, and catalog copy in this patriotic and celebratory light, exonerated its questionable present as both an industry-trailing, farm-implement firm as well as a foe of the politically minded farmer. The McCormicks' self-interested curation of history was only a slight variation of a trend of wealthy elites endeavoring to rescue their public reputations during the Gilded Age. As Americans questioned whether the wealthy were "robber barons" defrauding the nation or "captains of industry" leading the march of progress, the rich busily arranged the evidence to argue the latter. Unlike many others who might point toward their philanthropic efforts to define the meaning of their wealth, the McCormicks pointed to their father's invention as proof that they made their money the old-fashioned way—by earning it.

For as closely as the McCormicks sculpted their heritage to match conventional notions of national history, labor, and heroism in the late nineteenth century, once they formed the harvester trust with their rivals in 1902, the invention story became the pivot in an entirely realigned grand narrative of the national past. In this new chronology they reframed history within conceptions of cooperation and corporatization as the new hallmarks of progress. They countered prevalent claims that corporations were monopolist enemies of the common man, sapping opportunities for manly self-sufficient independence and competition while unfairly stealing the wealth of hardworking people. Instead, trusts were benevolent institutions, efficiently and predictably spreading the fruits of modernity and abundance around the world—to employees, customers, and public stockholders—while taming the threat of an increasingly volatile industrialized marketplace.

During the corporate-merger movement, the explanatory power of triumphal Jacksonian self-sufficient individualism became seemingly anachronistic amid the disorienting social, cultural, and economic upheaval of the Progressive Era. Among budding universities, reform crusades, and mushrooming government agencies, massive corporations played a leading role in industrializing, bureaucratizing, professionalizing, urbanizing, and interconnecting all of society while seemingly destroying the power of the individual. During the Great Merger movement of 1895 to 1904, 1,800 business merged into 157 corporations, restraining trade by design while extending their market grip across oceans and continents. This appeared to be not the robust labor of hardworking Americans but the financial manipulation of investors and banking masterminds looking to get rich on the backs of others by tightly orchestrating the marketplace.

These massive businesses came to dominate the nature of work life. As fewer and fewer people worked for themselves, more and more were employed by corporations on the factory floor or as new middle-class clerks, professionals, managers, and salesmen. Reflecting this shift away from the traditional entrepreneurial spirit, by 1910 salaried middle-class professionals outnumbered independent businessmen by 5,609,000 to 3,261,000. Ten years later, in 1920, the nation would have an urban majority population for the first time in its history, and the populace of independent farmers—those romantic, self-sufficient guardians of American democracy—would continue to shrink as their offspring sought professions and lives away from the land. At the same time, consumers began to lose their power to negotiate prices, as competition for their patronage disappeared in the merger movement. These transformations, hastened by large corporations, seemed utterly incongruous with traditional notions of U.S. history and identity, feeding populistic outcries for trust-busting, restoration of competitive markets, and a return to the old order.[2]

Advancing a new corporatized history became necessary for corporations to create credibility that explained away frightening social and economic changes as no more than the natural results of progress. From almost the beginning International Harvester's public relations history offered a vision of a unified modern society, in which farmers, workers, investors, and businessmen of all stripes cooperated to create a new middle-class prosperity for all to enjoy. The previous generations' priority on manly independence and free-market competition vanished wholesale, as did allusions to the cultural divisions between city and country, along with the sectional divides that had wrought the Civil War. Public relations and advertising campaigns became tools for widely distributing a sanctifying history of corporate inevitability to a disoriented and anxious public in the throes of the business revolution. Such historical contortions helped create space in the public mind to accommodate massive corporate entities as the natural result of progress. Moreover, they pushed Americans toward forming new "modern" identities, founded not on independent self-sufficient producerism but rather on their pursuit of consumer prosperity and middle-class stability as allies of progress within the corporate order.

International Harvester was not alone in reframing U.S. history as corporate preamble. In 1907 the United States Steel Corporation commissioned *The Romance of Steel*, which cast the history of the steel trust as the ongoing perfection of steel production and the altruistic rise of modern investor democracy, or "the story of a thousand millionaires." In this telling U.S. Steel's monopolistic domination was necessary to make steel cheaply and ensure that the United States would become a leader in spreading "steel-ribbed civilisations" around the world. Elements of a corporatized past became increasingly evident during the 1920s and 1930s at places like Greenfield Village, organized by Henry Ford, and Colonial Williamsburg, sponsored by John D. Rockefeller. Ford famously declared in 1916 that "history is more or less bunk," because it was a tradition out of touch with the revolutionary force of corporate modernity. At Greenfield Village, however, Ford curated his vision of the past, eliminating the history of political and social strife almost altogether and instead honoring the importance of technology and inventors in improving the standard of living of the common man. Moving in a different direction, Rockefeller's Colonial Williamsburg presented a romantic image of the rational organization and tidiness of monarchical authority in eighteenth-century Virginia, free of dirt, slavery, or any other form of exploitation. Predating the United States and its democratic and chaotic cultural impulses, Colonial Williamsburg provided a past that celebrated the exact same type of authority, organization, and predictability that Rockefeller and other financiers treasured in the modern corporation. In these instances, and others, history was a malleable cultural resource made to shroud new forms of order, power, and authority in the cloak of presumed national tradition.[3]

In the hands of able and connected moguls, corporatizing history proved to be a powerful tool. George Perkins, the trust lord who facilitated the International Harvester merger with the McCormicks, shared his version of the corporatized past with his "trust busting" friend Theodore Roosevelt, helping to convince the president not to pursue antitrust prosecution of the Harvester Company in 1907. Perkins's careful historical parsing to some degree was responsible for creating Roosevelt's articulation of "good" trusts serving the people and "bad" trusts driven by greed. In a clear departure from conventional understandings of the past and benevolent free-market forces, Perkins believed that the creation of massive corporations was motivated not by individualism and the "greed of man" but rather by the inevitable "working of natural causes-of evolution" and history toward the "universal" historical impulse to "cooperate." Corporations, brought about by human technology and capacity building, were the natural antidote to the "old destructive competition" that brought "suffering," most recently witnessed during the Panic of 1907. They benefited an ever-expanding pool of public owners across the nation, while stably "guaranteeing better wages and more steady employment to labor, with a more favorable price to the consumer." Perkins further argued that corporations were willing to pay handsomely for a whole new class of progressive-minded professionals that would perfect corporate operations and spread their benefits across the world.[4]

While advertising, public relations rhetoric, journalistic punditry, and speeches went to great lengths to explain the major changes in American life, they were not enough to "prove" the corporatized thrust of history on their own. Corporate claims to the past needed a new type of *professional* to do the work; those new foot soldiers of the Progressive Era's bureaucratic revolution. They required educated and accredited historians to scientifically and objectively countersign their historical ambitions. For their part, new historical professionals were eager to participate in the process, legitimize their profession, and formulate new identities as modern workers in step with the corporate revolution.

Working within this context the historical profession's push toward the "New History" was angling historical labor toward being relevant within the emerging modern order and synchronizing historical education with corporate needs. The leader of the New History movement, James Harvey Robinson, along with his peers, recognized the opportunity to legitimize the historical discipline by framing their intellectual labor in terms that were familiar to the rising corporation. Indeed, Robinson pressed his peers to advance historical inquiry relevant to contemporary life. Robinson denounced the older approach to scholarship—embodied by the famous phrase "history is past politics, and politics present history"—as narrow and melodramatic with "no assignable relation to our [society's] needs." Instead, Robinson believed history might be made relevant to the industrial class, transforming them into better "artisans" and citizens who would be able to "cooperate" with progressive leaders in "eliminating the evils from which they suffer." In a manner very similar to Perkins's vision for educated corporate professionals, Robinson held that historians could use their craft to "cooperate with and direct" modern forces of progress toward the "abolition of poverty and disease and war, and the promotion of happy and rational lives." Robinson's "new" historians were just the sort of progressive-minded professionals that corporations wanted and needed.[5]

In step with Robinson's vision, progressive historians responded by working to make their scholarship relevant to the public as well as solving pressing contemporary challenges in an effort to prove the value of their discipline. Corporations were only one factor in the modernizing order of Progressive Era America, alongside urbanization, immigration, bureaucratization, technological innovation, government growth, educational reform, and others. As has been established in other studies of the origins of public history, scholars in the early twentieth century eagerly hoped to make their efforts useful to reforming government policies surrounding labor, economics, agriculture, public works, and more.

On a parallel path *Harvesting History* has shown how historians such as Herbert Kellar, Salem Pattison, Reuben Thwaites, and Clarence Alvord and organizations like the Mississippi Valley Historical Association and Agricultural History Society, among others, sought to make history useful in the marketplace of big business. By making their historical efforts relevant to a wealthy patron and later a corporation, they could secure stability as well as the trappings of middle-class living. In that exchange their labor became useful and respected in the modern world. New professional historians built out the corporatized history scaffolded by International Harvester, George Perkins, and others, providing the necessary scholarship to intellectually fortify and naturalize the arrival of the corporate age.

Despite appearances, Robinson, Kellar, and the Mississippi Valley Historical Association members were not intellectual mercenaries. Rather, as an intellectual cohort, they were acutely aware of their economic context and cultural reality. Despite aspirations and posturing to the contrary, they were influenced by the world outside of their ivory tower. They both consciously and unconsciously synchronized their scholarship with the times in ways that were mostly complementary. Catering to the emerging corporate order would have been recognized as a logical continuation of patron-supported scholarship, which had roots in the nineteenth century. Many Gilded Age millionaires sought to soften their reputations as industrialists by philanthropically founding private universities and libraries. Universities such as Johns Hopkins, Vanderbilt, Stanford, and Carnegie Mellon and institutions such as the McCormick Theological Seminary and the Huntington, James J. Hill, and the Newberry Libraries, among many others, were all supported by individuals of means. In such a setting academics and administrators were familiar with the implicit or explicit strings-attached obligations that accompanied the support they eagerly sought.

Notions of intellectual freedom would solidify only later in the twentieth century, when significant support for higher education from federal and state funding sources offset the need for dutiful reliance on the wealthy elite. In a patron-oriented milieu, the sort of support that Herbert Kellar or the Mississippi Valley Historical Association were able to develop with the McCormicks and International Harvester would not have been shrouded in suspicion but praised as a mix of skilled advocacy and good fortune. A step further removed from this direct exchange, the "new historians" led by Robinson and others advocated for and advanced a historical practice that was engaged with modern forces in a manner not wholly contradictory or self-destructive. Through matching the cultural, economic, and political currents of the times, the historical discipline rode the rising tide of scientific research, education, and scholarship in the mid-twentieth century.[6]

Today's conflation of the corporate order with "free markets" has, in part, been the product of extended cultural campaigns to naturalize big business as a logical extension of deep-seated American values and history. Public relations' spin and the rhetoric of multinational corporations rarely boast about the truth of a business's origins in massive mergers or sophisticated financial acumen, nor do they bandy about legislated lobbying victories or government contracts as evidence of a company's public virtue. Instead, they obscure those abstract and questionable facets of their enterprise through promoting tales of innovation, new abundance, and improved service created by the corporation's sophisticated organization. Along these lines the image of a corporation is often softened by celebrating its "humble origins." In the same way that International Harvester trumpeted Cyrus McCormick's invention of the reaper in the family blacksmith shop as its genesis, companies like Amazon, Google, Walt Disney, and Hewlett-Packard, among many others, celebrate their supposed founding in garages by innovative, bootstrapping entrepreneurs. The garage start-up folktale serves to personify the corporation as the righteous extension of an individual's foresight and ingenuity while distracting from the far more important and complex story of how a corporation is made or molds the market. The ubiquitous patchwork of fictions cloak the machination of corporate-capitalism. Over a century removed from the Great Merger movement, the widespread cultural and historical subterfuge as well as the inertia of the economic order make alternatives and criticism difficult to imagine, let alone sustain in the national forum.

In the meantime succeeding generations of academic historians have endeavored to be detached from the corporate order as aloof critics of the regime rather than as educated professionals operating within its purview. During significant portions of the postwar collegiate boom, this comfortable approach to jobs came at little cost to the profession, as federal funding and enrollment steadily rose, allowing the discipline to drift away from the New History focus on economic relevance. In such a context cutting-edge scholarship was the seemingly meritocratic path to securing tenure-track jobs in the university for PhD historians, and everything short of that standard was either considered a personal failure or not considered at all. Beyond the litmus test of scholarship and employment, academic historians comfortably rested on the laurels of the middle-class cultural cache associated with professorship. This model, however, has faltered, as fewer students study history because they cannot see the applicability of the discipline to twenty-first-century careers and because secure tenure-track jobs are disappearing. Moreover, democratized publishing online has undermined the discipline's cultural cache, as its historical authority has precipitously declined in the public imagination. This certainly echoes the first Gilded Age, in which Americans fabricated and advanced whichever heritage narrative was most advantageous for themselves in a world where professional historians hardly existed.

Faced with such circumstances, Herbert Kellar and his peers offer us a useful source of inspiration. They recognized and leaned into the battles for historical and professional authority with lawyers, advertisers, public relations specialists, journalists, and creative writers. They knew that if they did not make a demonstration of their profession's value to employers in a competitive labor market, they would be only avocational history buffs rather than historical professionals. As part of that effort, they balanced scholarly virtues with pragmatic financial needs. Following in their footsteps, today's trained public historians have similarly placed emphasis on finding jobs wherever they can be found in the twenty-first-century economy as a necessary condition for doing good history.

As a byproduct of fortifying a single fiction as fact, Herbert Kellar probably did more than any other individual to document the history of agriculture and change in rural America. Despite being a historian for a corporation and an elite family, he created an archive that documented the experience of everyday people in the United States. A tireless proponent of local history and archival accessibility, he was also deeply involved in the New Deal's Federal Writers' Project's historical documentation campaigns. While he undoubtedly participated in advancing nefarious and bizarrely narrow goals, through his archival and professional efforts, he further enabled succeeding generations of historians to reinterpret the past through the lens of their own experience.

As any historiography supposes, the works of the preceding generations are artifacts of their times. Within that context of creation, however, historical works are also evidence of the aspirations of the discipline: to be accepted, to be influential, and, perhaps more quietly, to be economically valued as professionals in the workforce. The historical canon we have inherited bears the marks of the cultural politics of the past. The racial, social, and gendered politics and meaning of that canon can be more or less easily exposed through applying the appropriate analytical lens. Beyond this, however, the nature of basic "facts" is also suspect and can reveal depths of meaning beyond their seemingly obvious facade as things that actually happened or perhaps didn't happen at all. Approaching the inherited past with a view toward deciphering built-in contextual distortions of the facts provides an opportunity to read history against the grain. It can illuminate richer narratives than were intended by earlier curators of the historical record. Likewise, behind every archive is a story of the complex cultural, economic, and political anxieties, conflicts, and purposes of those who created them.

Notes

INTRODUCTION

1. Trouillot's *Silencing the Past* offers a strong theoretical framework for analyzing historical production built on examples of its political and cultural operation in Haitian history making.
2. Cyrus H. McCormick II, "Memoir," *In Memoriam: Cyrus Hall McCormick*, 1885, 1–23, box 396, Mss 1E, MIHCC.
3. C. McCormick II, "Memoir," 1885, box 396, Mss 1E, MIHCC.
4. Nettie Fowler McCormick to Anita McCormick Blaine, July 30, 1897, box 7, Mss 1B; Cyrus McCormick II to John Carlisle, January 6, 1897, reel 8, Mss 3C, MIHCC. Lowenthal's *Heritage Crusade* offers many examples of the difference between history as an inclusive, objective pursuit of studying change over time, and heritage as a celebratory, exclusive, and whitewashed use of the past.
5. Andreas's *History of Chicago* recognizes the important innovations of competing harvesting firms in Chicago, such as McCormick and Deering, within his encyclopedic volumes, suggesting a broader understanding of the reaper's evolution. Ardrey's *American Agricultural Implements* is the most important of these histories because it was commissioned by the National Association of Agricultural Implement Manufacturer as a consensus history of technological progress in response to the rising agrarian dissent from the National Farmers' Alliance and similar organizations. McCormick Harvester notably did not participate in the association, but its contributions to the larger project of harvester innovation is recognized in Ardrey's work, alongside many others. Bidwell and Falconer's *History of Agriculture* also recognizes this broader history of the reaper's origins. See also R. McCormick, *Memorial of Robert Hall*; and Lyons, *McCormick Reaper Legend*.
6. Hutchinson's *Cyrus Hall McCormick: Seed-Time* and *Cyrus Hall McCormick: Harvest* are the two volumes composing the supposedly authori-

tative account that sanctions Cyrus McCormick as the inventor of the reaper. Steward and Pound's *Reaper* is a history asserting the primacy of Obed Hussey's reaper, written by a former inventor for William Deering Company. Lyons's *McCormick Reaper Legend* covers the arguments for Robert McCormick. Rogin's *Introduction of Farm Machinery* and "Introduction of Farm Machinery" argue, using the same material as Hutchinson, that the evidence is "inconclusive" for determining that either Cyrus McCormick or Obed Hussey invented the reaper, which in turn casts doubt on any evidence for Robert McCormick as the inventor as well.

7. Hutchinson's *Cyrus Hall McCormick: Seed-Time* and Lyons's *McCormick Reaper Legend* both acknowledge Jo Anderson's participation in supporting the inventive work alongside the McCormicks. Indeed, in the 1880s Jo Anderson was interviewed by both sides of the McCormick family about who invented the reaper, and he acknowledged on separate occasions with separate interviewers that both had. No one asked him particularly about his role as an inventor, only as a bystander and witness to the McCormicks' inventive accomplishments.
8. The McCormick Agricultural Library is now at the Wisconsin Historical Society in Madison and renamed the McCormick–International Harvester Collection; many scholars have utilized the library for work in a variety of historiographies. Cronon's *Nature's Metropolis*, Cohen's *Making a New Deal*, Chandler's *Visible Hand*, Zunz's *Making America Corporate*, and Evans's *Bound in Twine* are a short sampling of some of the more prominent studies that have utilized the collection, but the full list includes scores more.
9. Zunz's *Making America Corporate* and Marchand's *Creating the Corporate Soul* are the most relevant to this book. Chandler's books on the evolution of "managerial capitalism," *Visible Hand* and *Strategy and Structure*, stand as the major works of the historical reimagination of business history and placement of labor at the center of the corporation-building project. This field has expanded to include the structural and cultural implications of international business, such as in Rosenberg's *Spreading the American Dream*, as well as the politics of the corporate managed economy, such as in Sklar's *Corporate Reconstruction*. Kwolek-Folland's *Engendering Business* textures Zunz's interpretation to demonstrate that corporations were capable of recruiting this workforce only because of a gendered business language that placed corporations within traditional

American family values. In the wake of the financial meltdown of 2008, Ott's *Wall Street* builds on Marchand to suggest that the 1920s emergence of popular stockholding was a corporate strategy to assuage hostility toward corporate wealth and undermine popular support for government regulation. These efforts utilized the language of "investor's democracy" to manipulate the discourses of producer citizenship and property.

10. Historians prior to the 1940s often acknowledged philanthropic support from wealthy benefactors but never considered how that support might subjectively shape their scholarship. Ross's "Generation of Prairie Historiography" and Krey's "History" both serve as strong examples of contemporary understandings of the historical profession in the 1930s and 1940s. Both consider the activities of academic historians, alongside those of amateur historians as well as public and private institutions. Underlying their perspectives is an uncritical knowledge that wealthy benefactors such as Andrew Carnegie and the McCormick family financed historical work. Later studies of the historical profession, such as Higham, Krieger, and Gilbert's *History* and Lord's *Keepers of the Past*, parse the historical profession apart to preserve the objective sanctity of professionalism. Higham does not discuss the influence of elite wealth on scholarship, while Lord considers the influence of wealth on institution building but not scholarly direction. Later historians, like Novick, continue this separation, outlining changes in historiographical trends in light of the cultural turn's emphasis on middle-class values, demonstrating how historians sought, defined, and refuted "objectivity." Novick suggests that historians accommodated mainstream American values and authorities to augment their reputations and financial opportunities, but his analysis of this point is brief (*That Noble Dream*, 61–85).
11. Conard, *Benjamin Shambaugh*; Lauck, *Lost Region*. Lauck coined the phrase "Prairie Historians" and has used the concept to reinvigorate interest in the history of the region. Tyrell, in *Historians in Public*, describes the larger civic and public engagement of the profession throughout the twentieth century.
12. Lauck, *Lost Region*.
13. Within these works International Harvester agents are referenced as a source of progressive discourse and pressure on rural agrarians. Danbom, in *Resisted Revolution*, argues that the rural progressive movement was pushed on rural farmers, beginning in the early 1900s, by the "agricul-

tural complex" combination of agribusiness, universities, and federal authorities. These groups, operating through Morrill Land-Grant University Extension Services, the Country Life movement, regional sales agents, and U.S. Department of Agriculture county agents, attempted to modernize rural production habits to create cheaper foodstuffs for urban consumers. Danbom suggests that these efforts succeed only in the years after World War I, because of patriotic production. Neth, in *Preserving the Family Farm*, argues that these rural habits changed only in the 1920s and 1930s, because of the progressive movement's discursive reframing of gender norms around access to the tools of modernity. Kline, in *Consumers in the Country*, suggests that New Deal agricultural policy, influenced by agribusiness, successfully marginalized nonmarket farming techniques through scarcity management and technological subsidization.

14. Bederman's *Manliness and Civilization* masterfully demonstrates that ideas about "civilization" functioned as a discourse of power around the turn of the past century, which operated through entwined notions of gender and race that signified morality and progress within Anglo-American hegemony. Bender's *American Abyss* takes this analysis a step further and suggests that the discourse of civilization offered a world-view of "industrial evolution," which explicitly organized all people on a spectrum of Darwinian evolution and history. This spectrum could be "naturally" understood and communicated through modes of living, production, and consumption. For Bender, then, material associations of labor, environment, and bodies can be understood as historical indices of the civilized order, which placed industrialization as the height of human progress opposite caveman savagery.
15. Marchand, *Advertising the American Dream*; Leach, *Land of Desire*; Lears, *Fables of Abundance*.

1. EVERY SALESMAN, A HISTORIAN

1. George H. Brewster to C. H. and L. J. McCormick, July 23 and 25, 1877, reel 176, Mss 2X, MIHCC.
2. Brewster to C. H and L. J. McCormick, June 23, 1877, reel 210, Mss 2X, MIHCC; "Railroad Construction in Minnesota," *Minneapolis Tribune*, January 21, 1872; Hutchinson, *Cyrus Hall McCormick: Harvest*, 536–72.
3. Samuel D. Peterson to C. H and L. J. McCormick, March 27, 1877, reel 209, Mss 2X, MIHCC; Tenth Census of the United States, 1880, NARA

microfilm publication T9, reel 616, New Ulm, Brown County MN, sheet 14D, accessed October 23, 2013, www.ancestry.com. Gjerde, in *Minds of the West*, argues there was a fundamental cultural difference between communal Catholic and Lutheran immigrants from northern Europe and American Yankee Protestants. These differences accounted for crucial divergences in all manner of social organizations, from politics to market orientation.

4. Peterson to C. H and L. J. McCormick, March 27, 1877, reel 209, Mss 2X, MIHCC.
5. Brewster to C. H and L. J. McCormick, February 9, 1877, reel 209; May 21 and July 9, 1877, reel 210; Peterson to C. H and L. J. McCormick, March 27, 1877, reel 209, Mss 2X, MIHCC; McCormick to Brewster, February 15, 1877, reel 173, Mss 1X, MIHCC. Peterson received the McCormick maximum of 10 percent commission on cash sales and 5 percent commission on "time" sales. He also received 2 percent for past-due notes, a commission reserved for general agents.
6. C. H. McCormick I to Brewster, February 3 and 20, 1877, and July 3, 1877, reel 173, Mss 1X, MIHCC. Brewster to C. H and L. J. McCormick, July 14, 21, and 25, 1877, reel 210, Mss 2X, MIHCC, provides a description of how Brewster went about starting binders in new territory and Peterson's success in Brown County.
7. Kammen, *Mystic Chords of Memory*, 132–62; Lears, *Something for Nothing*, 144–45.
8. Bederman, *Manliness and Civilization*, 25–26; Lears, *Something for Nothing*, 180–84.
9. Lears explores the perceived connections between personal character and morality, divine intention, and material outcomes (*Something for Nothing*, 59–60, 135–36, 139–40). Laird in particular discusses the importance of business success as an indication of moral character (*Advertising Progress*, 102–5). See also *Manliness and Civilization*, in which Bederman demonstrates how ideas about progress and civilization operated as a hegemonic cultural discourse of race, class, and gender during the era.
10. Scholarship as early as Marx's *Machine in the Garden* notes the seemingly visible nature of progress (197). Laird's *Advertising Progress* builds on Marx's work to argue that the physical sense of progress was a ubiquitous aspect of Gilded Age advertising (108–16). In a still more recent

study, Bender's *American Abyss* argues that Americans projected the cultural discourse of progress onto the landscape in their daily lives and believed degrees of civilization could be "read" by the discerning eye—for example, comparing the savage, filthy tenement to the civilized, clean Victorian home.

11. Laird, *Advertising Progress*, 101–54; Friedman, *Birth of a Salesman*, 37–43.
12. Friedman's *Birth of a Salesman* (53–55), Ristow's "Alfred T. Andreas," and Conzen's *Chicago Mapmakers* offer good introductions to the subscription map, atlas, and history industry during the second half of the nineteenth century.
13. Harrington, *How 'Tis Done*, 10, 20.
14. Harrington, *How 'Tis Done*, 28–29, 151, 153.
15. Harrington, *How 'Tis Done*, 16–18, 33, 148, 168.
16. Casper, *Constructing American Lives*, 291; Neill and Williams, *History of Dakota County*, 161. Casper's *Constructing American Lives* also analyzes the content of county histories, atlases, and mug books (291–300).
17. Casper, *Constructing American Lives*, 297.
18. Kammen, *Mystic Chords of Memory*, 132, 161–62; Townsend, *History's Babel*, 15.
19. Laird discusses tactics for associating business with progress but does not discuss the importance of history to this effort (*Advertising Progress*, 100–151). Lears discusses the use of "civilization" as a key advertising concept for "animating" objects but does not infer how it shaped Americans' historical imaginations (*Fables of Abundance*, 196–234). Spears's *100 Years* and Jaffee's *New Nation of Goods* both highlight the role of traveling salesmen and earlier itinerant peddlers during the nineteenth century in creating a national market for consumer goods, but neither discusses the use of historical narrative in creating that market.
20. Hutchinson notes that the *Farmers' Advance* began to be published in 1871, three years after the Champion firms of Ohio commenced printing a trade paper (*Cyrus Hall McCormick: Harvest*, 491–92). Unfortunately, few copies of this quarterly are extant.
21. C. H. M'Cormick, "M'Cormick's Patent Reaping and Mowing Machine!" January 1853, bulletin; C. H. McCormick, "McCormick's Reaping and Mowing Machines," 1859, annual catalog, transcription, box 1, Mss 5X, MIHCC.
22. C. McCormick, "Reaping and Mowing Machines," 1859, 8–9, box 1, Mss 5X, MIHCC.

23. C. McCormick, "Reaping and Mowing Machines," 1859, 8–15, box 1, Mss 5X, MIHCC.
24. C. McCormick, "Reaping and Mowing Machines," 1859, 10, box 1, Mss 5X, MIHCC.
25. C. McCormick, "Reaping and Mowing Machines," 1859, 1–2, box 1, Mss 5X, MIHCC.
26. C. McCormick, "Reaping and Mowing Machines," 1859, 2–4, box 1, Mss 5X, MIHCC.
27. C. McCormick, "Reaping and Mowing Machines," 1859, 4–5, box 1, Mss 5X, MIHCC.
28. C. McCormick, "Reaping and Mowing Machines," 1859, 5–8, 15–25, box 1, Mss 5X, MIHCC.
29. C. H. McCormick and Bros., "McCormick's Reaper and Mower," 1861, annual catalog, Mss 5X, 1; "McCormick's Prize Harvesters," 1868, annual catalog, Mss 5X, 1; D. M. Osborne and Company, *1878: The Twenty Second Annual Pamphlet*, 1878, Mss 10Z, MIHCC.
30. C. H. McCormick and Bros., "McCormick's Reaper and Mower"; "McCormick's Prize Harvesters," 1868, Mss 5X; C. H. McCormick and Bros. to Agents and Farmers of the Country, "McCormicks' New Reaper Works," January 10, 1873, box 15, Mss 2A, MIHCC. Hutchinson includes extensive information about Cyrus McCormick's stances on political as well as Presbyterian sectionalism, including his vain efforts before and during the Civil War to defuse the conflict (*Cyrus Hall McCormick: Harvest*, 3–63, 202–73, 308–59).
31. C. McCormick, "Reaping and Mowing Machines," 1859, 1, box 1, Mss 5X, MIHCC.
32. M. T. Grattan to McCormick, January 30 and February 7, 1877; Peterson to McCormick, March 27, 1877; E. M. Brooks to McCormick, January 10, 1877, reel 209; Brooks to McCormick, May 8, 1877, reel 210, Mss 2X; McCormick and Bro. to H. H. Johnson, November 11, 1868, reel 109, Mss 1X, MIHCC.
33. W. J. Hanna to H. B. Mack, December 8, 1868, reel 109, Mss 1X; C. H. McCormick and Bro's., "Private Circular to Agents," March 1867, box 1, Mss 5X, MIHCC.
34. Brooks to McCormick, March 3, 1877, reel 209, Mss 2X; John Edgar, "To the Agents for the McCormick Machines," June 23, 1869, box 1, Mss 5X; C. H. and L. J. McCormick, "Two Gold Medals at Vienna Awarded the McCor-

mick!" September 20, 1873, ad copy, box 50; Hanna to C. H. McCormick I, September 13, 1879, box 52, Mss 2A, MIHCC; Hutchinson, *Cyrus Hall McCormick: Harvest*, 491–92; Winder, *American Reaper*, 120–21.

35. C. H. McCormick and Bro's., "Private Circular to Agents"; Edgar, "To the Agents," June 23, 1869, box 1, Mss 5X, MIHCC. Edgar's letter makes clear that subagents should not extend credit to homesteaders, renters, those badly in debt, those who live on untitled property, those on railroad or school land, and those who were unknown in the district.
36. C. McCormick, "Reaping and Mowing Machines," 1859, 5, box 1, Mss 5X, MIHCC.
37. Every catalog in the second half of the nineteenth century included testimonials, which stated the quality of the machines as tools as well as their economic value. C. McCormick, "Reaping and Mowing Machines," 1859, 5, 15–25, box 1, Mss 5X, MIHCC; C. W. Shanto, "A Wonderful Success: Great Northwestern Exposition," September 1879, pamphlet, box 2, Mss 5X; S. S. Pease to McCormick, May 4, 1877, reel 210, Mss 2X; C. N. Frazier, "Reminiscences of C. N. Frazier, September 6, 1930," in *Harvester Reminiscences*, ed. Herbert Kellar, 1930, 3, box 1, Reaper Centennial Celebration Records, 1923–36, Mss 1Q, MIHCC.
38. W. C. Rivers, "The Great Exhibition: The American Department," *New York Daily Times*, October 3, 1851; Horace Greeley, "The Crystal Palace and Its Lessons," *Graham's American Monthly Magazine of Literature, Art and Fashion*, May 1852, 473; Hutchinson, *Cyrus Hall McCormick: Seed Time*, 385–94.
39. Edgar, "To the Agents," June 23, 1869, box 1, Mss 5X, MIHCC; Brooks to McCormick, July 11 and 12, 1877, reel 210, Mss 2X, MIHCC.
40. Blanke, *Sowing the American Dream*, 33–38.
41. Blanke, *Sowing the American Dream*, 33, 46–51.
42. Blanke, *Sowing the American Dream*, 47–48; "Scales for Reapers and Mowers," *Prairie Farmer*, August 1855.
43. Frazier, "Reminiscences of C. N. Frazier," 1930, 3, box 1, Mss 1Q, MIHCC; Edgar, "To the Agents," June 23, 1869, box 1, Mss 5X, MIHCC.
44. "Great Reaper Trial! A Grand Fizzle!" ca. 1874–79, circular; "The Rattle of the Reapers: The McCormick on the War Path!" June 1, 1882, circular, box 2, Mss 5X; "Grand Exhibition of Self-Binding Harvesters at Decatur, IL," ca. 1882; Lake Ransom, "All Agents Should Read This Carefully," June 13, 1878, box 31, Mss 10Z; Hanna to C. H. McCormick, September

13, 1879, box 52; Hanna to C. H. McCormick I, August 29, 1881, box 53, Mss 2A; C. M. Fullerton, "Reminiscences of C.M. Fullerton, September 5, 1930," in *Harvester Reminiscences*, ed. Herbert Kellar, 1930, 3, box 1, Mss 1Q, MIHCC.

45. "Three Great American Inventions," *Valley Farmer*, August, 1860; "Invention, the Ally of Civilization," *Scientific American*, February 13, 1864; "Horace Greeley's Lecture to the Mechanics," *Evening Bulletin* (San Francisco), August 19, 1859; Kellar, *Solon Robinson*, 1:87, 2:668, 682; *Chicago Daily Democrat*, December 23, 1851, quoted in Hutchinson, *Cyrus Hall McCormick: Seed-Time*, 271.

46. H. W. Bellows, "The Moral Significance of the Crystal Palace," *North American Review*, July 1854, 14, 24; "Machinery as a Gospel Worker," *Christian Examiner*, November 18, 1869, 2, 10, 13–14; J. A. James, "Preaching," *Millennial Harbinger Devoted to Primitive Christianity* 2, no. 1 (January 1859): 292.

47. Neill, *History of Houston County*, 490; Andreas, *Illustrated Historical Atlas*, 61.

48. Winder's *American Reaper* is a fantastic geographic analysis of "patent pools" in the harvester industry (37–64).

49. D. M. Osborne and Company, "Harvesting Machinery," 1879, annual catalog, box 31, Mss 10Z, 10; Fullerton, "Reminiscences of C. M. Fullerton," 1930, 3, box 1, Mss 1Q, MIHCC. Hutchinson's *Cyrus Hall McCormick: Harvest* describes the complexity of patent law, license relationships, and negotiations in great detail; however, it excludes the reality of product comparison in real time (536–72).

50. C. H. and L. J. McCormick, "C. H. and L. J. McCormick: Harvesting Machinery," 1879, annual catalog, box 2, Mss 5X; Walter A. Wood M. and R. M. Company, "Harvesting Machines Manufactured Exclusively by Walter A. Wood," 1882, annual catalog, box 42, 7; William Deering and Company, "Deering Twine Binders, Reapers and Mowers," 1884, annual catalog, box 14, Mss 10Z, MIHCC; "Another Self Binder," *American Farmer*, August 1879, 8; "Wire in Wheat," *Chicago Daily Tribune*, February 26, 1879, 7.

51. C. H. and L. J. McCormick, "C. H. and L. J. McCormick," 1879, annual catalog, box 2, Mss 5X, MIHCC.

52. McCormick and McCormick, "C. H. and L. J. McCormick," 1879, box 2, Mss 5X, MIHCC.

53. E. K. Butler to Cyrus Hall McCormick I, August 20, 1880; Butler to Cyrus Hall McCormick II, August 12, 1881; Hanna to McCormick II, August 19, 1881, box 53, Mss 2A, MIHCC; Hutchinson, *Cyrus Hall McCormick: Harvest*, 556. Laird details the evolution of advertising and suggests that professional advertisers did not emerge until the turn of the century. Indeed, McCormick did not hire its first advertising specialist until the summer of 1900 (*Advertising Progress*, 100–151).
54. McCormick Harvesting Machine Company, circular to agents, February 6, March 16, March 20, March 22, and March 29, 1880, reel 472, Mss 1X, MIHCC.
55. McCormick Harvesting Machine Company, circular to agents, May 31, October 8, December 18, 1880, reel 471, Mss 10Z; McCormick Harvesting Machine Company, "McCormick Harvesting Machine Co's Illustrated Annual Catalogue," 1881, fair ed. catalog, box 2, Mss 5X, MIHCC.
56. Lee Grady, "McCormick's Reaper at 100," *Wisconsin Magazine of History*, Spring 2001, 13–15; Orvell, *Real Thing*, 36–38; "Testing of the First Reaping Machine," 1883, advertising poster, WHI-2497, Wisconsin Historical Images, accessed June 3, 2022, http://www.wisconsinhistory.org/whi/; "A Historical Picture," *Western Rural*, May 12, 1883, box 2, Mss 5X, MIHCC.
57. D. M. Osborne and Company, "Twenty-Fourth Annual Greeting," 1880, annual catalog, box 31; William Deering, "The Leader Reapers, Deering Mowers and Droppers and Deering Self-Binding Harvesters," 1881, annual catalog, box 14, Mss 10Z, MIHCC.
58. McCormick Harvesting Machine Company, "McCormick Machines Illustrated, 1886," box 2, Mss 5X, MIHCC; McCormick Harvesting Machine Company, "The Improvements of Fifty-Five Years," 1886, advertising card, WHI-36208 and WHI-36369, Wisconsin Historical Images, accessed June 3, 2022, http://www.wisconsinhistory.org/whi/.
59. McCormick Harvesting Machine Company, "*Westward the Course of Empire [. . .]*," 1886, advertising poster, WHI-2496, Wisconsin Historical Images, accessed June 3, 2022, http://www.wisconsinhistory.org/whi/.
60. "The Ball Just Opened!" 1883; "Rattle of the Reapers"; H. R. Gould to Agents, June 14, 1884, box 2, Mss 5X, MIHCC; McCormick Harvesting Machine Company, *Battle of Shiloh*, 1885, poster, Library of Congress, digital ID: PGA 00540, accessed June 3, 2022, http://loc.gov/pictures/resource/pga.00540.
61. Deering and Company, "Deering Twine Binders," 1884, annual catalog, box 14, Mss 10Z, MIHCC; Walter A. Wood M. and H. M. Company,

"Harvesting Machines," 1882, annual catalog, box 42; Osborne and Company, "Twenty-Fourth Annual Greeting," 1880, annual catalog, box 31, MIHCC.

62. Hutchinson, *Cyrus Hall McCormick: Harvest*, 704; Winder, *American Reaper*, 106–14; Chandler, *Visible Hand*, 407–8.

2. PRODUCING INVENTION

1. Bederman, *Manliness and Civilization*, 31–41.
2. E. F. Baker to McCormick Harvesting Machine Company (hereafter McCormick HMC), May 12, 1893, reel 267, Mss 2X, MIHCC; Domosh, "'Civilized' Commerce."
3. R. B. Swift to Culver and Tracey, June 1, 1893, reel 336, Mss 1X; Daily to J. B. Heywood, June 16, 1893, reel 336, Mss 1X; McCormick II to W. Pretyman, June 27, 1893, reel 337, Mss 1X, MIHCC.
4. James B. Campbell, *World's Columbian Exposition Illustrated: Devoted to the Interests of the Columbian Exposition, Art and Literature*, 3 vols. (Chicago: World's Columbian Exposition, 1893): 156–57, transcription, box 2, Mss 6X, MIHCC.
5. Swift to Culver and Tracey, June 1, 1893, reel 336, Mss 1X; Campbell, *World's Columbian Exposition Illustrated*, 156–57, MIHCC.
6. Campbell, *World's Columbian Exposition Illustrated*, 156–57, MIHCC; Wisconsin Historical Society and McCormick HMC, "McCormick Display at Columbian Exposition," WHI-60572, Wisconsin Historical Images, accessed June 3, 2022, http://www.wisconsinhistory.org/whi/feature/mccormick/.
7. Campbell, *World's Columbian Exposition Illustrated*, 156–57, MIHCC.
8. Campbell, *World's Columbian Exposition Illustrated*, 156–57, MIHCC.
9. "Established 1831: Sixty-Second Annual Catalogue; McCormick Machines, 1893," box 3, McCormick HMC, Advertising Materials and Catalogs, Mss 5X, MIHCC; McCormick Harvesting Machine Company, "The McCormick Annual Catalog," 1893, WHI-29409, Wisconsin Historical Images, accessed June 3, 2022, http://www.wisconsinhistory.org/whi/feature/mccormick/.
10. Ardrey, *American Agricultural Implements*.
11. Winder, *American Reaper*, 105–44.
12. Clark Lane to Aultman, Miller and Company, February 10, 1897, box 1, John F. Steward Papers, Mss BJ; Clark Lane, "The First Reaper: BE IT KNOWN

and DISTINCTLY UNDERSTOOD THAT MCCORMICK DID NOT MAKE the FIRST REAPING MACHINE," *Farm Implement News*, October 9, 1893, box 1, Mss BJ; Russell Parsons to John Steward, December 30, 1896, box 1, Mss BJ; McCormick II to Nettie F. McCormick, May 8, 1893, reel 3, Mss 3C, MIHCC; "Congress of Inventors," *Chicago Tribune*, December 11, 1892.

13. William Deering and Company, *The Foreign Commissioners Visit the Northwest and Learn Why Bonanza Farming Pays*, 1894, Abraham Lincoln Presidential Library, Springfield IL.
14. The "harmony of interests" ideology is described by Wallace as a Christian industrialist response to radical producerism, justifying the economic order (*Rockdale*, 350). McMath and Hild outline the producer unity among populist farmers and laborers (McMath, *American Populism*, 50–82; Hild, *Greenbackers*).
15. A. Wallace, *Rockdale*, 243–46, 293–95, 394–97; Wilentz, *Chants Democratic*; Montgomery, *Fall of the House*.
16. Ozanne, *Century*, 3–28; Cyrus McCormick II to Day, March 10, 1886, box 11, Mss 8C; Cyrus McCormick II, "About the Committee," February 1886, box 11, Mss 8C, MIHCC.
17. "Will Control Their Own Business," 1886, box 3, Mss 5X, MIHCC.
18. Ozanne, *Century*, 3–28. During the 1894 Pullman Strike, McCormick II wrote about his worries that "our men" might be "drawn into crowds and mobs." McCormick II to N. F. McCormick, July 9, 11, 1894; McCormick II to Butler, July 13, 1894, reel 4, Mss 3C, MIHCC.
19. Hirsch, "Efforts of the Grange." The company's response to the Grangers, as well as to the National Farmers' Alliance cooperative price initiatives, was to quote slightly reduced prices for bulk purchases that did not include shipping. They then had their regional agents target the leaders of local alliances, offering a still lower price for that individual. In that way they systematically broke resistance by "drawing them away from the Alliances one by one." R. B. Swift to J. S. Wogan, May 20, 1890; Butler to M. D. Coffeen, April 25, 1891, reel 297, Mss 1X, MIHCC.
20. Ridge, *Ignatius Donnelly*, 247; Postel, *Populist Vision*, 126–33; Beinhauer, "Development of the Grange," 614; Carstensen and Roazen, "Foreign Markets"; Evans, *Bound in Twine*, 121–26.
21. Ridge, *Ignatius Donnelly*, 288; Donnelly, *Cyrus H. McCormick*, 65; George Brewster to C. H. and L. J. McCormick, July 4, 1877, reel 210, Mss 2X, MIHCC.

22. Butler to W. H. Town, May 31, 1890; Butler to N. B. Fulmer, June 28, 1890, reel 297, Mss 1X; Butler to Chas. F. Adams, June 16, 1893, reel 327, Mss 1X, MIHCC.
23. John D. Hicks, "Omaha Platform, July, 1892," in Hicks, *Populist Revolt*, 439–44.
24. O'Malley, *Face Value*, 124–61.
25. Walter A. Wood to C. H. McCormick II, December 5, 1889; H. J. Shields to William Deering and Company, December 23, 1890; C. H. McCormick II to Adriance Play and Company, January 10, 1891, telegraph; McCormick HMC to Agents, January 8, 1891, box 1, Mss W, MIHCC; "To Fight the Harvester Trust: Farmers of North Dakota Will Take Matter into Court," *New York Times*, January 7, 1891.
26. Plano Manufacturing Company, "Plano Manufacturing Co.," 1891, annual catalog, box 33, Mss 10Z, MIHCC.
27. Mallock, *Labour*; "Labor and Ability," *Chicago Daily Tribune*, November 11, 1894, 28; National Association, *Farm Implement News Daily*, 113.
28. "Established 1831: Fifty-Fourth Annual Catalogue: McCormick Machines, 1885"; "Established 1831: Fifty-Sixth Annual Catalogue: McCormick Machines, 1887"; "Bindlochine," 1892, box 3, Mss 5X, MIHCC.
29. "Annual Catalogue: McCormick Machines, 1887"; "Established 1831: Fifty-Seventh Annual Catalogue; McCormick Machines, 1888," box 3, Mss 5X, MIHCC.
30. Butler to S. B. Town, May 2, 1890, reel 297, Mss 1X, MIHCC; "Annual Catalogue: McCormick Machines, 1887," box 3, Mss 5X; A. Mayer to S. B. Town, June 10, 1893, reel 337, Mss 1X, MIHCC; Butler to S. W. Park, April 1, 1889, and May 13, 1890, reel 297, Mss 1X, MIHCC.
31. "Established 1831: Fifty Fourth Annual Catalogue: McCormick Machines, 1885"; "McCormick Harvesting Machine Company, 1893," annual catalog, box 3, Mss 5X, MIHCC.
32. "Established 1831: Fifty Ninth Year; The McCormick Annual Catalogue, 1890," box 3, Mss 5X, MIHCC; Wisconsin Historical Society and McCormick Harvesting Machine Company, "The McCormick Annual Catalog," 1890, WHI-86968, Wisconsin Historical Images, accessed June 3, 2022, http://www.wisconsinhistory.org/whi/feature/mccormick/.
33. "Established 1831," 1890, box 3, Mss 5X, MIHCC.
34. Butler to S. W. Park, May 13, 1890, reel 297, Mss 1X, MIHCC.

35. McCormick HMC, "The Farmers Grange Movement," 1889, box 3, Mss 5X, MIHCC.
36. The firm annually sent out prefabricated advertisement copy to their agents to post in local newspapers. In 1893 it sent out four sets of copy for agents to rotate in weekly readers. "McCormick Advertisements," April 20, 1893, box 3, Mss 5X, MIHCC.
37. "The Man for the Time," *Easter's Implement World*, February 28, 1893, box 134, Cyrus H. McCormick II, Subject Files, Mss 2C, MIHCC; "Farming in America," *Greater Chicago*, August 4, 1898, box 134, Mss 2C, MIHCC.
38. "Sixty-Third Annual Catalogue: McCormick Machines, 1894," box 3, Mss 5X, MIHCC; Wisconsin Historical Society and McCormick Harvesting Machine Company, "The McCormick Annual Catalog," 1894, WHI-4415, Wisconsin Historical Images, accessed June 3, 2022, http://www.wisconsinhistory.org/whi/feature/mccormick/.
39. "Sixty-Third Annual Catalogue," 5, 13, box 3, Mss 5X, MIHCC.
40. "Sixty-Third Annual Catalogue," 37, box 3, Mss 5X, MIHCC.
41. Bookwalter, *If Not Silver, What?*, 21–24.
42. *Lincoln Freie Presse* to McCormick II, July 4, 1896; McCormick II to *Lincoln Freie Presse*, July 8, 1896, box 11, Mss 8C, MIHCC; "M'Cormick Denounces Popocracy: He Looks upon Free Silver as a National Calamity," *Chicago Daily Tribune*, September 2, 1896, 3.
43. Butler to Sales Agents, August 17, 1896, box 11, Mss 8C, MIHCC "What Bryan's Election Would Mean," *Chicago Daily Tribune*, September 2, 1896, 6.
44. "Factory Men Hear Him: M'Kinley Speaks to Clubs from Springfield, O.," *Chicago Daily Tribune*, October 2, 1896, 3.
45. "New Silver Certificates: Beautiful Designs of the Bill Shortly to Be Issued, How This Change Has Taken Place," *New York Times*, March 1, 1896, 25. The "education" series included one-, two-, and five-dollar bills that were briefly in circulation. Pictures and a discussion of the "education" series artwork are in Hessler, *U.S. Essay*, 98–133.
46. McCormick II to Louis Dent, August 14, 1896, reel 7, Mss 3C, MIHCC.
47. McCormick II to George E. Adams, March 8, 1894, reel 4, Mss 3C, MIHCC.
48. "New $10 Silver Certificates: Will Bear Vignettes of C. H. McCormick and Eli Whitney," *Chicago Daily Tribune*, December 25, 1896, 8.

49. J. F. Steward to Walter A. Wood Mowing and Reaping Machine Company, January 13, 1897, box 1, Mss BJ; "Established 1831: Sixty-First Annual Catalogue; McCormick Machines, 1892," box 3, Mss 5X, 5; "Annual Catalog: McCormick Machines, 1892," 4, box 3, Mss 5X, MIHCC; McCormick Harvesting Machines Company, "Which Side Are You On?" 1888, advertising card, WHI-86304, Wisconsin Historical Images, accessed June 3, 2022, http://www.wisconsinhistory.org/whi/.
50. J. F. Steward to Ginn and Company, January 15, 1898, box 1, Mss BJ; Harvester Company to John Russell Parsons, December 31, 1896, box 1, Mss BJ, MIHCC.
51. Charles Deering et al. to John G. Carlisle, December 29, 1896, box 1, Mss BJ, MIHCC; Parsons to Steward, December 30, 1896; Parsons to Edward Murphy, December 30, 1896; Parsons to David Hill, January 2, 1897, box 1, Mss BJ, MIHCC.
52. Steward and Wood, "Advertisements on United States Bank Notes," box 1, Mss BJ, MIHCC.
53. McCormick II to Carlisle, January 6, 1897, reel 8, Mss 3C, MIHCC.
54. Steward to Deering, January 11, 1897, box 1, Mss BJ; J. G. Carlisle to C. M. Johnson, January 14, 1897, box 1, Mss BJ, MIHCC; "Gossips in a Flutter: Wife of Secretary Francis Breaks a Precedent," *Chicago Daily Tribune*, January 8, 1897, 8.
55. Deering Company, *Farm Machinery*, January 13, 1897, box 1, Mss BJ, MIHCC.
56. E. K. Reifsnider to Deering Harvester Company, January 18, 1897, box 1, Mss BJ; "Pounding the Same Old Straw," *Farmers' Advance*, May 1897, box 134, Mss 2C, MIHCC.
57. Steward, *Overlooked Pages*; Steward to Deering, January 13, 1897, box 1, Mss BJ, MIHCC; Rodney B. Swift, "Who Invented the Reaper," *Implement Age*, April 15, 1897, press clippings, box 134, Mss 2C; Louis Dent to Frances Smith, April 18, 1905, box 215, Mss 1E, MIHCC.
58. "Review of Recent Additions to Reaper History," *Implement Age*, April 29, 1897, box 134, Mss 2C; R. B. Swift, "To the Editor," November 2, 1898; "Correspondence from W. P. Nolan to J. F. Steward," November 21, 1898, box 64, Mss AC, MIHCC.
59. Deering Harvest Company, "Forty Harvest Seasons: 1858–1898," folder 740, box 95, Mss 6Z, MIHCC.
60. *Retrospective Report on the International Universal Exposition at Paris*, box 2, Mss 6X, 456–65; Stanley McCormick to Charles Richards Dodge, July

23, 1900, box 2; S. E. Morss to Harold McCormick, March 25, 1901, box 3, Stanley McCormick Papers, Mss 1G, MIHCC.

61. Harold McCormick to Stanley McCormick, August 15, 1900, box 2, Mss 1G, MIHCC; Winder, *American Reaper*, 18–19.
62. Nettie Fowler McCormick to C. H. McCormick II, September 16, 1897, October 4, 1897; N. McCormick to A. McCormick Blaine, July 30, 1897; Nettie Fowler McCormick to Earl Butler, September 22, 1897, box 7, Nettie Fowler McCormick Papers, Mss 1B, MIHCC.
63. McCormick Jr., "Memorandum on the Creation of International Harvester," August 13, 1902, box 30, Mss 2C; John D. Rockefeller Jr. to Harold McCormick, June 23, 1902, box 605; Edith Rockefeller McCormick to Anita McCormick Blaine, July 1903, box 453, Mss 1E, MIHCC.
64. Kramer attributes the 1897 shift from McCormick to Deering industrial authority to sales superiority in the harvester industry and the Deerings' successful vertical integration, which the McCormicks could not keep pace with financially. In light of the massive amount of investment capital available to the McCormicks from their close relationship with the Rockefellers, this explanation seems unlikely. The Deerings' public relations and history-advertising victory over the McCormicks warrants greater consideration in understanding the precipitous rise in the Deerings' market share and the McCormicks' move to seek a merger. See "Harvester and High Finance," 288–89.

3. HISTORICAL LABORERS

1. International Harvester, "McCormick Reaper Centennial Source Material (1831–1931)," 1931, 7, box 643, Mss 6Z, MIHCC.
2. Lyons, *McCormick Reaper Legend*; Hutchinson, *Cyrus Hall McCormick: Harvest*, 627–42.
3. Like any other professional group during the Progressive Era, academically trained historians need to be considered within their social and cultural context as trained laborers competing for jobs. This proposition becomes that much more dynamic when considering their pursuit of careers outside of the university within the emerging corporate order. The study of historical professionals can benefit by borrowing from the labor-oriented histories of capitalism and advertising. Lear, in *Fables of Abundance*, details the struggle of advertising professionals and artists to demonstrate the concrete value of their expertise in a cultural

climate that dismissed their labor as unnecessary and later in a corporate climate that undermined their identities as artists. Zunz, in *Making America Corporate*, points out that new professionals were anxious to stake their claim in the corporate order through proving their utility and initiating bureaucracy building to make the institution, and their jobs, viable for the long term.

4. Novick, *That Noble Dream*, 48–50.
5. Hutchinson, *Cyrus Hall McCormick: Harvest*, 37–63, 82; H. Greeley to W. L. Dayton, July 14, 1862, box 16, Mss 1A, MIHCC. Hutchinson devoted the second chapter of his second volume to exclusively discussing Cyrus McCormick's political activities leading up to and during the war. Footnote 50 on pages 56–57 in *Cyrus Hall McCormick: Harvest* discusses the intentional destruction of a letter from Cyrus McCormick I to J. E. Thompson, a former Buchanan cabinet member and Confederate associate in Canada.
6. William McCormick, quoted in Hounshell, *From the American System*, 166.
7. Hounshell details the antiquated mode of production at the reaper works, which had difficulty producing more complicated implements (*From the American System*, 153–88). Ozanne discusses the labor unrest at the McCormick works during the Civil War, including more than six strikes, which are conspicuously absent from most of the company's histories (*Century*, 5). Lerner covers the McCormicks' response to monetary inflation during the war, a problem that got so out of hand that at one point William McCormick proposed suspending production of reapers all together ("Investment Uncertainty"). Olmstead and Rhode touch on the increased number of firms producing reapers during the Civil War ("Beyond the Threshold," 27–28). Gates looks into the contributions of agriculture to the Civil War and puts the production of reapers at 250,000 for the five-year period of the war (*Agriculture*, 233–34).
8. Gies, "Great Reaper War." Hutchinson, in *Cyrus Hall McCormick: Seed-Time*, covers the legal and competitive aspects of the reaper wars extensively in six chapters.
9. Lincoln and Stanton met in 1855, when they both worked as lawyers for John Manny in defense of a patent-infringement accusation brought by McCormick. Stanton's skillful litigation in this case is what is said to have convinced Lincoln to appoint him secretary of war and more immediately convinced McCormick to make him his lawyer. This story

frequently shows up in McCormick's histories (Levene, "Lincoln and McCormick," 98–99).

10. Levene, "Lincoln and McCormick," 101n27; Flower, *Edwin McMasters Stanton*, 114.
11. Flower, *Edwin McMasters Stanton*, 114.
12. Edwin Stanton et al., "Argument for the Applicant," in Patent Office Records, *McCormick Extension Case: Patent of 1847*, 36:260, Mss 4X, MIHCC.
13. "One of the People," "The Reaper Man and Seceasion [*sic*]," letter to the editor, *Chicago Tribune*, January 28, 1861, 2.
14. Dent to F. Smith, April 18, 1905, box 215, Mss 1E; Stanley McCormick to Dodge, July 23, 1900; Stanley McCormick to Bonet Maury, January 31, 1900, box 2, Mss 1G, MIHCC.
15. Harold F. McCormick to S. E. Morss, March 23, 1901, box 2; Stanley McCormick, "Interview at Commissioner Peck's Office," October 24, 1899, box 1, Mss 1G; Cyrus McCormick II to Salem Pattison, August 8, 1900, box 121, Mss 2C, MIHCC.
16. Harold McCormick to Stanley McCormick, August 15, 1900; Stanley McCormick, "Copies of Correspondence to and from Mr. James Deering," July 27, 1900, box 2, Mss 1G, MIHCC. These ten pages of transcribed letters demonstrate the McCormick plan of abrasively questioning the evidentiary base for the Deering exhibit. It is most striking that only a fraction of their protests regard their father's machine specifically.
17. "McCormick Biographical Association," charter 1900, box 453, Mss 1E; Cyrus McCormick II to Anita Blaine, June 28, 1900, box 121, Mss 2C, MIHCC.
18. Cyrus McCormick II to Frances Smith, September 26, 1907, box 4, Mss 6X, MIHCC. On the other hand, in 1909, they paid $500 to the James T. White Publishing Company to "correct" an article in the *National Cyclopedia of American Biography*, which credited Robert McCormick with the invention of the reaper. MBA meeting minutes, June 4, 1909, box 3, Mss AA, MIHCC. A similar instance is mentioned in Lyons, *McCormick Reaper Legend*, 200, claiming that the MBA spent $4,000 to correct an entry in the *Encyclopedia of American Manufacturers*. Pattison to Anita McCormick Blaine, February 5, 1901; Salem Pattison, "Report to the Members of the McCormick Biographical Association," April 16, 1903, box 363, Mss 1E, MIHCC.

19. For comparison to another emerging profession, Harold McCormick hired the company's first advertising professional that same year at $2,500 for half-time labor. Harold McCormick to Clifford Wild, October 10, 1900, box 121, Mss 2C; Salem Pattison to Cyrus McCormick II, December 28, 1900, box 363, Mss 1E; Pattison to Harold McCormick, October 1, 1898, box 2, Mss 1F, MIHCC; "Cornell Alumni Notes," *Cornell Alumni News*, January 27, 1901, accessed January 13, 2014, http://dspace.library.cornell.edu/handle/1813/3158.
20. Salem Pattison, "Report of Salem G. Pattison to Mrs. Emmons Blaine, Secretary Biographical Association," October 26, 1900, box 363, Mss 1E; Salem Pattison to Stanley McCormick, June 15, 1900; Cyrus McCormick II to Stanley McCormick, May 10, 1900, box 2, Mss 1G; Cyrus McCormick II to Pattison, July 5, 1900, box 121, Mss 2C, MIHCC; Pattison, *McCormick Extension Case*.
21. Pattison, "Report of Salem G. Pattison," October 26, 1900; Salem Pattison to Anita McCormick Blaine, October 21, 1901, box 363, Mss 1E, MIHCC.
22. Pattison to McCormick Blaine, September 26, 1902; Pattison, "Report of Salem G. Pattison," October 26, 1900; Pattison, "Report of Salem G. Pattison," April 16, 1903, box 363, Mss 1E, MIHCC.
23. Pattison, "Report of Salem G. Pattison," October 26, 1900; Salem Pattison to David Schaff, August 18, 1900; Pattison to Cyrus McCormick II, May 11, 1902; Pattison to Cyrus McCormick II, October 19, 1905, box 1, Mss AA, MIHCC.
24. Beyond his work as a historian, Pattison spent substantial time as a university administrator at Carthage College, Hastings College, and Taylor University before joining the McCormick Biographical Association in 1900. However, after his time with the McCormicks, he worked for insurance companies from 1903 to 1908, before again becoming a university administrator at Westminster College and ultimately a professor of history at Coe College by 1914. "Personal," *Indiana School Journal* 37 (1892): 455; Salem Pattison to C. H. McCormick II, April 16, 1915, box 363, Mss 1E, MIHCC; Justin Price, "2010 Reconnaissance Survey of the Pillar of Fire Structures and Historical Context," 2010, cultural resource study, Metropolitan State College of Denver, accessed February 13, 2014, http://www.ci.westminster.co.us/Portals/0/Repository/Documents/ExploreWestminster/Pillar%20of%20Fire%20survey

%20Report%20%28add%20appendices%29.pdf; "Cornell Alumni Notes."

25. Cyrus McCormick II to Anita McCormick Blaine, October 8, 1900; Pattison to Cyrus McCormick II, September 7, 1900, box 121, Mss 2C; Pattison to McCormick Blaine, October 26, 1900, and December 3, 1900, box 363, Mss 1E, MIHCC.
26. Salem Pattison to Anita Blaine McCormick, September 27, 1900; Pattison, "Report of Salem G. Pattison," October 26, 1900; Pattison to Cyrus McCormick II, December 28, 1900, box 363, Mss 1E, MIHCC.
27. Cyrus McCormick II to Pattison, August 17, 1900, box 121, Mss 2C; David Schaff to Salem Pattison, August 1, 1900, box 4, Mss AA; Pattison to McCormick Blaine, April 16, 1903, box 363, Mss 1E, MIHCC.
28. Watson, "Carnegie Ladies, Lady Carnegies," 168–69.
29. "Gift for a Hall of Fame: New York University to Commemorate Great Americans," *New York Times*, March 6, 1900, 12; "The Hall of Fame," *New York Times*, October 12, 1905, 8; "Memorial Day Exercises," *New York Times*, May 30, 1901, 12. The Hall of Fame still stands to this day on what is now the campus of Bronx Community College and is open to the public for tours. "Hall of Fame of Great Americans," Bronx Community College, accessed December 1, 2010, http://www.bcc.cuny.edu/halloffame/.
30. S. G. Pattison to D. S. Schaff, August 6, 1900, in Frances Smith, compiled documents on the Hall of Fame, May 11, 1910, 2, box 4, Mss AA, MIHCC.
31. Pattison to Schaff, August 18, 1900, in Smith, compiled documents, 3–3.5, box 4, Mss AA, MIHCC.
32. "Names for Hall of Fame," *New York Times*, October 11, 1900, in Smith, compiled documents, 14, box 4, Mss AA, MIHCC.
33. Harold McCormick to W. H. P. Faunce, n.d. [but in response to a letter from August 30, 1904]; Faunce to H. McCormick, September 7, 1904, in Smith, compiled documents, 6, box 4, Mss AA, MIHCC; H. McCormick to Faunce, September 15, 1904, box 4, Mss AA, MIHCC.
34. C. H. McCormick II, memorandum, December 5, 1904, in Smith, compiled documents, 8–9, box 4, Mss AA, MIHCC.
35. Robert Parkinson, invoice to C. H. McCormick II, November 30, 1911, box 355, Mss 2C, MIHCC.
36. Ardrey, *American Agricultural Implements*; Robert L. Ardrey to Harold McCormick, April 1, 1901, box 323, Mss 1E, MIHCC.

37. Ardrey to H. McCormick, April 1, 1901, box 323, Mss 1E; "Material Taken East by Mr. Cyrus H. McCormick in Re: Hall of Fame," March 7, 1905, box 1, Mss AA, MIHCC.
38. Frank Abial Flower to Salem Pattison, May 27, 1900, box 453, Mss 1E, MIHCC.
39. Flower to Pattison, May 27, 1900, box 453, Mss 1E, MIHCC.
40. Flower, *Edwin McMasters Stanton*, 79; Flower to Pattison, May 27, 1900, box 453; Pattison to McCormick Blaine, February 5, 1901; Pattison, "Report to the Members," 2, box 363, Mss 1E, MIHCC.
41. Stanley McCormick to Members of the Biographical Association, March 3, 1905, box 398, Mss 1E, MIHCC.
42. Cyrus McCormick II to Nettie Fowler McCormick, February 18, 1905; Cyrus McCormick II to the Members of the Biographical Association, March 16, 1905, box 398, Mss 1E; C. H. McCormick II to Stanley McCormick, March 18, 1905, box 1, Mss AA, MIHCC.
43. Cyrus McCormick II, memorandum, March 18, 1905, box 1, Mss AA; Frederick Jackson Turner to Cyrus McCormick II, March 20, 1905, box 398, Mss 1E, MIHCC.
44. C. McCormick II to the Members, March 27, 1905, box 398, Mss 1E, MIHCC.
45. C. H. McCormick II, memorandum to the Members of the Biographical Association, March 27, 1905, box 1, Mss AA, MIHCC; C. H. McCormick II to Turner, March 22, 1905, box 2, Wis Mss VJ, RGTP; Turner, *Reuben Gold Thwaites*; Lauck, "Prairie Historians."
46. C. McCormick II to the Members, March 27, 1900, box 398, Mss 1E; "Material Taken East," box 1, Mss AA, MIHCC; C. McCormick II, "Memoir," 1885, 1–23, box 396, Mss 1E, MIHCC.
47. Cyrus McCormick II to Reuben Thwaites, April 14, 1905, box 2; Salem Pattison to Reuben Thwaites, April 22, 1905, Wis Mss VJ, RGTP.
48. Pattison to Thwaites, May 11, 1905; Thwaites to Pattison, April 25, 1905, box 2, Wis Mss VJ, RGTP.
49. Thwaites, "Cyrus Hall McCormick," 255.
50. C. H. McCormick to N. F. McCormick, April 13, 1905, box 1, Mss AA; Robert Parkinson to Cyrus McCormick II, April 11, 1905, box 398, Mss 1E, MIHCC.
51. International Harvester Company, "Memorandum of Material to Be Sent to Commissioner Smith," April 10, 1907, box 37, Mss 2C, MIHCC;

Ozanne, *Century*, 71–72; Casson, "The Romance of the Reaper," *Everybody's Magazine* 17, no. 6 (December 1907): 755–66; Casson, *Romance of the Reaper*, 45; Casson, *Romance of Steel.*

52. Frances Smith to Members of the Biographical Association, June 4, 1908; Cyrus McCormick II, memorandum, January 25, 1909, box 2, Mss AA, MIHCC.

53. Harold McCormick to F. Smith, February 26, 1909; C. H. McCormick II, memorandum, January 23, 1909, box 3; F. Smith, memorandum, December 3, 1908; F. Smith to the Members of the Biographical Association, June 4, 1908, box 2, Mss AA, MIHCC.

54. N. F. McCormick to F. G. Brown and A. C. McClurg Publishers, May 26, 1908; F. Smith to C. H. McCormick II, April 30, 1909, in Smith, compiled documents, box 4, Mss AA, MIHCC.

55. In addition to its own article commemorating Cyrus Hall McCormick, International Harvester's magazine published twelve excerpts from prominent newspapers and magazines that were also about McCormick. "Echoes from the Press," *Harvester World* 1, no. 3 (December 1909): 2–4.

56. Nolan R. Best, "Cyrus Hall McCormick," *Harvester World* 1, no. 3 (December 1909): 1–2. The secretary of the Illinois State Board of Agriculture, J. K. Dickirson, discusses the ceremonial plans at Champaign for the Farmer's Hall of Fame and also invited Cyrus H. McCormick to contribute an essay to a volume that the state board was preparing on the value of the reaper. This is a great example of other groups producing the MBA's version of history unsolicited. Dickirson to MBA, 1909, box 3, Mss AA; F. Smith, memorandum, December 3, 1908, box 2, Mss AA, MIHCC.

57. McCormick and Shields, *Robert McCormick, Inventor*; R. H. McCormick II to C.H McCormick II, October 18, 1910, box 4, Mss AA, MIHCC; "Poe Gets a Place in Hall of Fame," *New York Times*, October 22, 1910, 1.

58. Herbert Kellar to H. L. Boyle, March 21, 1941, Special Reports File: "Civil War, Influence of the Reaper upon, Compiled 1924," March 1943, box 2, Mss AD, MIHCC. In this report Kellar explains to an interested International Harvester employee why the McCormick company did so poorly during the Civil War—a history never acknowledged in the works he produced for the family or International Harvester. C. McCormick, *Century of the Reaper*, 63; Herbert Kellar to C. H. McCormick II, Anita McCormick Blaine, and Harold McCormick, February 3, 1932; "General

Report of the MHA for the Period January 1, 1931 to January 30, 1932," 11, box 35, Mss AC, MIHCC; International Harvester, "History and Development of International Harvester," 1976, 6, box 477, Mss 6Z, MIHCC.

59. Kellar to C. H. McCormick II, April 12, 1930, box 9, Mss AC, MIHCC.
60. Paxson, *Civil War*, 59; Schlesinger, *Political and Social History*, 185.
61. Longstreet, *Chicago*, 39; Lewis, *Chicago*, 93; Clark, *Farms and Farmers*, 190; R. McLaughlin, *Heartland*, 89; Ebeling, *Fruited Plain*, 167; Theobald, "Lion of the Hour," 41; Bruce, *History of Virginia*, 532.

4. REALIGNING HISTORY

1. "Chautauqua Proves a Great Success," *Glenwood Opinion*, August 22, 1907; "Chautauqua Is in Full Blast," *Glenwood Opinion*, August 10, 1911; "Glenwood Chautauq'a Begins Saturday," *Glenwood Opinion*, August 4, 1913; Canning, *Most American Thing*, 71–97.
2. "Glenwood Chautauq'a Begins Saturday"; "Glenwood Chautauqua," *Glenwood Opinion*, August 14, 1913; "The Chautauqua Closed Last Saturday Evening," *Glenwood Opinion*, August 18, 1913.
3. "Glenwood Chautauqua Begins Saturday"; "Chautauqua Closed"; Sanders, *Roots of Reform*, 1–9.
4. "Chautauqua Closed Last Saturday"; International Harvester Company of America, "The Dawn of Plenty," 1913, 5, 17, 32, folder 4200, Mss 6Z, MIHCC.
5. "Chautauqua Closed Last Saturday"; "The Dawn of Plenty Grows," *Harvester World* 4, no. 8 (August 1913): 4.
6. Building on Marchand, *Creating the Corporate Soul*, this chapter investigates the means through which corporate imagery was spread and sustained. The use of imagery recalling history, a service ethic, welfare capitalism, patriotism, and the corporation as community member were all common corporate public relations strategies in the early twentieth century, as Marchand identifies. What is unique about this study is that International Harvester seized on established and foundling education institutions, such as the lyceum, the chautauqua, the emerging public school, and the historical profession as a means to covertly spread those images.
7. Ozanne, *Century*, 71–72; "Judson's Address to State Grange," *Glenwood Opinion*, January 1, 1905; "The Farmer's Greatest Enemy," *Southern Mercury*, November 24, 1904; "The Harvester Merger," *Southern Mercury*,

October 22, 1903; *Missouri v. International Harvester Company of America*, Defense Brief, Supreme Court of Missouri, 5–6, box 7, M2001-144, MIHCC.

8. Wiebe, in *Search for Order*, discusses the major social transitions and migrations of the Gilded Age and Progressive Era that accompanied the corporatization and modernization of the economy. Neth, in *Preserving the Family Farm*, describes the impact of these transitions on the farm family through both social and gender analyses.
9. Ozanne, *Century*, 71–161; "Making Cripples and Dodging Taxes," *Collier's Weekly*, April 18, 1908; "Where Harvester $2-a-Day Families Live," *Day Book*, April 17, 1914, 28.
10. Cyrus McCormick II to George Perkins, June 19, 1905, box 1, M2002-052; Cyrus McCormick II, memorandum of conference held at the Manhattan Hotel, February 15, 1907; Cyrus McCormick II, memorandum, April 1, 1907; C. S. Funk to Cyrus McCormick II, March 27, 1907, box 37, Mss 2C; "The International Harvester Case: A Compilation," vol. 29, 31, Mss 3Z, MIHCC; "Harvester Company Meets All Charges: Files Brief in Answer to Missouri Ouster Suit Begun There in 1907," *Harvester World* 1, no. 9 (June 1910): 1; "Kentucky," *Harvester World* 2, no. 14 (November 1911): 16; "Playing Politics with Business," reprinted editorial, *Harvester World* 3, no. 5 (May 1912): 2–4; "Workings of Harvester Trust," *Bismarck Daily Tribune*, February 7, 1907; *United States v. International Harvester Company and Others*, "Petition in Equity" (U.S. District Court, Saint Paul, 1912), 2, 8–9, 40–43; Cyrus H. McCormick II, "President Cyrus H. McCormick's Letter to the Harvester Family," *Harvester World* 9, no. 10 (October 1918): 2–3. International Harvester lost the suit in the Saint Paul District Court in 1914. After the case was appealed to the U.S. Supreme Court and argued twice, it was settled out of court with a compromise that forced International Harvester to sell off its smaller assets but allowed it to keep the McCormick and Deering lines together.
11. Ozanne, in *Century*, and Marchand, in *Creating the Corporate Soul*, discuss International Harvester's welfare programs as public relations enterprises. Fitzgerald, in *Every Farm a Factory*, and Danbom, in *Resisted Revolution*, reflect on the cultural dispute between farmers and corporations as well as the environmental impact of agronomic education. Evans, in *Bound in Twine*, considers how the company created materials

that culturally sanctioned their twine monopoly in the mid-1910s but does not reflect on the company's larger cultural education project.

12. M. R. D. Owings to R. C. Haskins, November 21, 1912, box 151; International Harvester Advertising Department, "Instructions and Suggestions," 40, box 325, Mss 6Z, MIHCC.
13. M. R. D. Owings, "Current Advertising" and "Prospy at the Bat," *Harvester World* 1, no. 1 (October 1909); International Harvester Company, *Prospy*, 1909, poster, WHI-4625, Wisconsin Historical Images, accessed February 27, 2014, http://www.wisconsinhistory.org/whi/advancedSearch.asp.
14. "A Delightful Allegory on the Uses of Farm Machines," *Herald of Gospel Liberty*, September 30, 1909, 28; "A Delightful Allegory on the Uses of Farm Machines," *Better Fruit* 4, no. 4 (October 1909): 42; International Harvester Company, *Glimpses of Thrift-Land*.
15. Bederman, *Manliness and Civilization*.
16. Owings to Haskins, June 19, 1913, box 33, Mss 6Z, MIHCC; "A New Department," *Harvester World* 4, no. 1 (January 1913): 16.
17. Owings to Haskins, November 21, 1912, box 151; Mss 6Z, MIHCC; "New Department."
18. Cyrus McCormick II, "The International Harvester Company and the Farmer from 1902 until 1912," December 29, 1912, box 748, Mss 6Z, MIHCC.
19. Edwin L. Barker, "Holden Leaves Iowa," *Harvester World* 3, no. 12 (December 1912): 24–25; International Harvester Company, "Campaign Budgets: Agricultural Extension Department," 1914, box 74; C. McCormick II, "International Harvester Company"; Cyrus McCormick II, "The Coming Problem of Agricultural Development," reprinted from *Farm Machinery*, December 31, 1912, box 3, Mss 5Z, MIHCC.
20. Barker, "Holden Leaves Iowa"; E. L. Barker, "Batting It Up to Our Own Family," *Harvester World* 4, no. 10 (October 1913): 12.
21. Editorial, *The Lyceumite and Talent* 5, no. 7 (June 1907): 20; "Guy Standing and Theodore Roberts, 'The Right of Way': Plays and Players," *Chicago Daily Tribune*, January 5, 1908; "Funny Men in a League," *Chicago Daily Tribune*, September 4, 1903; "Christmas for the Deaf and Dumb," *Chicago Daily Tribune*, December 25, 1895; "Masonic Roof Temple Garden," classified ad, *Chicago Daily Tribune*, July 30, 1894, 8; Edwin Lincoln Barker, "Dirty Hands: A Clean Comedy in Three Acts," script,

1932; "Middletown: A Play in Three Acts," script, 1934; F.W.H. to P. G. Holden, "IHC Service Bureau Employees," January 31, 1914, box 151, Mss 6Z, MIHCC; Sandburg, *Great and Glorious Romance*; Tapia, *Circuit Chautauqua*, 43–44. Sandburg and Tapia describe the great midwestern poet and author Carl Sandburg and his experience working for Barker as the advertising manager at the *Lyceumite*.

22. Canning, *Most American Thing*, 2, 21, 76, 82; Tapia, *Circuit Chautauqua*, 43–44; Rieser, *Chautauqua Movement*, 269–74.
23. F.W.H. to Holden, "IHC Service Bureau Employees"; "Report of Service Bureau Meeting," November 25, 1912, box 151; Owings to Haskins, June 19, 1913, box 33, Mss 6Z, MIHCC; "The Harvester Company at the Chautauqua," *Lyceumite and Talent*, July 1911, 34.
24. Barker, *Story of Bread*, 1, 4, 17.
25. Barker, *Story of Bread*, 17.
26. Barker, *Story of Bread*, 16–17, 23, 25, 29.
27. Barker, *Story of Bread*, 1, 21–22.
28. Barker, *Story of Bread*, 21–22, 28.
29. Harold McCormick, reprinted speech, June 19, 1912, *Harvester World* 3, no. 7 (1912); Advertising Department to Harold McCormick, 1912, box 28, Mss 1F, MIHCC.
30. IHC Service Bureau, *The Dawn of Plenty: A Dramalogue with Motion Pictures, Colored Views, Pictorial Effect* (Chicago: Crown Press, 1913), 2, souvenir program, box 150, Mss 6Z, MIHCC; Grace Marian Smith, "Service Bureau Work in Public Schools," *Harvester World* 3, no. 4 (April 1912): 10–11; "School Work in Iowa," *Harvester World* 3, no. 9 (September 1912): 6; "Booklet Circulation," *Harvester World* 4, no. 8 (August 1913): 4.
31. "What the Bureau Is Doing," *Harvester World* 4, no. 7 (July 1913): 12–13; Danbom, *Resisted Revolution*, 51–58; Barron, *Mixed Harvest*, 43–77.
32. International Harvester Advertising Department, "Instructions and Suggestions," 50; "Harvester Company at the Chautauquas," 34.
33. International Harvester Advertising Department, "Instructions and Suggestions," 50; Edwin Barker, "Getting into Swing," *Harvester World* 5, no. 11 (November 1914): 15; "The Harvester Trust Will Teach Farmers How to Make More Money for It," *Day Book*, November 16, 1912, 7; "How about Your Town," *Harvester World* 5, no. 5 (May 1914): 5.
34. International Harvester Company, "Dawn of Plenty," 1913, 44, folder 4200, Mss 6Z, MIHCC; International Harvester Company of America,

"The Dawn of Power," 1913; International Harvester Company of America, "The Dawn of Commerce," 1913, folder 4200, Mss 6z, MIHCC.

35. International Harvester Company, "Dawn of Power," 1, folder 4200, Mss 6z, MIHCC.

36. International Harvester Company, "Dawn of Plenty," 1913, 11, 14, 44–48, folder 4200, Mss 6z, MIHCC; International Harvester Company, "Dawn of Power," 2, 5, 40, folder 4200, Mss 6z, MIHCC.

37. International Harvester Company, "Dawn of Plenty," 1913, 39–41, folder 4200, Mss 6z, MIHCC; International Harvester Company, "Dawn of Power," 27–29, folder 4200, Mss 6z, MIHCC; International Harvester Company, "Dawn of Commerce," folder 4200, Mss 6z, MIHCC; Lears, *Fables of Abundance*, 196–234.

38. International Harvester Company, "Dawn of Commerce," 6, folder 4200, Mss 6z, MIHCC.

39. International Harvester Company, "Dawn of Commerce," 21, 28, 30, 43–43, folder 4200, Mss 6z, MIHCC.

40. International Harvester Company, "Dawn of Commerce," 7, 29, 31–32, 39, 4, folder 4200, Mss 6z, MIHCC.

41. "The Dawn of Plenty," *Harvester World* 4, no. 6 (June 1913): 17; Advertising Department, "Suggestions for Advertising and Creating Interest in 'The Dawn of Plenty,'" 1913; Advertising Department, "Professor P. G. Holden Says—," promotional postcard, box 4, Mss 5z; International Harvester Advertising Department, "Instructions and Suggestions," 50, box 325, Mss 6z, MIHCC.

42. "The Dawn of Plenty," *Harvester World* 4, no. 6 (June 1913): 16; "Summer Lecture Tour," *Harvester World* 4, no. 7 (July 1914): 12; "The Dawn of Plenty Grows," *Harvester World* 5, no. 8 (August 1914): 4; "Do You Know," *Harvester World* 4, no. 10 (October 1913): 12; "Chronicles of the Dawn of Plenty," *Harvester World* 6, no. 1 (January 1915): 21; "Something New: A Course of Lectures," *Harvester World* 4, no. 4 (April 1914): 5; "How about Your Town?"; "IHC Plans for an Alfalfa Campaign," *Harvester World* 4, no. 4 (April 1913): 4–5; E. L. Barker, "Meeting the Crows in Utah and Idaho," *Harvester World* 4, no. 5 (May 1913): 6–7.

43. "The Dawn of Plenty," *Harvester World* 4, no. 12 (December 1913): 5; "Frank Stockdale Talks to Ags in Morrow Hall," *Daily Illini*, November 9, 1912, 1; "Institute and Short Course," *Sycamore True Republican*, January

31, 1914, 1; F.W.H. to Holden, "IHC Service Bureau Employees," box 151, Mss 6Z, MIHCC.

44. "Harvester Trust Will Teach"; Cyrus H. McCormick II to Herbert Casson, January 26, 1914, box 36, Mss 2C; Owings to Haskings, June 19, 1913, box 33; Advertising Department, "Boo Hoo Don't Want to Stay Here," cartoon sketch, box 151, Mss 6Z, MIHCC.
45. Greeno, *Obed Hussey.*
46. "International Harvester Case," 29:31, Mss 3Z, MIHCC.
47. Robert Hall McCormick II to Harold McCormick, December 21, 1910; Cyrus McCormick II, "Memorandum of Conference between Anita McCormick Blaine, Cyrus Adams and Cyrus McCormick II," April 18, 1911, box 399, Mss 1E; Cyrus Bentley to Harold McCormick, July 15, 1911; Bentley to Cyrus McCormick II, April 24, 1911, box 20, Mss AB; Bentley to C. McCormick II, June 4, 1915, box 55, Mss 1E, MIHCC.
48. Francis Steuert to Louis Dent, January 5, 1911; Cyrus Bentley to Anita McCormick Blaine, October 10, 1911, receipt, box 20, Mss AB; Bentley to C. McCormick II, Nettie McCormick, Anita McCormick Blaine, and Harold McCormick, March 31, 1911; Cyrus Bentley, interview questions, August 13, 1912, box 4, Mss AA; Cyrus Bentley to John Latane, December 17, 1914, box 20, Mss AB; Cyrus Bentley to Anita McCormick Blaine, August 1, 1912, box 54; F. A. Steuert to T. B. Gorton, November 16, 1914, box 400, Mss 1E, MIHCC.
49. Cyrus Bentley, "Memorandum on the Story of Bread," June 20, 1911, box 20, Mss AB, MIHCC.
50. Cyrus Bentley to Anita Blaine McCormick, July 3, 1915, box 55, Mss 1E; Cyrus McCormick II to McCormick Blaine, August 4, 1915, box 400, Mss 1E, MIHCC.
51. "Introduction to Book Is Written by Prof. Alvord," *Daily Illini*, March 23, 1915; F. A. Steuert to M. H. Jaynes, January 25, 1914, box 150, Cyrus Hall McCormick II Subject Files, Mss 1C, MIHCC.
52. Sellers, "Before We Were Members"; Tyrell, "Public at the Creation," 23.
53. Clarence Alvord to Clarence Paine, March 15, 1912, and November 8, 1913, box 21; Clarence Paine, "The Meetings of the MVHA," December 30, 1912, 4–10; Clarence Paine, "Report of the Secretary-Treasurer of the MVHA," May 8, 1913, 1, box 1, Mss 27, OAH.
54. Alvord to Paine, January 27, 1914, February 25, 1914, and June 24, 1914; Clarence Paine to Clarence Alvord, June 29, 1914, box 21; Clarence

Paine to Notre Dame, February 26, 1914, box 79, Mss 27, OAH; Cyrus McCormick II, folder "University of Illinois Donation Files, 1914–1931," no. 9:116, box 26, Mss 5C, MIHCC. The latter is composed mostly of papers regarding the MVHA and *Review*. The misleading label on the file indicates that McCormick always perceived his contribution to the *Review* (which was financially managed from Lincoln, Nebraska, by Clarence Paine) as a relationship with Clarence Alvord, who worked at the University of Illinois. To this point he probably stopped contributing in 1931, because Alvord had passed away in 1928, just after McCormick had committed to a three-year guarantor renewal.

55. Alvord to Paine, May 20, 1914, box 21, Mss 27, OAH; Paine, "Report"; Bentley to C. McCormick II, March 31, 1920; list of potential biographers, n.d., box 2, Mss 9C, MIHCC.
56. "Dawn of Plenty-Motion Pictures," *Daily Illini*, January 24, 1914; "Dawn of Plenty: Moving Picture," *Daily Illini*, January 14, 1914; "Last Day Mid-Winter Fair," *Daily Illini*, February 14, 1914; "Frank Stockdale Talks"; "Large Numbers Enroll in Short Course," *Daily Illini*, January 21, 1914; Novick, *That Noble Dream*, 61–85.
57. Clarence Alvord to Cyrus McCormick II, February 23, 1914; Mississippi Valley Historical Association, *Mississippi Valley Historical Review*, 1914, circular, box 150, Mss 1C, MIHCC.
58. Correspondence, boxes 21–24, Mss 27, OAH, demonstrate that support for the *Review* from Julius Rosenwald, Joy Morton, H. J. Patten, Calvin Dawes, Frank Lowden, the University of Chicago, and Northwestern University was secured after McCormick committed to the effort. While they do not specifically mention McCormick, this connection can be inferred from their inclusion in the same social circles, most specifically the membership of the social elite in the Commercial Club of Chicago. H. Horowitz, *Culture and the City*.
59. Cyrus Bentley, "Interview between W.N.C. Carlton and Cyrus Bentley," May 27, 1915, box 55, Mss 1E; D. C. Munro to H. Kellar, June 26, 1915, box 23, Mss AC, MIHCC; Kellar, "The Minnesota State Archives: Their Character, Condition and Historical Value," *Minnesota History Bulletin* 1 (1915–16): 37–53. Kellar had received his undergraduate degree from the University of Chicago and done graduate work at the University of Wisconsin-Madison. He had been a student of Dana Munro's, who had

been a close colleague of Reuben Thwaites and who had let Kellar know about the opening with the McCormick family.

60. "Industrialogues Discontinued," *Harvester World* 6, no. 2 (February 1915): 2; F.W.H. to Holden, "IHC Service Bureau Employees," box 151, Mss 6Z, MIHCC.
61. "Everett Busy," *Northwestern Worker* (Everett WA), June 1, 1916; A. McLaughlin, *History*, 320; Muzzey, *American History*, 289.

5. HERBERT ANTHONY KELLAR

1. Herbert Kellar to Harold McCormick, March 27, 1931, box 2, Mss 1Q, 1; Kellar to Anita McCormick Blaine, Cyrus McCormick II, and Harold McCormick, May 2, 1932, 1, box 11, Mss AB, MIHCC.
2. Kellar to H. McCormick, March 27, 1931; Cyrus McCormick II to Harold McCormick, April 10, 1931; Judson Stone to Cyrus McCormick II, May 7, 1931, box 2, Mss 1Q; Kellar to McCormick Blaine, C. McCormick II, and H. McCormick, May 2, 1932, 3, box 11, Mss AB, MIHCC.
3. Kellar to McCormick Blaine, C. McCormick II, and H. McCormick, May 2, 1932, 3, box 11; Frederick Lewton to Kellar, April 27, 1932, box 10, Mss AB; "The Fifth Annual Meeting of the Agricultural History Society," June 2, 1923, minutes, 7, box 86, Mss AC, MIHCC; "Notes and Comments."
4. Kellar to McCormick Blaine, C. McCormick II, and H. McCormick, May 2, 1932, 2–6, box 11, Mss AB, MIHCC.
5. Kellar to McCormick Blaine, C. McCormick II, and H. McCormick, May 2, 1932, 6; May 4, 1932; Cyrus McCormick II to McCormick Blaine and Harold McCormick, May 14, 1932, box 11, Mss AB; Harold McCormick to Cyrus McCormick II and Anita McCormick Blaine, February 19, 1931, box 1, Mss 1Q, MIHCC.
6. Kellar to McCormick Blaine, C. McCormick II, and H. McCormick, May 2, 1932, 3–4, box 11; Lewton to Kellar, April 27, 1932, box 10, Mss AB, MIHCC.
7. Kellar to McCormick Blaine, C. McCormick II, and H. McCormick, May 2, 1932, 8–13; May 17, 1932, box 11, MIHCC.
8. Cyrus McCormick II to McCormick Blaine and Harold McCormick, May 14, 1932; Kellar to McCormick Blaine, C. McCormick II, and H. McCormick, May 2, 1932, 5, box 11; Herbert Kellar, "Report on Trip to the Smithsonian Institution, Washington, D.C., May 13–29, 1934," box 15, Mss AB, MIHCC.

9. While not officially a part of International Harvester, Kellar's collection and knowledge were utilized as a company resource. He offered the same services as later corporate archives to inform advertising, public relations, policy, and legal decisions. Indeed, Kellar and his McCormick Agricultural Library provided both inspiration and a model for the "first" U.S. corporate archive in 1937, at the Firestone Tire and Rubber Company. Mooney, "Practice of History"; William D. Overman to Herbert Kellar, December 1, 1937, box 135, Mss AC, MIHCC; Conard, *Benjamin Shambaugh*; Tyrell, "Public at the Creation"; Lauck, *Lost Region*, 13–52.
10. Harrison, *Timeless Affair*.
11. Bentley, "Interview between W. N. C. Carlton"; Bentley to McCormick Blaine, August 10, 1915, box 55, Anita McCormick Blaine Papers, Mss 1E; Cyrus McCormick II to Dana C. Munro, June 24, 1915, box 5, Mss 9C, MIHCC.
12. "Historical News and Comments"; George Vincent to Kellar, November 17, 1914, box 1, Mss AC; Bentley to McCormick Blaine, August 2, 1915, box 55, Mss 1E, MIHCC.
13. Kellar to Bentley, September 8, 1915, box 23; Herbert Kellar, "The McCormick Records and State, Local, and Regional History," n.d., box 19, Mss AC, MIHCC.
14. Cyrus Bentley, "Outline of Work for the Historical Association," 1915, box 1, Mss AB, MIHCC.
15. Kellar to McCormick Blaine, January 17, 1916, box 34, Mss AC, MIHCC.
16. Herbert Kellar, memorandum, March 9, 1916, box 5, Mss 9C, MIHCC.
17. Cyrus McCormick II to McCormick Blaine, March 10, 1916; Cyrus McCormick II, "Leads to Follow Up for Docket"; "Memos," March 8, 1916, box 5, Mss 9C; C. McCormick II to H. McCormick, May 26, 1914, box 400, Mss 1E; Herbert Kellar to Richard Bentley, January 8, 1956, box 31, Mss AB, MIHCC.
18. Bentley to C. McCormick II, "Special Report on Kellar," November 23, 1923, box 2, Mss 9C, MIHCC.
19. Kellar to McCormick Blaine, report, June 14, 1916; report, September 23, 1913, box 34, Mss AC, MIHCC.
20. Kellar to Bentley, January 19, 1918, box 1; Kellar to Bentley, June 16, 1919, Mss AB; Kellar to McCormick Blaine, January 17, 1916, and May 4, 1916, box 34; Kellar to Bentley, November 30, 1916, box 23, Mss AC, MIHCC.

21. Kellar to Bentley, January 19, 1918, box 1, Mss AB; Kellar to Bentley, April 9, 1919, box 34, Mss AC, MIHCC; Schmidt, "Economic History," 9.
22. Kellar to Bentley, June 15, 1918, box 34, Mss AC, MIHCC.
23. Kellar to McCormick Blaine, September 25, 1918, box 34, Mss AC; Kellar to Bentley, December 10, 1918, box 1; Kellar to Bentley, June 16, 1919, box 2, Mss AB; Kellar to Bentley, November 17, 1923, box 4, Mss 9C, MIHCC.
24. Kellar to McCormick Blaine, September 25, 1918; Kellar to Bentley, April 23, 1917, and May 2, 1917, box 34; Kellar to Bentley, March 22, 1918, box 23; Herbert Kellar, "Notes on Trip," April 24–May 2, 1929, box 109, Mss AC; Kellar to Bentley, December 10, 1918, box 1; Clarence Alvord to Kellar, April 19, 1922, box 30, Mss AB; Clara Paine to Cyrus McCormick II, April 7, 1920, and October 25, 1920; Kellar to C. S. Stilwell, April 25, 1922, box 26, Mss 5C, MIHCC.
25. Kellar to Bentley, December 23, 1916, box 23; Kellar to McCormick Blaine, August 21, 1916; Kellar to Bentley, May 2, 1917, box 34, Mss AC; "News and Comments."
26. Kellar to Bentley, May 2, 1917, and July 26, 1917, box 34, Mss AC, MIHCC.
27. Kellar to Bentley, June 16, 1919, box 2; Kellar to Bentley, January 18, 1918, box 1, Mss AB, MIHCC.
28. Rasmussen, "Growth of Agricultural History"; Peterson, "Agricultural History."
29. Kellar to Cyrus McCormick II, April 12, 1930, box 9, Mss AB; Kellar to Waldemar Kempffert, March 13, 1929, box 134, Mss AC, MIHCC; Hirsch, "Efforts of the Grange."
30. Lauck, *Lost Region*, 29–30; Barker, *Story of Bread*.
31. Tyrell, *Historians in Public*, 165–68; Nils A. Olsen to Kellar, May 25, 1921, box 84; "Fifth Annual Meeting," box 86, Mss AC, MIHCC.
32. Herbert Kellar, "Agricultural Surveys," 1923 speech, AHS annual meeting; Kellar to O. C. Stine, October 27, 1927, box 84; "Minutes of the Meeting of the Executive Committee of the Agricultural History Society," October 18, 1927; "Notes on Meeting of Agricultural History," December 29, 1927, box 86; Kellar, "McCormick Records," box 19, Mss AC, MIHCC.
33. Krey notes that Kellar's work and theory of history were one of the best examples of historians making their craft a "practical" social tool ("History," 11–12).
34. Krey, "History," 11–12.

35. Herbert Kellar, "Suggestions for the Organization of the McCormick Agricultural Library, 1922–1944," April 1, 1922; "Estimates of Annual Cost of Suggestions for the Organization of the McCormick Agricultural Library, 1922–1944," April 21, 1922, box 5, Mss 9C, MIHCC.
36. Kellar to Bentley, April 3, 1922, and January 5, 1925; Cyrus Bentley, "Memorandum, Re: Organization of the Historical Library," May 19, 1922, box 5; Bentley to C. McCormick II, November 23, 1923, box 2, Mss 9C, MIHCC.
37. Kellar to Bentley, May 17, 1926, box 35, Mss AC, MIHCC.
38. Kane, "Manuscript Collecting," 41–43.
39. Kane, "Manuscript Collecting," 41–43.
40. Norton, "Herbert Anthony Kellar"; Ulrich Phillips to Kellar, May 12, 1956, box 137, Mss AC, MIHCC.
41. Kellar to Bentley, June 6, 1926, box 25; Kellar to Bentley, March 19, 1921; Kellar to Steuert, March 22, 1921, box 45; Kellar, "Agricultural Surveys," box 86, Mss AC, MIHCC.
42. Novick, *That Noble Dream*, 92–97; Kellar to Alderman, February 14, 1928, box 133, Mss AC, MIHCC.
43. Kellar, "Agricultural Surveys," box 86; Herbert Kellar, "Report of the Committee on Co-operation in Historical Work," June 10, 1924, box 107, Mss AC, MVHA, MIHCC.
44. Kellar to Bentley, May 17, 1926, and June 5, 1926, box 25; Kellar to Mr. House, March 29, 1919, box 45, Mss AC, MIHCC; Kane, "Manuscript Collecting," 41–43.
45. Don Peters to Kellar, November 11, 1926; February 23, 1927; September 22, 1927; November 13, 1930; May 7, 1931; Kellar to Peters, November 14, 1926, box 45, Mss AC, MIHCC.
46. Van Tassel and Tinsley, "Historical Organizations," 140; Norton, "Herbert Anthony Kellar," 151; Kellar to Bentley, June 6, 1926, box 25, Mss AC, MIHCC.
47. Kellar to Bentley, April 10, 1926, and April 17, 1926, box 25, Mss AC; Bentley to C. McCormick II, October 14, 1926, box 59, Mss 1E, MIHCC.
48. Kellar to Bentley, July 13, 1926, box 6, Mss AB; Kellar to Bentley, June 6, 1926, box 25, Mss AC; Bentley to Kellar, July 16, 1926, box 59, Mss 1E; Bentley to C. McCormick II, quarterly report, July 1926, box 59, Mss 1E, MIHCC. The report includes a summary of the correspondence between Kellar and himself as well as his reflections on Kellar's work.

49. Bentley to C. McCormick II, July 1926; October 15, 1926, box 59, Mss 1E; Kellar to C. McCormick II, April 12, 1930; Cyrus McCormick II to Kellar, April 17, 1930; Kellar to Bentley, April 14, 1930; Cyrus McCormick II to Bentley, April 15, 1930, box 9, Mss AB, MIHCC.
50. Kellar to C. McCormick II, April 12, 1930, box 9, Mss AB; Kellar to Bentley, July 12, 1927, box 35; Kellar to Phillips, August 27, 1926, box 137, Mss AC, MIHCC. Boxes 137 and 25 Mss AC are, respectively, focused on Ulrich B. Phillips correspondence (mostly regarding manuscript collecting and dealing) and Kellar's hunts in Virginia.
51. Kellar to Ulrich Phillips, January 27, 1928; Phillips to Kellar, May 26, 1926, and February 28, 1927, box 137; Kellar to Dr. Alderman, February 14, 1926, box 133; Kellar to Clarence Brigham (AAS), October 16, 1926; Claribel Barnett (USDA) to Kellar, October 27, 1926, box 25; Kellar to W. F. Boyd (Duke), October 16, 1926; Kellar to Franklin Riley (Washington and Lee), January 31, 1927; Kellar to P. L. Winsor (Illinois), May 27, 1927; Kellar to the Business Historical Society, August 24, 1927; Harry Clemmons (Virginia) to Kellar, November 22, 1928, box 45, Mss AC, MIHCC
52. Herbert Kellar, "A Proposed Staff and Organization for the Work of the Historical Association," August 25, 1924, box 5, Mss 9C, MIHCC.
53. Cyrus McCormick II to McCormick Blaine and Harold McCormick, June 19, 1925; Bentley to Kellar, April 29, 1925; Kellar to Bentley, June 13, 1925; Cyrus McCormick III to Cyrus McCormick II, February 25, 1930, box 1, Mss 9C, MIHCC.
54. A ubiquitous feature of Kellar's reports to Bentley beginning in 1922 was his progress on the outline and the number of note cards he had completed. Bentley to C. McCormick II, March 31, 1920, and November 23, 1923, box 2; Kellar to Bentley, December 21, 1923, box 4; Kellar to Bentley, November 26, 1924; December 11, 1925; April 27, 1927, box 5, Mss 9C; Bentley to C. McCormick II, Harold McCormick, Anita McCormick Blaine, July 30, 1925; Cyrus Bentley, "The Invention of the McCormick Reaper," page proofs, R. R. Donnelly and Sons, 1930, box 21, Mss AB, MIHCC.
55. Cyrus McCormick II to Cyrus Bentley, October 17, 1919; Dana Munro to Cyrus McCormick II, September 2, 1919; James Franklin James to Cyrus McCormick II, January 17, 1921; Cyrus McCormick II, memorandum on meeting with Frederic Paxson, June 6, 1921, box 401, Mss 1E; C. McCormick II to Bentley, January 30, 1923; Yale University Press, "The New

Historians: A Booklet about the Authors of the Chronicles of America Series"; "Meeting of the McCormick Historical Association with Arthur Cole," December 31, 1921; "Analysis of Suggested Historians to Date," May 11, 1920; Bentley to C. McCormick II, March 31, 1920, box 2, Mss 9C; Cyrus McCormick II to McCormick Blaine, June 30, 1927, box 28, Mss 2C, MIHCC.

56. Bentley to Kellar, May 18, 1922, and April 25, 1922; Bentley, "Memorandum, Re: Mr. Kellar's Search for a Biographer," May 18, 1922; Kellar to Bentley, April 24, 1922, and May 4, 1922, box 2, Mss 9C, MIHCC.

57. Bentley to C. McCormick II, March 22, 1927; C. McCormick II to Bentley, March 25, 1927; Anita McCormick Blaine to Cyrus McCormick II, March 22, 1927; H. McCormick to C. McCormick II, March 28, 1927; William Dodd to Cyrus McCormick II, April 8, 1927, box 7, Mss AB; memorandum of conference attended by William Dodd, Harold McCormick, and Cyrus Bentley, May 21, 1927; Cyrus McCormick II to Mr. Stilwell, May 22, 1927; H. McCormick to C. McCormick II, May 23, 1927; Cyrus McCormick II to McCormick Blaine, June 30, 1927, box 28, Mss 2C, MIHCC.

58. Cyrus McCormick II, "Memorandum," February 16, 1927; Harold McCormick to Stilwell, June 9, 1927, box 7; Bentley to C. McCormick II, October 1, 1929, box 8, Mss AB; Dodd to C. McCormick II, July 19, 1928; December 24, 1928; May 10, 1932; Cyrus McCormick II to Dodd, September 5, 1928, and May 26, 1932; Bentley to Cyrus McCormick II, Anita McCormick Blaine, and Harold McCormick, January 11, 1929, box 20, Mss 5C, MIHCC.

59. "Historical Association: Receipts and Disbursements," January 9, 1928; C. McCormick II to Dodd, December 28, 1927, box 7; Dodd to Bentley, January 15, 1930, and January 28, 1930; Bentley to C. McCormick II, January 16, 1930, box 20, Mss AB, MIHCC.

60. Hutchinson, *Cyrus Hall McCormick: Seed-Time*, 99–125.

61. Bentley to C. McCormick II, December 4, 1928, box 7; Bentley to Dodd, January 13, 1930, box 20, Mss AB, MIHCC.

62. S. B. White to Cyrus McCormick III, April 9, 1927, box 1, M2002-049; Don Gridley, "History as a Factor in Good-Will Advertising," *Printers' Ink Monthly*, January 1926, 44–45, 133–34; James True, "Advertising the Fair of the Iron Horse," *Printers' Ink*, November 3, 1927; James Murray to Cyrus McCormick II, November 17, 1926; Cyrus McCormick II to Edward Hungerford, November 20, 1928; Hungerford to C. McCormick II, November 22, 1922, box 1, Mss 1Q, MIHCC.

63. E. S. Simpson to George Ranney, "McCormick Reaper Centennial," April 6, 1928, box 7, Mss AB.

64. Kellar to Bentley, December 21, 1923, box 4; Alice Kroeschell to Bentley, March 5, 1925, box 5, Mss 9C; Kellar to R. E. Kenny, February 23, 1927; H. P. Doolittle to Kellar, December 30, 1927, box 7, Mss AB, MIHCC.

65. Kellar to Kenny, May 9, 1927; Kenny to Kellar, May 13, 1927, box 7, Mss AB, MIHCC.

66. S. B. White, memorandum, August 24, 1928; Bentley to C. McCormick II, September 29, 1928, box 7; Kenny to Kellar, February 20, 1928; Kellar to Bentley, February 12, 1929; May 11, 1929; June 7, 1929; Anita McCormick, memorandum, June 7, 1929; Hebert Kellar, "Comment on the IHC Scenario: *Romance of the Reaper*," June 4, 1929, box 8, Mss AB; Kellar to Stilwell, September 18, 1928; Kellar to Cyrus McCormick II, "List of Points: Film," June 12, 1929, box 1, Mss 1Q, MIHCC.

67. Cyrus McCormick II, memorandum on centenary, December 20, 1928; Alex Legge to Harold McCormick, June 12, 1929; H. McCormick to C. McCormick II, June 17, 1929; White to Harold McCormick, May 13, 1929; C. McCormick II to H. McCormick, June 12, 1929, box 1, Mss 1Q, MIHCC.

68. Kellar to Bentley, August 1, 1929, box 8, Mss AB; Kellar to U. B. Phillips, July 24, 1929, box 137, Mss AC; White to Kellar, June 12, 1931, box 3, Mss 1Q, MIHCC.

69. Anita Blaine McCormick to Cyrus McCormick II, June 14, 1930, box 1, Mss 1Q, MIHCC; International Harvester Company, *The Romance of the Reaper*, 1930, film, Wisconsin Digital Collection, accessed May 7, 2014, http://content.wisconsinhistory.org/cdm/singleitem/collection/p15932coll3/id/0/rec/1.

70. International Harvester Company, *Romance of the Reaper*.

71. International Harvester Company, *Romance of the Reaper*; C. D. Harnsberger to Kellar, October 6, 1919, box 3, Mss 9C; International Harvester, "The Reaper Takes Form," 1931, poster, box 3, Mss 2Q, MIHCC.

72. McCormick Blaine to C. McCormick II, June 14, 1930, box 1, Mss 1Q, MIHCC.

73. International Harvester Centennial Committee and Sub-committee Meeting, July 28, 1930, minutes, box 1; H. C. Pemberton to IHC, June 30, 1931, box 3; A. C. Seyfarth to Kellar, October 1, 1930, box 4, Mss 1Q; C. McCormick II to Bentley, May 14, 1930, box 1, Mss 2Q; Herbert Kellar to

Cyrus McCormick II, Anita McCormick Blaine, and Harold McCormick, report on 1931, February 3, 1932, box 35, Mss AC; Kellar to C. McCormick II, October 28, 1930, box 9, Mss AB; "McCormick Reaper Centennial Source Book," 1931, box 643, IHC Corporate Archives Central File, Mss 6Z, MIHCC; C. McCormick III, *Century of the Reaper*.

74. C. McCormick III to C. McCormick II, February 25 and 26, 1930, box 38, Mss AB; Herbert Kellar, "Family Centennial Committee Report," box 1, Mss 2Q, MIHCC.

75. Kellar to Judson Stone, February 16, 1931, box 1, Mss 1Q, MIHCC.

76. Kellar, "Family Centennial Committee Report," box 1, Mss 2Q; "Conference," February 17, 1931, minutes, box 1, Mss 1Q, MIHCC.

77. Kellar, "Family Centennial Committee Report," box 1, Mss 2Q; IHC to Cyrus McCormick II, February 11, 1931; "Meeting of the Centennial Committee and Sub-committee," July 28, 1930, minutes, box 1; Harold McCormick to Anita McCormick Blaine, March 31, 1931, box 2; Hans Emch to Cyrus McCormick III, July 27, 1931, box 3; Mss 1Q; Herbert Kellar to Anita McCormick Blaine, Harold McCormick, and Cyrus McCormick II, "Report on 1931," February 3, 1932, box 35, Mss AB; American Society of Agricultural Engineers, "Pageant Portraying the Evolution and Development of Grain Harvesting Machinery," July 24, 1931, program, box 1, M2002-049, MIHCC. Mss 4Q is composed of four boxes of centennial reports submitted to the company by dealerships about their local celebrations, including the information about the number of people that attended and saw the movie, how many medallions were distributed, local advertising efforts, and other miscellaneous details about promotion endeavors.

78. Kellar, "Family Centennial Committee Report"; Advertising Department, "Free Distribution of Book, 'The Century of Progress,'" March 12, 1931, box 1, Mss 2Q; IHC to C. McCormick II, February 11, 1931; "Meeting of the Centennial Committee," box 1, Mss 1Q, MIHCC.

79. "Meeting of the Centennial Committee," box 1, Mss 1Q, MIHCC; Herbert Kellar, "McCormick Family Centennial Committee Estimate of Expenses," June 17, 1931, box 3, Mss 1Q, MIHCC.

80. Bentley to C. McCormick, May 1, 1926, box 55, Mss 1E; Herbert Kellar, individual income tax return, 1925, box 9, Mss AC, MIHCC.

81. Cyrus McCormick II, Anita McCormick Blaine, and Harold McCormick to Herbert Kellar, July 6, 1932; "Excerpts of Meeting Minutes, Relat-

ing to the Historical Association," September 1, 1932, box 11, Mss AC, MIHCC.

82. Cyrus Hall McCormick had still not been elected to the Hall of Fame when elections ceased and it went defunct in 1976. Bruce Barton to F. A. Steuert, June 18, 1935, and August 13, 1935, box 39; minutes, conference of F. A. Steuert, Herbert Kellar, and Bruce Barton, May 14, 1936; Herbert Kellar, "Report Concerning Interview with Bruce Barton," May 14, 1936; Barton to Steuert, June 4, 1936, box 40, McCormick Historical Association Records, Mss AB, MIHCC.
83. Herbert Kellar, "Report on Survey of Institutions with Respect to the Possible Acquisition of the Collections of the McCormick Historical Association," December 1, 1950; Lucille Kellar to Stella Roderick, February 15, 1952, box 43, Herbert Kellar Papers, Mss AC, MIHCC.
84. Van Tassel and Tinsley, "Historical Organizations"; Bauer, "Public Archives"; Rasmussen, "Growth of Agricultural History"; Herbert Kellar, "Memorandum upon the Status of Historical Activities in the United States in Recent Years," January 1939, box 19, Mss AC, MIHCC. This memo was read at the 1939 AHA meeting as a sort of "call to arms" for the profession to devote more attention to training historians for jobs outside of academic settings, which focused on public education.
85. Herbert Kellar, "Living Agricultural Museums," presentation at the National Agricultural Jefferson Bicentenary Committee, April 13, 1944, box 86, Mss AC, MIHCC (boxes 34–48 of the McCormick Historical Association Papers, Mss AC, contain the extensive documentation of the Walnut Grove restoration during the late 1930s); Alexander, "Historical Restoration."
86. Smiley, "W.P.A. Historical Records Survey."
87. Younger, "Foundations."
88. Lyons, *McCormick Reaper Legend*; Frank Tuttle, "Review: *The McCormick Reaper Legend* by Norbert Lyons," *Business History Review* 30 (December 1956): 497–99; Kellar to McCormick Blaine, C. McCormick II, and H. McCormick, September 21, 1932, box 9, Mss AB, MIHCC.

CONCLUSION

1. Herbert Kellar, "The Organization and Preservation of Manuscript Collections in the McCormick Historical Association Library," address

to the American Library Association, June 15, 1938, box 19, Mss AC, MIHCC.

2. Levy, *Freaks of Fortune*, 274; Muncy, "Trustbusting and White Manhood," 24–25.
3. Casson, *Romance of Steel*, 365–66; M. Wallace, *Mickey Mouse History*, 9–15.
4. Levy, *Freaks of Fortune*, 299–303; Perkins, "Modern Corporation," 156–58, 168.
5. Robinson, *New History*, 8, 22, 165, 263, 265.
6. Tyrell, *Historians in Public*.

Bibliography

ARCHIVES AND MANUSCRIPT MATERIALS

MIHCC. McCormick–International Harvester Company Collection. Wisconsin State Historical Society, Madison.

OAH. Organization of American Historians Records. Ruth Lilly Special Collections and Archives. Indiana University–Purdue University Indianapolis.

RGTP. Reuben Gold Thwaites Papers. Wisconsin State Historical Society, Madison.

PUBLISHED WORKS

Alexander, Edward. "Historical Restoration." In Hesseltine and McNeil, *In Support of Clio*, 195–214.

Andreas, Alfred T. *History of Chicago: From Its Earliest Period to the Present Time*. Vols. 1–3. Chicago: Andreas, 1884–86.

———. *An Illustrated Historical Atlas of the State of Minnesota*. Chicago: Andreas, 1874.

Ardrey, Robert. *American Agricultural Implements: A Review of Invention and Development in the Agricultural Implement Industry of the United States*. Chicago, 1894.

Barker, Edwin Lincoln. *The Creeds of Great Business Men*. Chicago: International Harvester Company of America, 1913.

———. *The Story of Bread*. Chicago: International Harvester Company of America, 1911.

———. *The Story of Twine*. Chicago: International Harvester Company of America, 1912.

Barron, Hal. *Mixed Harvest: The Second Great Transformation in the Rural North, 1870–1930*. Chapel Hill: University of North Carolina Press, 1997.

Bauer, G. Philip. "Public Archives in the United States." In Hesseltine and McNeil, *In Support of Clio*, 49–76.

Bederman, Gail. *Manliness and Civilization: A Cultural History of Gender and Race in the United States, 1880–1917*. Chicago: University of Chicago Press, 1995.

Beinhauer, Myrtle. "Development of the Grange in Iowa, 1868–1930." *Annals of Iowa* 34, no. 8 (Spring 1959): 597–618.

Bender, Daniel E. *American Abyss: Savagery and Civilization in the Age of Industry*. Ithaca: Cornell University Press, 2009.

Bidwell, Percy, and John Falconer. *History of Agriculture in the Northern United States, 1620–1860*. Washington DC: Carnegie Institution of Washington, 1925.

Billias, George Athan, and Gerald N. Grob, eds. *American History: Retrospect and Prospect*. New York: Free Press, 1971.

Blanke, David. *Sowing the American Dream: How Consumer Culture Took Root in the Rural Midwest*. Athens: Ohio University Press, 2000.

Bookwalter, John W. *If Not Silver, What?* Springfield OH: Bookwalter, 1896.

Brinkley, Alan. *The End of Reform*. New York: Knopf, 1995.

———. *The Unfinished Nation: A Concise History of the American People*. 5th ed. Boston: McGraw Hill, 2008.

Bruce, Philip. *History of Virginia*. Vol. 2. New York: American Historical Society, 1924.

Canning, Charlotte. *The Most American Thing in America: Circuit Chautauqua as Performance*. Iowa City: University of Iowa Press, 2005.

Carstensen, Fred, and Diane Roazen. "Foreign Markets, Domestic Initiative, and the Emergence of a Monocrop Economy: The Yucatecan Experience, 1825–1903." *Hispanic American Historical Review* 72 (November 1992): 555–92.

Casper, Scott E. *Constructing American Lives: Biography and Culture in Nineteenth-Century America*. Chapel Hill: University of North Carolina Press, 1999.

Casson, Herbert. *Cyrus Hall McCormick: His Life and Work*. Chicago: McClurg, 1909.

———. *The Romance of Steel: The Story of a Thousand Millionaires*. New York: Barnes, 1907.

———. *The Romance of the Reaper*. New York: Doubleday, Page, 1908.

Chandler, Alfred. *Strategy and Structure: Chapters in the History of American Industrial Enterprise*. Cambridge MA: MIT Press, 1972.

———. *The Visible Hand: The Managerial Revolution in American Business*. Cambridge MA: Belknap, 1977.

Clark, William Horace. *Farms and Farmers: The Story of American Agriculture*. New York: Page, 1945.

Cohen, Lizabeth. *Making a New Deal*. New York: Cambridge University Press, 1995.

Conard, Rebecca. *Benjamin Shambaugh and the Intellectual Foundations of Public History*. Iowa City: University of Iowa Press, 2002.

Conzen, Michael P., ed. *Chicago Mapmakers*. Chicago: Chicago Historical Society, 1984.

Cronon, William. *Nature's Metropolis: Chicago and the Great West*. New York: Norton, 1991.

Danbom, David. *The Resisted Revolution: Urban America and the Industrialization of Agriculture, 1900–1930*. Ames: Iowa State University Press, 1979.

Domosh, Mona. "A 'Civilized' Commerce: Gender, 'Race,' and Empire at the 1893 Chicago Exposition." *Cultural Geographies* 9 (April 2002): 181–201.

Donnelly, Ignatius. *Cyrus H. McCormick and Leander J. McCormick, Partners as C. H. and L. J. McCormick, Appellants, vs. Ignatius Donnelly, Respondent [. . .]*. Hastings MN: Hall, 1884.

Ebeling, Walter. *The Fruited Plain: The Story of American Agriculture*. Berkeley: University of California Press, 1979.

Evans, Sterling. *Bound in Twine: The History and Ecology of the Henequen-Wheat Complex for Mexico and the American and Canadian Plains, 1880–1950*. College Station: Texas A&M University Press, 2007.

Fitzgerald, Deborah. *Every Farm a Factory: The Industrial Ideal in American Agriculture*. New Haven: Yale University Press, 2010.

Flower, Frank Abial. *Edwin McMasters Stanton: The Autocrat of Rebellion, Emancipation, and Reconstruction*. New York: Wilson, 1905.

Foner, Eric. *Give Me Liberty! An American History*. Vol. 1. 3rd ed. New York: Norton, 2012.

Friedman, Walter. *Birth of a Salesman: The Transformation of Selling in America*. Cambridge MA: Harvard University Press, 2004.

"Front Matter." *Mississippi Valley Historical Review* 1, no. 1 (1914) to 17, no. 4 (1931).

Gates, Paul. *Agriculture and the Civil War*. New York: Knopf, 1965.

Gies, Joseph. "The Great Reaper War." *American Heritage of Invention and Technology* 5, no. 3 (1989): 20–28.

Gjerde, Jon. *The Minds of the West: Ethnocultural Evolution in the Rural Middle West, 1830–1917*. Chapel Hill: University of North Carolina Press, 1997.

Greeno, Follett Lamberton, ed. *Obed Hussey, Who, of All Inventors, Made Bread Cheap*. Rochester: Rochester Herald, 1912.

Harrington, Bates. *How 'Tis Done*. 2nd ed. 1879. Reprint, Syracuse NY: Pattison, 1890.

Harrison, Gilbert. *A Timeless Affair: The Life of Anita McCormick Blaine*. Chicago: University of Chicago Press, 1979.

Hesseltine, William, and Donald McNeil, eds. *In Support of Clio: Essay in Memory of Herbert A. Kellar*. Madison: State Historical Society of Wisconsin, 1958.

Hessler, Gene. *U.S. Essay, Proof, and Specimen Notes*. Portage OH: BNR, 1979.

Hicks, John D. *The Populist Revolt*. Lincoln: University of Nebraska Press, 1961.

Higham, John, Leonard Krieger, and Felix Gilbert. *History: The Development of Historical Studies in the United States*. Englewood Cliffs NJ: Prentice-Hall, 1965.

Hild, Matthew. *Greenbackers, Knights of Labor, and Populists: Farm-Labor Insurgency in the Late-Nineteenth-Century South*. Athens: University of Georgia Press, 2007.

Hirsch, Arthur. "Efforts of the Grange in the Middle West to Control the Price of Farm Machinery, 1870–1880." *Mississippi Valley Historical Review* 15 (1929): 473–96.

"Historical News and Comments." *Mississippi Valley Historical Review* 42 (1955): 598–99.

Horowitz, Helen Lefkowitz. *Culture and the City: Cultural Philanthropy in Chicago from the 1880s to 1917*. Lexington: University Press of Kentucky, 1976.

Hounshell, David. *From the American System to Mass Production, 1800–1932: The Development of Manufacturing Technology in the United States*. Baltimore: Johns Hopkins University Press, 1984.

Howe, Daniel Walker. *What Hath God Wrought: The Transformation of America, 1815–1848*. New York: Oxford University Press, 2007.

Hutchinson, William T. *Cyrus Hall McCormick: Harvest, 1857–1884*. New York: Century, 1935.

———. *Cyrus Hall McCormick: Seed-Time, 1808–1856*. New York: Century, 1930.

International Harvester Company. *Glimpses of Thrift-Land*. Chicago: International Harvester Company, 1909.

Jaffee, David. *A New Nation of Goods: The Material Culture of Early America*. Philadelphia: University of Pennsylvania Press, 2010.

Jones, Arnita A., and Philip L. Cantelon, eds. *Corporate Archives and History: Making the Past Work*. Malabar FL: Krieger, 1993.

Kammen, Michael. *The Mystic Chords of Memory: The Transformation of Tradition in American Culture*. New York: Vintage Books: 1991.

Kane, Lucille. "Manuscript Collecting." In Hesseltine and McNeil, *In Support of Clio*, 29–48.

Kellar, Herbert, ed. *Solon Robinson: Pioneer and Agriculturalist*. 2 vols. Indianapolis: Indiana Historical Bureau, 1936.

Kline, Ronald. *Consumers in the Country: Technology and Social Change in Rural America*. Baltimore: Johns Hopkins University Press, 2000.

Kramer, Helen. "Harvester and High Finance: Formation of the International Harvester Company." *Business History Review* 38 (1964): 283–301.

Krey, August. "History in the Machine Age." *Minnesota History* 14 (1933): 3–29.

Kwolek-Folland, Angel. *Engendering Business: Men and Women in the Corporate Office, 1870–1930*. Baltimore: Johns Hopkins University Press, 1994.

Laird, Pamela. *Advertising Progress: American Business and the Rise of Consumer Marketing*. Baltimore: Johns Hopkins University Press, 1998.

Lakwete, Angela. *Inventing the Cotton Gin*. Baltimore: Johns Hopkins University Press, 2003.

Lauck, Jon K. *The Lost Region: Toward a Revival of Midwestern History*. Iowa City: University of Iowa Press, 2013.

———. "The Prairie Historians and the Foundations of Midwestern History." *Annals of Iowa* 71 (2012): 137–73.

Leach, William. *Land of Desire: Merchants, Power, and the Rise of a New American Culture*. New York: Pantheon Books, 1993.

Lears, Jackson. *Fables of Abundance: A Cultural History of Advertising in America*. New York: Basic Books, 1995.

———. *Something for Nothing: Luck in America*. New York: Viking, 2003.

Lerner, Eugene. "Investment Uncertainty during the Civil War: A Note on the McCormick Brothers." *Journal of Economic History* 16, no. 1 (1956): 34–40.

Levene, Byron. "Lincoln and McCormick: Two Emancipators." *Wisconsin Magazine of History* 42, no. 2 (1959): 97–101.

Levy, Jonathan. *Freaks of Fortune: The Emerging World of Capitalism and Risk in America*. Cambridge MA: Harvard University Press, 2012.

Lewis, Lloyd. *Chicago: The History of Its Reputation*. New York: Harcourt, Brace, 1929.

Longstreet, Stephen. *Chicago: 1860–1919*. New York: McKay, 1973.

Lord, Clifford L. *Keepers of the Past*. Chapel Hill: University of North Carolina Press, 1965.

Lowenthal, David. *The Heritage Crusade and the Spoils of History*. New York: Cambridge University Press, 1998.

Lyons, Norbert. *The McCormick Reaper Legend: The True Story of a Great Invention*. New York: Exposition, 1955.

Mallock, William H. *Labour and the Popular Welfare*. London: Black, 1893.

Marchand, Roland. *Advertising the American Dream: Making Way for Modernity, 1920–1940*. Berkeley: University of California Press, 1985.

———. *Creating the Corporate Soul: The Rise of Public Relations and Corporate Imagery in American Big Business*. Berkeley: University of California Press, 1998.

Marx, Leo. *The Machine in the Garden: Technology and the Pastoral Ideal in America*. New York: Oxford University Press, 1964.

McCormick, Cyrus Hall, III. *The Century of the Reaper*. New York: Houghton Mifflin, 1931.

McCormick, Robert Hall. *Memorial of Robert Hall McCormick: Being a Brief History; Life, Character and Inventions, Including the History of the McCormick Reaper*. Chicago: Barnard and Gunthrop, 1885.

McCormick, Robert Hall, and James Shields. *Robert McCormick, Inventor*. Chicago, 1910.

McLaughlin, Andrew. *A History of the United States for the Schools*. New York: Appleton, 1911.

McLaughlin, Robert. *The Heartland*. New York: Time, 1967.

McMath, Robert C. *American Populism: A Social History, 1877–1898*. New York: Hill and Wang, 1993.

Montgomery, David. *The Fall of the House of Labor*. New York: Cambridge University Press, 1987.

Mooney, Phillip. "The Practice of History in Corporate America: Business Archives in the United States." In Jones and Cantelon, *Corporate Archives and History*, 9–20.

Muncy, Robyn. "Trustbusting and White Manhood in America, 1898–1914." *American Studies* 38, no. 3 (Fall 1997): 21–42.

Muzzey, David. *An American History*. Boston: Ginn, 1911.

National Association of Agricultural Implement Manufacturers. *Farm Implement News Daily: Official Report of the Annual Convention*. Chicago: National Association of Agricultural Implement Manufacturers, 1894.

Neill, Edward. *History of Houston County*. Minneapolis: Minnesota Historical Company, 1882.

Neill, Edward, and J. Fletcher Williams. *History of Dakota County and the City of Hastings Including the Explorers and Pioneers of Minnesota*. Minneapolis: North Star, 1881.

Neth, Mary. *Preserving the Family Farm: Women, Community and the Foundations of Agribusiness in the Midwest, 1900–1940*. Baltimore: Johns Hopkins University Press, 1995.

"News and Comments." *Mississippi Valley Historical Review* 8 (1921): 297–98.

Norton, Margaret. "Herbert Anthony Kellar, 1887–1955." *American Archivist* 19 (1956): 151–53.

"Notes and Comments." *Agricultural History* 2, no. 2 (1928): 103–4.

Novick, Peter. *That Noble Dream: The "Objectivity Question" and the American Historical Profession*. Cambridge: Cambridge University Press, 1998.

Olmstead, Alan, and Paul W. Rhode. "Beyond the Threshold: An Analysis of the Characteristics and Behavior of Early Reaper Adopters." *Journal of Economic History* 55, no. 1 (1995): 27–57.

O'Malley, Michael. *Face Value: The Entwined Histories of Money and Race in America*. Chicago: University of Chicago Press, 2012.

Orvell, Miles. *The Real Thing: Imitation and Authenticity in American Culture, 1880–1940*. Chapel Hill: University of North Carolina Press, 1989.

Ott, Julia. *When Wall Street Met Main Street: The Quest for an Investors' Democracy*. Cambridge MA: Harvard University Press, 2011.

Ozanne, Robert. *A Century of Labor-Management Relations at McCormick and International Harvester*. Madison: University of Wisconsin Press, 1967.

Paine, Clarence. "Report of the Secretary-Treasurer." *Proceedings of the Mississippi Valley Historical Association* 7 (1913–14): 35–36.

Pattison, Salem G. *The McCormick Extension Case of 1848, and Other Matter Related to the Invention of 1831*. Chicago: Donnelly, 1900.

Paxson, Frederic. *The Civil War*. New York: Holt, 1911.

Perkins, George. "The Modern Corporation." In *The Currency Problem and the Current Financial Situation: A Series of Addresses Delivered at Columbia University, 1907–1908*, 153–70. New York: Columbia University Press, 1908.

Peterson, Arthur G. "The Agricultural History Society's First Quarter Century." *Agricultural History* 19 (1945): 193–203.

Postel, Charles. *The Populist Vision*. New York: Oxford University Press, 2007.

Rasmussen, Wayne "The Growth of Agricultural History." In Hesseltine and McNeil, *In Support of Clio*, 153–72.

Ridge, Martin. *Ignatius Donnelly: Portrait of a Politician*. Chicago: University of Chicago Press, 1962.

Rieser, Andrew. *The Chautauqua Movement*. New York: Columbia University Press, 2003.

Ristow, Walter T. "Alfred T. Andreas and His Minnesota Atlas." *Minnesota History* 40 (1966): 120–29.

Robinson, James Harvey. *The New History: Essays Illustrating the Modern Historical Outlook*. New York: Macmillan, 1912.

Rogin, Leo. *The Introduction of Farm Machinery*. Berkeley: University of California Press, 1931.

———. "The Introduction of Farm Machinery: A Reply." *Journal of Political Economy* 40, no. 5 (October 1932): 695–96.

Rosenberg, Emily S. *Spreading the American Dream: American Economic and Cultural Expansion, 1890–1945*. New York: Hill and Wang, 1982.

Rosovsky, Henry, ed. *Industrialization in America in Two Systems*. New York: Wiley, 1966.

Ross, Earle D. "A Generation of Prairie Historiography." *Mississippi Valley Historical Review* 33 (December 1946): 391–410.

Sandburg, Helga. *A Great and Glorious Romance*. New York: Harcourt Brace Jovanovich, 1978.

Sanders, Elizabeth. *Roots of Reform: Farmers, Workers, and the American State, 1877–1917*. Chicago: University of Chicago Press, 1999.

Schlesinger, Arthur M. *Political and Social History of the United States, 1829–1925*. New York: Macmillan, 1925.

Schmidt, Louis. "The Economic History of American Agriculture as a Field of Study." *Historical Outlook* 10 (January 1919): 8–12.

Sellers, James L. "Before We Were Members: The MVHA." *Mississippi Valley Historical Review* 40, no. 1 (June 1953): 494–518.

Sklar, Richard. *The Corporate Reconstruction of American Capitalism, 1890–1916*. New York: Cambridge University Press, 1988.

Smiley, David. "The W.P.A. Historical Records Survey." In Hesseltine and McNeil, *In Support of Clio*, 3–28.

Spears, Timothy. *100 Years on the Road: The Traveling Salesman in American Culture*. New Haven: Yale University Press, 1995.

Steward, John. *Overlooked Pages of Reaper History*. Chicago, 1897.

Steward, John, and Arthur Pound. *The Reaper: A History of the Efforts of Those Who Justly May Be Said to Have Made Bread Cheap*. New York: Greenberg, 1931.

Swift, Rodney B. *Who Invented the Reaper? An Answer to the Protest Statement Said to Have Been Filed at the Treasury Department*. Chicago, 1897.

Tapia, John. *Circuit Chautauqua*. Jefferson NC: McFarland, 1997.

Theobald, Mary Miley. "Lion of the Hour." *Virginia Living Magazine* 7, no. 4 (2009).

Thwaites, Reuben. "Cyrus Hall McCormick and the Reaper." In *Proceedings of the Annual Meeting of the State Historical Society of Wisconsin*, 234–59. Madison: State Historical Society of Wisconsin, 1908.

Townsend, Robert. *History's Babel: Scholarship, Professionalization, and the Historical Enterprise in the United States, 1880–1940*. Chicago: University of Chicago Press, 2013.

Trouillot, Michel-Rolph. *Silencing the Past: Power and the Production of History*. Boston: Beacon, 1995.

Turner, Frederick Jackson. *Reuben Gold Thwaites: Memorial Address*. Madison: State Historical Society of Wisconsin, 1914.

Tyrell, Ian. *Historians in Public: The Practice of American History, 1890–1970*. Chicago: University of Chicago Press, 2005.

———. "Public at the Creation: Place, Memory, and Historical Practice in the Mississippi Valley Historical Association, 1907–1950." *Journal of American History* 94, no. 1 (June 2007): 19–46.

Van Tassel, David, and James Tinsley. "Historical Organizations as Aids to History." In Hesseltine and McNeil, *In Support of Clio*, 127–52.

Wallace, Anthony. *Rockdale: The Growth of an American Village in the Early Industrial Revolution*. New York: Knopf, 1978.

Wallace, Mike. *Mickey Mouse History and Other Essays on American Memory*. Philadelphia: Temple University Press, 1996.

Watson, Paula. "Carnegie Ladies, Lady Carnegies: Women and the Building of Libraries." *Libraries and Culture* 31, no. 1 (1996): 159–96.

Wiebe, Robert H. *The Search for Order, 1877–1920*. New York: Hill and Wang, 1967.

Wilentz, Sean. *Chants Democratic: New York City and the Rise of the American Working Class, 1788–1850*. New York: Oxford University Press, 1984.

Winder, Gordon. *The American Reaper: Harvesting Networks and Technology, 1830–1910*. London: Ashgate, 2012.

Younger, Richard. "Foundations and the Study of History." In Hesseltine and McNeil, *In Support of Clio*, 107–26.

Zunz, Olivier. *Making America Corporate, 1870–1920*. Chicago: University of Chicago Press, 1990.

Index

Printed in the USA
CPSIA information can be obtained
at www.ICGtesting.com
LVHW042142081223
765719LV00004B/78